PING-PONG
DIPLOMACY

ALSO BY NICHOLAS GRIFFIN

Dizzy City: A Novel

Caucasus: A Journey to the Land between Christianity and Islam

The Masquerade

The House of Sight and Shadow: A Novel

The Requiem Shark: A Novel

NICHOLAS GRIFFIN

PING-PONG DIPLOMACY

Ivor Montagu and the Astonishing
Story Behind the Game That
Changed the World

SIMON &
SCHUSTER

London · New York · Sydney · Toronto · New Delhi

A CBS COMPANY

First published in USA by Scribner, a division of Simon & Schuster Inc., 2014

First published in Great Britain by Simon & Schuster UK Ltd, 2014
A CBS Company

1 3 5 7 9 10 8 6 4 2

Simon & Schuster UK Ltd
1st Floor
222 Gray's Inn Road
London WC1X 8HB

Simon & Schuster Australia, Sydney
Simon & Schuster India, New Delhi

www.simonandschuster.co.uk

A CIP catalogue record for this book is available from the British Library.

Hardback ISBN 978-0-85720-734-0
Trade Paperback ISBN: 978-0-85720-735-7
ebook ISBN 978-0-85720-737-1

Printed and bound by CPI Group (UK) Ltd, Croydon, CR0 4YY

Photo insert credits: All four photographs on page 1 by permission of the People's
History Museum. Page 2 top and page 4 middle and bottom courtesy of the ETTA.
Page 2 middle left, middle right, and bottom; page 3 bottom; page 4 top; and
page 5 middle and bottom left courtesy of the ITTF Museum. Page 3 top and middle,
page 5 top, and page 8 bottom courtesy of Eastfoto. Page 5 bottom right courtesy of
William J Cunningham. All three photographs on page 6 courtesy of Getty Images.
Page 7 top and bottom and all three photographs on page 8 copyright
Malcolm R Anderson. Page 7 middle courtesy of Newscom.

For Tomás and Eva

Contents

Contents

PART THREE | East Meets West

Contents

PART FOUR | Aftermath

Author's Note

Nowadays, Chinese names are transliterated into English using the Pinyin system. In this book, I've used Pinyin almost everywhere, except where it seemed to me that the names were so familiar in Wade–Giles (e.g., Chiang Kai-shek) that using Pinyin would only confuse matters.

Also, where organisations have gone through minor name changes over the years, I've stuck with the one most pertinent for the time period this book covers. For example, today's USATT was once the USTTA (United States Table Tennis Association).

Ping-Pong Diplomacy

Prologue

The world champions were dead. As the best players gathered at the 1969 World Table Tennis Championships, the rumour circulated that the Chinese men's team, which had total dominance in the sport, had been paraded in front of tens of thousands of Chairman Mao's Red Guards. They had been screamed at, spat at, locked up, and tortured. They had been shot as spies. They had been strung up on trees by a vast teenage mob. As their dead bodies twirled back and forth at the ends of ropes, the cadavers came to rest with their bulbous eyes turned toward Taiwan or Hong Kong – a sure sign that they weren't faithful followers of Chairman Mao but traitors to Chinese Communism. It was nearly impossible to believe, yet the rumour was rooted in truth.

Why should a sports team be put through such hell? The only answer was that table tennis in China wasn't considered a sport at all. In the West, sports were mere entertainment. In China, all forms of culture had become political. Sports were 'a form of war waged for world revolution,' explained a member of the country's table tennis squad.

When the surviving team members reconvened at the 1971 World Championships in Japan, the political implications became clear. The Americans, a team of odds and ends, were also present in Nagoya. At a diplomatic level, a meeting between the two countries was considered impossible. Mao would have been torn down by the leftist radicals of his party for approaching the Americans directly, just as Richard Nixon would have been accused of treason

1

by the Republican right for holding out an olive branch to the Chinese. But the first steps between the two distant nations weren't carried out by politicians; they were conducted by Ping-Pong players.

That April, one of America's better players, a long-haired hippie, accidentally wandered onto the Chinese table tennis team's bus. He shook hands with the best player in the world. They swapped gifts. An invitation was extended, casually from team to team, and within forty-eight hours, a group made up entirely of table tennis players was touching down in Beijing – the first official American delegation since Mao had taken power in 1949. To the Americans it was a serendipitous moment. To the Chinese it was a carefully managed conclusion to years of work. It was the sport's finest moment, the initial step in what would be known as Ping-Pong diplomacy.

But Ping-Pong, that seemingly innocuous game of fraternity houses and suburban basements, had a much deeper history than many Westerners assume. It was never simply a game to the man who first wrote down its rules, the Honorable Ivor Montagu. Montagu, son of an English baron, was the forgotten architect of Ping-Pong diplomacy. As an eighteen-year-old student at Cambridge in the 1920s, before he joined the Communist Party against his father's wishes, Montagu codified Ping-Pong. Convinced that the sport could spread Communism throughout the world, he founded the International Table Tennis Federation, eventually engineering its path to Mao's China. He is the reason – the only reason – that 300 million Chinese play table tennis every week.

Montagu also had a secondary job: spying for the Soviet Union.

The real history of table tennis is a bizarre tale of espionage, aggravation, and reconciliation, of murder, revenge, and exquisite diplomacy. This is the story of how Ivor Montagu molded the game, and how the Chinese came to embrace it and then shaped it into a subtle instrument of foreign policy. Chairman Mao was fond of quoting 'Let foreign things serve China.' Little has served China as effectively as Montagu's very British game of table tennis.

PART ONE | The West

CHAPTER 1 | # Not-So-Humble Beginnings

At four years old, the future Communist agent Ivor Montagu stared out of his nursery window in Kensington Court, London, awaiting the Princess of Wales. He expected a gilded carriage, a woman wrapped in ermine and lit by jewels. He was brushed and combed by his nanny, then 'dragged downstairs and set astride a footstool.'

The Princess of Wales wore a plain grey suit and arrived by car. Years later, the Princess, by then the Queen of England, would write to Montagu's mother to commiserate about her son's scandalous marriage. For now, it was Montagu who suffered the deep disappointment. His only recollection on leaving the drawing room was that of having 'felt thoroughly cheated.'

That one of his mother's closest friends was May, Princess of Wales, wasn't particularly surprising in the Montagu household. The Montagus were among the wealthiest families in England, raised to the nobility thanks to generous contributions to political parties by Samuel Montagu, the family patriarch.

Ivor Montagu's father, the eldest son, had inherited the London house. Fires burned day and night throughout the winters, 'casting a warmth and amber glow that added to the sense of comfort and luxury.' Generals, admirals, royalty, and ministers all visited, passing under the cut-glass chandeliers and padding across thick carpets. In turn, the family visited the great and good, including a stop at 10 Downing Street, where young Ivor played in the garden while his father met with the prime minister.

5

In the south of England, the family maintained two great houses, Townhill and South Stoneham, where Ivor Montagu would spend much of his childhood. In the summers, the houses would play a cricket match against each other. Footmen would face off between the wickets. Montagu played long stop, undisturbed in the daisies while his older brothers reaped applause at bat.

On New Year's Eve, he would be forced to attend the Servants' Ball at Townhill, where his mother would break the ice by leading off in dance with either the butler or the head gardener. The rest of the staff would stand awkwardly with their families around the edge of the ballroom, waiting their turn. Montagu, who professed a deep hatred of being 'touched by either sex,' would still have to fill his dance card until, on one inspired New Year's Eve morning, he picked up a large rock and 'solemnly . . . dropped it from about waist high on my big toe,' earning an exemption from the ball. It was an early sign of his determination to do things the hard way.

There was no road map for Ivor Montagu. His future decisions would cross continents and political systems. From Hollywood to Hong Kong, Montagu would build bridges between radical ideas and the people ready to receive them. He'd risk his life on several occasions, share secrets with assassins, live in lies, and weave his way safely through two wars, until finally his own secret was discovered.

If Ivor Montagu's beginnings were all velvet knee pants and frilly baby bonnets, his grandfather's were modest. As Montagu would later put it, if you looked among the books in the family library, 'the thin one was the family pedigree.' It contained a coat of arms and then his father, his grandfather, and 'nothing else.' That was an exaggeration, though the Montagus' rise to nobility was rapid. Ivor's grandfather, Montagu Samuel, was born to an observant Jew in Liverpool in 1832. By the time he was twenty-one, he had founded his own bank, which thrived under a near-monopoly in Britain's foreign exchange transactions. There were offices dotted around the world, within and beyond the borders of the British Empire.

His first name change took him from Montagu Samuel to Samuel Montagu. Thanks to hefty contributions to political parties, he next added the title of Lord Swaythling, a name borrowed from a village between the family's two Hampshire estates. He'd have preferred

Lord Montagu, but the current Lord Montagu would agree to share his name only if Lord Swaythling would share his money.

Although he'd anglicised his name, he hadn't forgotten his Jewish roots. Lord Swaythling gave generously to Jews escaping pogroms in 1880s Russia and to numerous charities near his Hampshire home. As a member of the Houses of Parliament for fifteen years, he carried a deep love of Prime Minister Gladstone's version of England but never forgot his own childhood, when he'd fought 'with young bigots of other faiths.' Anti-Semitism was a virus that could emerge in any country. Hilaire Belloc, the brilliant politician, poet and satirist in chief, couldn't resist a passing shot:

> *Lord Swaythling, whom the people knew,*
> *And loved, as Samuel Montagu,*
> *Is known unto the fiends of hell*
> *As Mr Moses Samuel.*

There was nothing fiendish about Lord Swaythling. He built temples, poorhouses, schools for the teaching of Hebrew. On his death in 1911, the poor streamed out from the slums of London's East End to follow in the wake of his funeral procession. Ivor Montagu, almost seven, was kitted out in a black velvet suit and a ceremonial sword but was not allowed to join the throng following the cortege. Three miles divided the last carriage from the hearse. Streets from Camden Town to Bayswater were closed as the police kept the black-coated traffic moving.

Lord Swaythling had died a millionaire, one of only a handful in England. Much of the land, money, and other interests were left to Ivor's father – the second Baron Swaythling. Ivor had two older brothers and a baby sister, all guaranteed healthy inheritances as long as they married within their faith. There would be no title waiting for him. He was and would remain the Honorable Ivor Montagu.

The family followed an established pattern. Money made in the cities would be paraded in the countryside. Part of being a good Victorian was to embrace land and sport of all kinds. Father was a keen shot and a member of the Middlesex Cricket Club (MCC). Stuart, the oldest of the three brothers, was a rugby player obsessed with breeding cows. Ewen was good at pretty much everything.

Ivor had the desire but not the talent to get involved. He was the boy with glasses keeping score, the umpire, the referee trotting up and down the sidelines with a whistle in his hand. But there was one game he could play: table tennis. Before he was six, he had petitioned his father to get a table for the house in London, and there it sat on the vast landing, overlooking the front hall. When he wasn't playing on it, it was cleared and used for bridge by his father and his friends, the foreign secretary and the home secretary.

The year of Ivor's birth, 1904, was also considered the year that Ping-Pong had died. For a short time, Britain had been creating and exporting games at an extraordinary rate. Football, rugby, cricket, tennis, hockey, billiards, and badminton spread across the British Empire and beyond. At the turn of the century, table tennis had become a full-blown fad and had sped across the world – not as an organised sport; more as an after-dinner amusement, to be mixed with a brandy or a port and flirtatious chitchat with the opposite sex. It was called gossima, whiff-whaff, table tennis, but Ping-Pong, a name trademarked by Jaques & Son, was the most popular name. Much was written about watching girls on their hands and knees searching for balls under sofas and side tables. There were Ping-Pong parties, tournaments, picnics, and even Ping-Pong poetry. 'Pingpongitis' captured the happy mood:

> Oh what's this very funny game, Pray tell me, if you please,
> That looks like tennis, feels like golf, And sounds like
>   Cantonese. . . .
> What, that's the game, That's known to fame
> As Ping-Pong, Ping-Pong, Ping-Pong Ping.

That's one of the better ones. Within the same volume, you can feel the zeitgeist itching to move on. 'The Ping-Pong face, too well we know it; But please, oh please, won't someone kill, The puling, punning Ping-Pong poet.'

The game's origins were hotly contested. It was devised by the British Army in India, Malaysia, or Asia Minor, in a mess hall, cavalry club, or pavilion. The balls were carved from champagne corks. The bats were the lids of cigar boxes. Beneath all the creation myths lurked the frivolity that would irk its adherents for the next hundred years. Ping-Pong was for boys (and girls!), it could be played sober (or drunk!), you could hit the ball with a book (or a hairbrush!), in the billiard room, or even in the kitchen.

While other sports developed teams, trophies, leagues, and stadia, Ping-Pong suffered from a lack of coherence. Arguments erupted frequently because no official rules had been written. So, as one future world champion would lament, Ping-Pong 'suffered no slow lingering agonies, but burst like a soap bubble into nothingness from one day to the next.'

That same year of 1904, when Ping-Pong expired and Ivor Montagu was born, the Russo-Japanese War began. China wasn't yet ready to stand up; it still had another half century of humiliation ahead of it and was already deeply scarred thanks to losses to the British in the Opium Wars and to Japan in 1895. But in 1904 Japan did something considered impossible for an Asian country. It confronted a European power and then defeated it. Two Russian ships were crippled in Port Arthur early in the war after their crews had been surprised during a game of table tennis. 'Apparently the Ping-Pong nets were up, all taut and ready: it was only the torpedo nets that had been forgotten.'

Ivor's father, the second Baron Swaythling, was fascinated by the Japanese victory. The *Financial Times* would write in his obituary that he, 'like all great men, had no hobbies outside of his passion for work.' But there was one, an obsession with Japan that would in turn prove crucial in his son's adventures in Asia. Lord Swaythling wasn't the only foreigner amazed by Japan's victory. China's future leaders, Mao Zedong and Zhou Enlai, still young students, considered it a key moment in their development. It led them to wonder: If Japan was capable of such a victory, what could a unified China do? But few saw how quickly the repercussions of Japan's victory would rock the world. Russia's defeat was a fatal slash at Tsarism – it would struggle on for just a few years until the rise of Communism heralded the Russian Revolution. The moment would inspire such disparate men as Mao Zedong and Ivor Montagu, though their approaches could not have been more different.

CHAPTER 2 | **Gentlemanly Rebel**

By 1917 Ivor Montagu's oldest brother and his cousins were at war on the other side of the English Channel. To the thirteen-year-old, it seemed he was missing out on a thrilling adventure. The closest the teenager would come to combat was witnessing the first ever Zeppelin raid over London as he blithely walked through arcing shrapnel with his Brownie camera held high.

Air aces would land at Townhill, and on the weekends the family would drive down to look at the warships in Portsmouth Harbour. Many of the footmen were mobilised into the military, so Montagu laid out great sheets of white linoleum in one of their empty apartments and started charting out the sea battles according to his own algorithms. Only in a family as well connected as the Montagus would the Admiral of the Fleet visit. He spent 'several hours on hands and knees with the small boy' and then astonished the Montagu family by inviting Ivor to give a lecture on his system at the Naval Staff College.

Montagu kept up his studies at his new school, Westminster, where he was forced into an Eton suit and top hat. After school, he'd leave the hat at the lost luggage office in St James's Park underground station and pick up his light coat and cloth cap. It was a half-hearted attempt to pass as a member of the working class, betrayed by his favourite accessory, an ebony silver-headed cane.

The path from the underground station to school took him directly past the offices of the Fabian Society in Tothill Street. That spring, he paused before the window to peer at a pamphlet that he thought 'appropriate to me'; George Bernard Shaw's *Socialism for Millionaires*. Socialism, he decided, was 'the only plausible explanation of man's history and the processes of the universe.' It was a big leap for a young aristocrat to make, but for Montagu it was a sure foundation that he would construct the rest of his life around. Instead of helping his mother organise his messy notes for his upcoming lecture on war games, he told her that he had become a pacifist and would cancel his engagement.

By October 1917, as the bloody details of the Russian Revolution filtered through the British press, Montagu noticed that a kind of fear had entered the public consciousness. Was revolution contagious? Would his mother's friend, Queen Mary, soon suffer the same fate as the tsarina and end up executed by radicals? Montagu watched the incessant marches that filed past his school, just steps from the Houses of Parliament and his father's seat in the House of Lords.

One night, finished with his classes, Montagu emerged from school into a scuffle between charging policemen and unemployed war veterans. He was knocked to the ground and watched a policeman crack a banner from a man's hand. Montagu swung his cane and brought the policeman down. Had the policeman tried to identify his attacker in the melee, the least likely suspect would have been the retreating schoolboy, the Honorable Ivor Montagu. From the beginning, Montagu understood that his class offered a thick smokescreen of protection, one that would linger around him for decades. He walked home to the mansion in Kensington Court and said nothing of the afternoon's events to his father.

At fifteen, the precocious schoolboy passed the entrance exam to Cambridge University, but his chosen college, King's, asked him to wait two years before beginning university. Tall and slightly hunched, with a tendency to wear his glasses halfway down his nose, Montagu busied himself with a mixture of zoology and politics. He studied botany and biology at the Royal College of Science, eating at the same small restaurant every day his chosen fare of 'minestrone and wobbly pink blancmange.' Through his father's connections, he met the heads of the British Museum and the Royal Geographic Society. Another family friend, the head of London Zoo, allowed Montagu to spend a night on the zoo grounds listening to the wolves howl at the lions and the lions roar at the wolves.

His rebellious streak remained hidden. On weekends down at Townhill, he'd sneak out to canvass his father's tenants in support of the Labour Party; back in London during the week, he befriended socialist sympathisers HG Wells and George Bernard Shaw. To prove his commitment, he helped the British Socialist Party by volunteering to hide a consignment of Lenin's booklet *State and Revolution*. They were being sought by Scotland Yard. He put them on the landing at home, right by the Ping-Pong table. The sense of openness would be Montagu's way of hiding in plain sight throughout his life.

He was still honing his skills. A speech he was writing to present at the British Socialist Party was discovered by the butler and handed to his parents. Lord Swaythling asked him to leave the party at once and forbade him to spend any more family money on political memberships. Montagu decided that being a child was like being a 'worker without a union.' From then on, he wrote, he began to repay his family's love 'with wariness.'

Finally arriving at Cambridge, he revelled in being away from his family. A compulsive joiner of clubs, he also founded two: the Cheese Eaters' Society, where he led the charge to try to find whale's milk cheese; and the Spillikins, a left-wing society where they talked about the rise of Communism and wore black ties with little red dots.

The one thing he didn't do at Cambridge was study. 'Quite frankly,' he wrote, success there depended entirely on extracurricular activities, and the ones that he 'went a-whoring after' were 'politics, art, sport (and) new friends.' Montagu understood that team sports dominated university campuses and he longed for the associated popularity. After failed attempts at football and tennis, Montagu had a eureka moment: Ping-Pong. Using a portion of his allowance, he had two tables made to order. It was a recourse only a very wealthy undergraduate could take, but over the next fifty years it would be hard to find a fellow Communist who would have begrudged the extravagance for the effect his decision would have on the greater world.

Montagu's first tournament amazed him: 140 players registered. Ping-Pong wasn't dead after all. Montagu saw a player in a wheelchair beat Cambridge University's finest runner. Montagu lost in an early round, then watched the field thin out. Cambridge's best chess player beat its top tennis player in the final. Immediately, Montagu organised a team to challenge Oxford University and captained it to a thirty-one–five victory. All five losses were Montagu's. Within a year, Montagu, not yet eighteen years old, was chairman of the national Ping Pong Association.

A Manchester businessman, already interested in resurrecting the game, had heard of Montagu's efforts and approached him, glad of 'Oxbridge' support to help draw up rules and regulations. Montagu was in his element. As the whistle-blower, umpire, and organiser, he was allowed to write the rules of the sport. The fundamentals would remain intact for the next forty years and be translated into dozens of languages.

Yet, almost immediately, there was a problem. Setting up a few small tournaments under the name of the new Ping-Pong Association, Montagu and his associates had failed to realise that the words themselves were trademarked. 'Ping Pong' belonged to the famed toy manufacturer Jaques & Son, which insisted that its equipment should now be used at all events. Jaques representatives called a meeting at which Montagu surprised them by dissolving the Ping-Pong Association, then immediately re-forming the group as the Table Tennis Association in an adjacent room – an early foray into defending an ideology against the forces of capitalism.

The reasons Montagu began to pay attention to the game, he later wrote, 'were political. . . . I saw in Table Tennis a sport particularly suited to the lower paid . . . there could be little profit in it, no income to reward wide advertising, nothing therefore to attract the press. . . . I plunged into the game as a crusade.' Ping-Pong was also a game small enough for Montagu to control. He would use it to connect Communist countries to the West and to promote his political agenda. It would also be the perfect cover for an agent like Montagu to visit the centres of the Communist world.

One advantage that was unknown to Montagu in the 1920s is that table tennis is also the best sport for the brain. Not only does it fire up the same neurons as any other ball sport, but it excites the areas of the brain that deal with strategy and emotion. It is 'chess on steroids.' One of the keys is the distance you stand from your opponent. Across the nine feet of a table-tennis table, 'it's much more intense because you can interpret facial expressions.' The lack of distance is what makes the game so absorbing. The advantage has always been with players like Montagu who learn to disguise their emotions.

CHAPTER 3 | # Roast Beef and Russia

Montagu bounced between London and Cambridge, itching to get to Russia, studying just enough to keep moving toward his university degree. He heard about a Soviet trade union delegation visiting England and immediately invited them down to Cambridge with one eye 'on a possible future zoological visit to Russia.' It turned out that a visa could easily be arranged if Montagu wished to visit as a zoologist.

Montagu, not yet a card-carrying Communist but already thinking like one, knew that all culture, whether sport, literature, or film, should serve the people. The question was how to make inroads into British culture. Ping-Pong was one way, and he quickly settled on film as a second. Using another family friend, the owner of the *Times*, he secured an assignment to go to Berlin, then considered by some to be the world's capital of film. He had a fascinating time, never wrote a word, but decided on his return to London to found the Film Society. Instead of eternal subjection to English and American box office fodder, the British public would now be exposed to 'high art' – alongside a heavy dose of Communist propaganda. Producers would donate a copy of their films to the Film Society, and the Film Society would host free screenings. He brought in his friends as shareholders, almost all left-wing intellectuals, in a group where Cambridge met London: science fiction writer HG Wells, playwright George Bernard Shaw, film director Anthony Asquith, the son of Prime Minister Herbert Asquith, and JBS Haldane, one of the most distinguished scientists in Britain.

On the day he turned twenty-one, Montagu left for Russia. He spent the final eight weeks before his departure taking an intensive Berlitz language course. His father made one last, desperate attempt to convince his son to stay put, treating him to lunch of a 'juicy roast beef and crackly roast potatoes.' Lord Swaythling confessed that he and other bankers 'employed a network of informants in Russia' and that Montagu would be seized by Communists as soon as he crossed the border. When Montagu showed no signs of changing his mind, Lord Swaythling told him that he was also 'certain to catch plague.'

Montagu's overt mission was to look for specimens of the Prometheus mouse, a sightless vole endemic to the Caucasus Mountains. In reality, his first stop was Moscow, which is rather like leaving Birmingham for Manchester and stopping by London.

Supposedly the surest way to cure someone of Communism was to send them to Soviet Russia; there were few whose ideals could withstand the dour reality. To Montagu, Soviet Russia was intoxicating. In Moscow, he collected hunting licenses, tried to secure films for the Film Society, joined the slow-moving queue to look at Lenin's waxen corpse, was taken to the Bolshoi Ballet, and visited a film studio to watch a sci-fi production complete with 'futuristic costumes and a comic Russian accordion player who stimulated the downtrodden Martians to revolt.'

When Montagu finally arrived in the North Caucasus, his dreams of a Soviet Russian paradise were challenged. Children swarmed his train, begging for money. Montagu had little to give. He sat by his open window, cutting his pencils into pieces and passing them out to the clasping hands.

Once the expedition started digging for Prometheus mice, they found that the voles moved quickly in the mountain heat. Montagu bought a straw hat like the ones the local donkeys wore and dug for a day or two, before resorting to a strictly capitalist scheme, offering to pay one ruble for every vole brought to him. They were inundated by 'optimistic peasants' who continued to send sacks of voles long after they had left town.

Montagu was a poor collector of zoological specimens. First he caged the voles together, but they fought viciously until only eight or nine remained. On the train back to Moscow, three of the voles escaped. Montagu had to ask a squad of Russian soldiers to surround the carriage to catch the runaways. By the time he reached London, all the voles had died.

Montagu returned to England desperate to get more deeply involved in the world of Communism. He took the first step by joining the Society for Cultural Relations (SCR), hoping it would act as a signal flare for his rising interest. One thing was certain. Montagu was not going to become a first-rate zoologist. A dog he adopted first caused a car crash in front of his house, then expired 'thoroughly infested with worms.' There was also a 'Sicilian polecat who died of galloping consumption' and a marten he tried to take care of until it 'bit off its own feet in a cage.'

The first few Ping-Pong tournaments he had organised were well attended, but could that lead to a full-time job? He decided to work in the film business. One of his first jobs was to help a producer friend edit the work of a man named Alfred Hitchcock. Two weeks of recutting *The Lodger* secured Montagu a decade-long working friendship with the director and gave Hitchcock his breakthrough hit.

One morning, a few months after his return from the Soviet Union, a messenger tracked Montagu down in his tiny film office. The matter was urgent: an order to visit Bob Stewart, Communist Party stalwart. It would be many years before Stewart's full involvement with Moscow was known. Soon, Stewart would build a radio transmitter in Wimbledon that would give him direct access to orders from the Kremlin. Less than a decade later, he'd have other Cambridge graduates under his control: the five most famous spies of the coming Cold War. But for the moment, he had standing in front of him a puzzled Ivor Montagu.

Stewart handed Ivor Montagu a letter. It was from the Communist International, better known as the Comintern, created to spread Communist propaganda, an organisation that was riddled with spies and double and triple agents.

'How soon can you leave?' asked Stewart.

'I suppose I could leave tonight,' said Montagu. Stewart suddenly 'became so stern as to be almost conspiratorial.' He pointed at Montagu's letter. 'Don't show it to anyone.' Montagu might not have known it yet, but 'a letter of this kind carries in Soviet Russia the weight of a decree.'

Only months after his return to London, Montagu was speeding across European railways back to Moscow. The only thing he had forgotten to pack in his desperate rush was his rubber-coated Ping-Pong paddle. But what possible use could a paddle have on vital Comintern business?

Arriving in Moscow, not a penny left in his pocket, he found no one to meet him; the entourage had been waiting for Lord Sway-thling's son at the first-class carriages. Montagu spilled out of the hard seats and wandered confused around Moscow. When, finally, he showed up at the Trade Union Building, there was a 'great relief' balancing their irritation that it had taken him so long to get there. Moscow was preparing for the annual celebration of their October revolution and Montagu was asked to stay. What, he asked, should I do? Wait, said the functionary, then added on Montagu's way out of the room, 'There is something else you can do. . . . I hear you play table tennis.'

Montagu spent the week battling a 'series of the keenest players' in all of Russia, who, he suspected, had been brought in to impress him. He wired his new girlfriend back in England urging her to ship his paddle to Moscow at once.

His treatment in Moscow was even better than last time. He attended the parade in Red Square, sitting close to Stalin in the VIP section. At the Bolshoi Theatre he watched Vyacheslav Molotov give a lengthy report from the gallery. The great man, Stalin, sat three rows in front. Obviously, Ivor Montagu was being groomed, but for what exactly? Could it really be Ping-Pong?

It turned out to be film. The Film Society was to be a funnel that ran straight from Moscow to London, through which Russia was going to pump its finest propaganda productions. Montagu would be their man in London. That, at least, is what Montagu confessed in his unpublished notebooks. His extensive travels and the vast grounds he covered for the Comintern in the coming years showed that, very simply, he was Moscow's man.

From now on, Montagu would be drawn deeper and deeper into

the Comintern, befriending some of its most notorious spies and assassins. Not only would he never deny them, he'd be among the most enthusiastic volunteers the Soviets had ever stumbled across, willing to bend all of his talents in film, journalism, and table tennis to the Communist cause. In turn, perhaps as homage to their new disciple, a Ping-Pong craze swept across Russia in Montagu's wake. All culture, Montagu knew, had a propaganda value, but how should it be unleashed on an unsuspecting Western world?

CHAPTER 4 | The Dangers of Derision

Every decision that Montagu made, in both his personal and business life, passed through the prism of his politics. In Ping-Pong it was direct. In order to help him regulate and spread the sport, he chose a man named WJ Pope. Before his life in Ping-Pong, Pope had worked for the National Union of Railwaymen. He had learned the game inside a jail in Bradford, where he'd spent most of the Great War as a conscientious objector.

If Montagu wanted to think of Ping-Pong in terms of the Comintern, where Communist culture crossed borders, then the sport had to grow large enough to hold international matches. By the mid-1920s, Montagu had created a lot of interest in the game, mostly by promoting a national championship through the *Daily Mirror*. The event, which promised a car for winning the men's singles and a mink coat for the ladies, had drawn thirty thousand entrants. From 1926 onward, Pope had the task of giving direction to the enthusiasm, guiding the creation of hundreds of local clubs that mirrored the organisation of the trade unions. In December 1926, Montagu and Pope decided to bring in national teams from across the Continent for a European championship. They would need to build tiered seating in the Memorial Hall in Farringdon for the tournament, but luckily, Ivor Montagu had three hundred pounds left from his grandfather's will to cover the cost. Montagu was never shy with his money. When he had made up his mind, he went all-in with his bets.

Come December, Montagu and Pope had fully converted the Farringdon Street site into an arena with four tables standing in the middle. The place was packed with Hungarians, Slovaks, French, and Germans, and a group of eight Indian students. Montagu quickly recalibrated the event as a world championship. Ping-Pong turned out to be not a parlour game, but a fully-fledged sport. How else to explain the numbers? Three thousand paying customers the first day, more than ten thousand in total? This was something to build upon.

Montagu's parents were proud 'to see (their) wayward son take an interest in something non-political.' The championship cup was paid for by his mother but chosen by his father, who took him into the bullion room at Samuel Montagu and Co. to select 'a fine fat-bellied design in old English style.' It cost thirty-five pounds and to this day carries the family name: 'The Swaythling Cup.'

Now that table tennis had a world championship, it was decided that while the organisers were all in London, they should create a federation to ensure it survived. The first meeting of the International Table Tennis Federation (ITTF) took place in the library of Kensington Court, the Montagu family home. Montagu's fellow Ping-Pong devotees got the message. If table tennis was to move from a promising beginning, it would be because of one man's influence and money – twenty-two-year-old Ivor Montagu. He was promptly elected president of the federation by all present, a position he would hold for more than forty years.

Table tennis now had a federation and a large following, but did it have respect? The *Times* suggested that the game could be improved by using a curtain rod instead of a net. 'Can you imagine the training' of Montagu's table tennis players? asked another newspaper. 'The long route-marches to give them endurance, the physical jerks to teach them how to crawl under the piano for the ball, the skipping to develop the ankles so that they can leap about like fun. It might almost be worthwhile forming a Ping-Pong Army to institute conscription.' The journalist saved his lowest blow for last. 'A rumour comes through, as I write, there is a great surge onwards in the training of tiddly winks athletes, who have been inspired by this noble example.'

At the time when Ping-Pong was teetering between sport and

punch line, Ivor Montagu met his future wife, Eileen Hellstern. She was known to all as Hell. From his parents' perspective, Montagu couldn't have made a worse choice. Hell was a divorced mother of one, the daughter of a maker of surgical shoes. Her mother had been institutionalised shortly after her father's death. A full two years after they had met, Montagu and Hell married secretly at St Giles's Registry Office.

The same month that his son married, Lord Swaythling made a friendly overture to Montagu, offering to go to a football game with him. Montagu was so moved that he felt a sudden desire to confess.

'Father,' said Montagu. 'I want to tell you that I'm married.'

His father stared at him. 'Who is she?'

'Nobody you'd know,' said Montagu, giving a brief description of his bride.

His father was stunned into silence. After a while, he looked up at Montagu and asked, 'Is she a Jewess?' She was indeed. 'Why did you have to marry her? Is she going to have a baby?'

To Lord Swaythling, Montagu's marriage was 'an irredeemable calamity.' His mother entered the room in her dressing gown, and Ivor Montagu watched her stoop to console his father. He walked downstairs and let himself out.

The story ran from Los Angeles to New York and made the front pages of all the London papers. 'BARON'S SON WEDS SECRE-TARY,' roared London's *Evening Standard*. For a week, the newly-weds were on the run from the press, using makeup and a wardrobe department borrowed from Montagu's film contacts. They sneaked into and out of apartments over fire escapes and rooftops. Eventually, Montagu took the advice of a friend, snapped a beautiful picture of Hell, and handed it to Fleet Street. She made the front page for one more day, and then the story died.

His mother received dozens of condolence notes. She made the mistake of leaving them out, allowing Montagu time to leaf through until he found the shortest, which he committed to memory. The Queen had sent a one-liner. 'Gladys I feel for you. May.' Lord Swaythling held his silence with his son but called in his lawyer to change his will.

The newlyweds spent a quick honeymoon in Sicily, where Hell

came down with paratyphoid fever and Montagu with jaundice. Hell's sickness peaked during her tense first dinner at Kensington Court. A doctor was called, and to their horror, he ordered Hell confined to a guest bedroom and her new husband to a nursing home. Lady Swaythling took care of her. His lordship would come back from work and sit silently for ten minutes in his daughter-in-law's room, saying nothing, then rise and leave. As Hell convalesced, Lady Swaythling warmed to her. She would arrive with old dresses from her wardrobe that she thought Hell could make use of.

Within the week, Lady Swaythling was showing every sign of welcoming Hell into the family, though her approaches were still filtered through the class system that so upset her son. One evening, sitting by Hell's bedside, Lady Swaythling asked Hell if she would mind changing her manner of speaking. 'I would pay,' explained Lady Swaythling, for 'lessons to change your accent . . . you know darling, when I'm abroad, I always try to learn a little of other people's languages.' When Montagu finally reappeared, more or less recovered from his jaundice, his father took him aside to tell him that he should regard them 'as reconciled.' Perhaps they would like to visit Townhill one weekend?

During that weekend, the fifty-three-year-old Lord Swaythling went fishing and caught a chill. Back in London, the King's physician was consulted, but his lordship slipped into a coma. He was dead within days. 'The family,' wrote Montagu, 'would not be the same.' His mother told him that his father had thought he'd judged Ivor's marriage too quickly. But when the will was read, Montagu found that his father's thaw was not reflected there. Montagu's share of the inheritance had been reduced by 'three fifths,' a sum that Montagu would always refer to as 'the curious fraction.'

As the 1920s were coming to an end, Communism itself was in the middle of a shattering rift. Leon Trotsky, one of the fathers of the revolution and founder of the Red Army, had faced off against Stalin for control of Soviet Russia and lost. Trotsky was protected twenty-four hours a day in exile by Turkish police officers. Montagu would visit Trotsky after the 1929 World Table Tennis Championships in Hungary. As usual, Ping-Pong wasn't to be far from politics.

CHAPTER 5 | Table Tennis and Trotsky

Montagu began his journey to the Hungarian capital of Budapest alongside a very young English table tennis team. It included a bright nineteen-year-old named Fred Perry, still the last Englishman to win Wimbledon. Montagu noted 'his bright-red face and his boundless self-confidence.' Montagu himself was only twenty-four. 'I doubt,' he wrote, 'whether so young a team have ever represented England at anything.'

Montagu had brought the game to cosmopolitan Budapest for the simple reason that if England was the birth mother of table tennis, then Hungary was her only surviving child. The level of play certainly indicated so. No foreigner had ever won a tournament there. Ping-Pong's status in Hungary equalled England's thirst for cricket or America's for baseball.

The popularity of the game wasn't lost on Hungarian politicians. Hungary's ruler, Admiral Miklós Horthy, sent Montagu a note letting him know that he would attend the finals. Montagu was suitably disgusted. He professed that he didn't 'approve of political leaders trying to show off at international sporting events . . . constitutional monarchs, perhaps, neutral officials such as mayors or ministers of sport were inoffensive, but dictators or prime ministers who were identified with controversial public events – certainly not. It imposes a totally unwarranted embarrassment on the sportsmen whose prowess they exploit to court popularity.' Montagu's position depended entirely on the political leanings of the leader.

The rest of the field watched Perry with amazement. 'The greatest attacking stroke we have seen,' wrote one foreign expert, 'is Perry's forehand drive.' Dressed in long, white trousers and sneakers that he wore out during the tournament, Montagu's young protégé began to clear the field in men's singles.

Perry was the older finalist, up against a 'short, stocky expressionless' local teenager named Szabados. The great hall was packed with three thousand people, thick with 'cabinet ministers like Christmas trees in evening dress' and a crowd 'oozing into every exit.' Students roamed the streets outside, singing patriotic songs in support of Szabados. To get Perry safely inside, Montagu had to smuggle him in through a coal chute in the back of the building.

Montagu was the nonplaying captain. It didn't matter that Perry had the best forehand in the world. Szabados retrieved the ball from farther and farther behind the table, a full thirty-five feet, the longest returns Montagu had ever seen. Then Perry tried a drop shot. It inched over. Szabados roared in and reached it just before it touched the table, only to see Perry blast it past him again. Perry won. The crowd stood and cheered 'for more than ten minutes.'

The news was splashed across Hungarian papers but found no traction back in England. 'I have finished now with serious table tennis,' Perry wrote to his father, retiring as champion. He returned to England and went to work on his tennis strokes. But Montagu had learned something vital: table tennis could attract the attention of a country's elite politicians. Now he turned toward Turkey.

In July Montagu had written to Trotsky, introducing himself as a 'zoologist by profession' who had 'taken part in the labour movement since 1918.' His trip to Turkey would find him spending a night with the man who had helped turn the world upside down. Trotsky lived in constant fear of assassination by Stalin, yet Ivor Montagu, a secret Stalinist at the beck and call of the Kremlin, was staying in his house. Trotsky ended their late evening by passing Montagu a loaded revolver and telling him to put it under his pillow. Montagu was many things, but not a killer. He barely slept, 'terrified that the gun would go off.' At dawn, accompanied by two policemen assigned for Trotsky's protection, they went fishing.

Montagu would confess privately that Trotsky was notable for 'charm that resides in a perfect frankness, an eager unaffectedness of manner. The two policemen, the fisherman, and the aged and courteous gardener are manifestly his devoted friends.'

Trotsky's two policemen rowed for them, laughing at Montagu's efforts in the heavy seas. The sea grew rougher and rougher, Montagu greener and greener. It took Trotsky a while to recognise that the situation was becoming dangerous. Soon Montagu was curled up at the bottom of the little boat as they rose and plummeted down raking waves and the policemen rowed for their lives between 'monstrous rocks.'

Montagu's admiration for Trotsky dried up on his return to England. Soon he would join the Communist Party of Great Britain officially. This remained highly unusual, not because Montagu was a wealthy aristocrat, but because he was British. In 1930, with Britain's population at 40 million, the nation's Communist Party had 2,550 members.

Trotsky was sanguine about the articles Montagu published based on their conversations. During their late-night talk, Trotsky had told the young man, 'We can only be right with and by the Party, for history has provided no other way of being in the right.' Now he knew what Montagu really was, a declared Stalinist who avowed that true Communism was whatever Moscow said it was.

CHAPTER 6 | Culture and the Coming War

By 1937, Montagu had the support of the new King as patron of the English Table Tennis Association. Better than that, the King had adopted the game, playing in Buckingham Palace until he had 'perfected a special shot of his own . . . declared by those who have been his opponents to be unplayable.' He had become one of the game's 'keenest devotees.'

That same year found the new Queen walking through the British Industries Fair at Olympia and 'showing very great interest in the modern table tennis equipment' while marvelling at 'its present day popularity.' Her mother-in-law, Queen Mary, was still a regular visitor to the Montagu household, and the table tennis table on the main landing had not gone unnoticed by Her Majesty. Montagu's mother, Lady Swaythling, had also done her bit for the sport, playing a match against boxing champion Joe Beckett and winning. 'In the winter evenings,' she wrote, 'table tennis is a distinct asset to people who suffer from cold in the extremities.'

Ivor Montagu was by now also one of the busiest men in the world of British film. Having started the Film Society and continuing to import the work of the finest Soviet filmmakers, he was also in lockstep with perhaps the best young director working in England, Alfred Hitchcock. Hitchcock's coterie would meet for 'hate parties,' where they'd dissect that week's releases. Ivor Montagu was at the centre of the group – Hitchcock had great regard for his understanding of narrative. Their shared credits include the

26

best of Hitchcock's movies on spies – *The Thirty-Nine Steps, Sabotage, The Man Who Knew Too Much*, and *The Secret Agent*.

In retrospect, the situation seems unbelievable, almost comical. Montagu and Hitchcock would sit up into the small hours. Hitchcock had his favourite book, *Plotto*, a primer on the pace of plotting, on his lap. There, giving him advice, sat the unremarkable Ivor Montagu, now a little tubby around the middle, black glasses halfway down his nose, a shabby gentleman braced against his fall from the aristocracy by a secure income, encouraging Hitchcock to weave outlandish plots into ordinary settings.

At the same time, Montagu was embedded in the Comintern's accelerated quest to spread propaganda. He made his way to America, lunched with family friend Franklin Roosevelt, met up with Soviet filmmaker Sergei Eisenstein, and pitched their distinctly left-wing scripts to Los Angeles studios. The two men took a meeting with Samuel Goldwyn, who was looking for 'something like *Potemkin* only a little cheaper, for Ronald Colman.'

Eventually Paramount bit, and for a few months, Montagu and Eisenstein wrote happily together. They would drive into Beverly Hills with their new friend Charlie Chaplin, teaching him Russian swearwords to shout out the window at the old White Russian generals standing stiffly in their new roles as parking valets. Even then Montagu was followed. He's a 'clever Moscow propagandist' warned the US Department of Labor, who 'devotes the whole of his energies and not inconsiderable intellect to the fomentation of industrial revolt. . . . Believe nothing he says or anything that may be said to you in his favour. . . . Deport him bag and baggage.'

Hollywood soon listened. Eisenstein was called a 'red dog' in the press, and Paramount was accused of 'having betrayed the United States.' There was no work left for the writing partners. The precarious situation in Europe drew Montagu straight home to England, while Eisenstein headed south to direct a film in Mexico. Hitler's threatening speeches, Germany's burgeoning arms production, and reports of Nazi behaviour horrified the left. The British secret services wouldn't be able to confirm until the summer of 1940 that Montagu had begun spying, but Montagu's familiarity with those at the centre of the Comintern's activity across the world was already a deep concern to British intelligence.

The man through whom Communist propaganda poured into Europe was named Willi Munzenberg, the Red Millionaire, who as a teenager had dined at Lenin's table. Montagu first met Munzenberg in Berlin in 1924, where Munzenberg provided the young Englishman with a long list of introductions for his very first trip to Moscow. Munzenberg was in charge of all covert operations in the West, appointed by Lenin himself. He had not only set up a large number of front organisations, but he'd also invented the concept of front organisations, including the Friends of the Soviet Union, which Montagu had immediately joined on his return from Russia. The British intelligence agents in MI5 watched as money flowed from Munzenberg to Montagu but could not figure out what Montagu was doing with it.

Even in 1933, British public sentiment was at odds with its government's passive approach to the rise of Fascism on the Continent. It was a heady opportunity for Communists like Montagu, who suddenly found themselves having more in common with the general public in Britain. The idea that the survivors of the Great War would have to send their own children to fight Germany once more was deeply disturbing.

The first tremors of the coming war were felt in Spain. In the mid-1930s, Spain's civil war became the front line in the battle between Fascism and Communism. Naturally Montagu was there, this time with a documentary film team. It was a testing ground for both the German and Russian militaries and was riddled with spies to a preposterous extent – preposterous, but never funny; the penalty was too stiff. A Nazi death list had recently been found with thirty-three names on it; Munzenberg was at the top. 'If you meet one of them, kill him,' instructed the list. The danger for men like Montagu was spelled out in the second sentence. 'And if he is a Jew, break every bone in his body.'

Russian intelligence officers were everywhere, dividing their time between analysing their enemies and their supposed allies. Members of the International Brigades associated with Trotskyism had a strange way of ending up in mass graves well back from the front line, victims of mini-purges conducted by Stalinist officers. Montagu managed to avoid being murdered by the Soviet state, but Munzenberg would end up garroted beneath an oak tree near a

French internment camp in the summer of 1940, victim of a pair of agents of the People's Commissariat for Internal Affairs, known by its Russian acronym, NKVD. That same summer Montagu's erstwhile friend Trotsky, now exiled to Mexico, received an ice pick to the brain from another NKVD agent.

Once the Spanish government became genuinely concerned that it might be toppled by Franco, it deferred to Stalin on all matters. The first thing that went East was Spain's gold. Stalin, at his own leisure and at inflated prices, supplied Spain with second-rate weaponry and armaments. Spanish gold ended up in many places that had nothing to do with the Spanish struggle, including Central China, where Ivor Montagu's future partners in Ping-Pong, the Red Chinese, were locked in their own struggle for dominance.

All of this was done with an even more cynical intention in mind. Stalin would soon be making a pact with the most hated of enemies, Adolf Hitler, the very man who had driven young anti-fascists to Spain in the first place. There were many challenges to the pure of heart in Communism, but 1939's Treaty of Non-Aggression between Russia and Germany was the most startling. Montagu would toe the party line: that it was a necessary manoeuvre on Stalin's behalf to avoid being caught between two fronts.

Montagu patrolled the Spanish front lines, where he produced and directed two pro-Soviet documentaries, carrying letters of introduction written by the highest-ranking Soviet agents. Montagu's 1936 production, *Defence of Madrid*, was crude in comparison to his work with Hitchcock, but it had urgency, thanks to the rawness of the footage. His crew was up early one morning, shaving in their hotel bathrooms, when they heard 'the sound of a descending bomb.' The building next door was destroyed. They watched from the window as the dead and dying were pulled from the rubble.

Montagu appeared on camera in Madrid, standing in front of the Duke of Alba's palace, searching for proof that Franco was being directly supported by Hitler's Germany. Shells poured overhead as the camera shivered from the explosions. Montagu stooped to cradle an unexploded device and turned it slowly to show the German markings to the camera. Suddenly, another shell came whining over his head. Montagu panicked and threw himself to the ground, his bulk landing directly on the shell. He stood up, dusted himself off, and later recorded it as 'one of my luckier and certainly one of my more foolish moments.' Years later, he would fall out with Alfred Hitchcock over inserting a similar moment in the film *Saboteur*, which climaxes with an unintended explosion.

There were many who thought of Ivor Montagu as a Pollyanna who wandered through the darkest times, a naïf who closed his eyes to the horrors being committed in the name of Communism and somehow managed to preserve his blind faith until the end of his life. For a man of Montagu's intelligence, this image was a disservice. From his very first trip to Moscow, Montagu involved himself with the leaders of the Communist world. He could play the fool, play his class card or his race card, but he remained a Communist all his life. The bloodshed that he witnessed in the name of Communism, he excused and dismissed as inevitable. What was a betrayal of a family, of a country, compared to the betrayal of the people? What was one more war if it was the last war?

| **Suspect**

Also in Spain was Montagu's old friend JBS Haldane, whom he'd first met on the streets of Cambridge when they were the only two people out in the streets on election night, booing a Conservative victory. Haldane, a 'massive, towering' man whose receding hairline only emphasised his enormous forehead, used to come to Montagu's parties wearing a floppy hat, sit down on a swivel chair, and declare himself the king of Scotland. Soon, they'd be partners in espionage. By the 1930s, Haldane had long been considered among the country's pre-eminent scientists. Like Montagu, he had made a successful transition from an aristocratic education to a socialist sensibility. As Captain of the School at Eton College, he had regarded his fellow students 'quite rightly, as intellectually sub-human.' A few years older than Montagu, he had fought in the trenches of the Great War and had found the experience 'enjoyable, which most of my companions did not.' Among his soldiers, he had a reputation as a genial lunatic. Field Marshal Douglas Haig had called him 'the bravest and the dirtiest officer.'

In 1915, Haldane's leg was shredded by steel splinters during a raid, and he was picked up behind the lines in an ambulance driven by the Prince of Wales. The Prince 'turned to him and commented "Oh, it's you"'; they had last met in Oxford, almost exactly a year before. Just as with Montagu, the assumption that Haldane was part of the establishment would give him extraordinary leeway to act against it.

In 1918, Haldane had started working for military intelligence, a relationship that would continue on and off for twenty-five years. In the early twenties, he taught at Cambridge, living openly with his mistress and insisting on using his own body for all of his medical experiments, including the ingestion of hydrochloric acid and calcium chloride. The result of one of these experiments was 'intense diarrhoea, followed by constipation due to the formation of a large hard fecal mass. There was great general discomfort, pains in the head, limbs and back, and disturbed nights . . . the experiment was not unpleasant.'

Like Montagu, Haldane had appeared in Moscow in 1926 and then headed to Spain at the invitation of her government at the outbreak of war. The Republican government hoped for advice on potential gas attacks that Franco might instigate through his German connections. Instead, Haldane's experience in Spain turned him into one of the world's experts on air defence, making him invaluable first to the British government and then as a spy for Soviet Russia.

On a November afternoon in 1936, Haldane was sitting on a park bench in Madrid when an air raid alarm sounded. The park emptied until the only two remaining were Haldane, determined to gather first-hand data, and an elderly woman sharing his bench. Haldane smiled at her after the end of the raid, only to see that she had been killed instantly by a bomb splinter. It shocked him much more than the horrors he'd experienced in the trenches because he knew he 'had so many things to do.'

In between the intrigue and near-death moments, Montagu hadn't forgotten about the importance of table tennis. It was his great fortune that MI5 was totally confused by his strange obsession. Montagu had one particular secret admirer, Colonel Valentine Vivian, the first head of MI5's counter-espionage unit. He was as close as anyone to tripping Montagu up, but became distracted by Montagu's involvement with table tennis.

It was testament to how seriously MI5 took Montagu that Vivian should personally inquire into his case. The first report to the colonel was almost apologetic, convinced that there was something sinister in Montagu's relationship with a Hungarian named Zoltan Mechlovits:

The reason of our tentative interest in these people will appear to
you rather quaint. They write interminably to Ivor Montagu about
table tennis and the trying out of table tennis balls. The exercise
of his occupation over a period of many months has so eaten into
Zoltan Mechlovits' time that he has informed Montagu that he
cannot go on with it. . . . [E]ven in England, which is not noted for
sanity in this respect, we find it hard to believe that a gentleman can
spend weeks upon weeks upon weeks testing table tennis balls. . . .
[W]e should be grateful if you could tell us whether the individuals in Budapest I have named to you are known to be queer in any
other way.

It says little for table tennis's impact that MI5 was unable to dis-
cover that Mechlovits had actually won the World Table Tennis
Championships less than five years before. He'd even starred in
Ivor Montagu's first-ever directorial effort, a slow-motion, silent
short of table tennis players showing off their finest strokes. The
Hungarian police were also stumped by the correspondence but
saw no link between Mechlovits and Communism.

Both intelligence reports missed the connection. During the Bol-
shevik Revolution, Mechlovits had been a prisoner of war serving
a sentence in Siberia. Liberated, he had made his way back to Hungary through Moscow, where he had 'declined an offer by Lenin to
stay and help organise the young republic's sport.' Montagu must
have been inspired by this. Lenin had known of table tennis, knew
one of the world's top players, and had been willing to include
the game in the spread of Soviet sport before Montagu had even
arrived at Cambridge. What was that but further proof that table
tennis was destined to blossom in a Communist society?

Vivian wasn't willing to give up on Montagu quite yet. He
remained convinced that table tennis was a cover for something
darker. What if the problem didn't lie with these Hungarian Jews?
What if it could be traced through Montagu to Germany? Were the
Communists communicating in code? If so, what were they saying?

MI5 intercepted an angry letter from a German reproaching
Montagu for not 'having answered him about the Hanno-ball, also
for not answering about . . . net stretchers.' It was absurd but also
lucky for Montagu. When Montagu was working in film to spread

Communism, the authorities centred on his table tennis obsession. When he advocated table tennis to spread Communism, they
eyed the Film Society. When he spied on his country, they missed it
entirely.

March 1936 saw Montagu travel from the front lines of Spain
to the World Championships in Prague, a seamless transition. It
spared him his usual trip with the rest of the English team, who
travelled third-class, including AJ Wilmott, a university don who
had invented a 'sleeping harness' that he 'attached to the rack
above, and then under his armpits, and finally under his chin,' leaving him 'all trussed up like a horse.'

Montagu arrived just in time for the opening dinner; an elegant
affair with tables for each nation marked by their national flags.
'Just after the triumphant entry of the Hungarians, the Hon. Ivor
Montagu, President of the ITTF, rose to make a welcome speech and
to declare the tournament open.' The future men's singles champion, Richard Bergmann, remembered that the chairman 'spoke in
English, French and German, and I was much impressed at such a
scintillating display. I sat agog and thought Mr Montagu a miracle
of human wisdom and knowledge.'

Montagu watched the renowned Romanian chiseller, Arnon
Paneth, from the front row. 'Pushing' or 'chiselling' was the dull-
est form of the game; playing to stay in a point, not to win it. It
was entirely possible, as Paneth had been proving in Prague, that a
game could be won without ever playing a single offensive stroke,
an anathema to spectators. From the initial enthusiasm table tennis
had stirred up, those crowds of eight and ten thousand were beginning to thin as men and women of mediocre talent adopted chiselling to survive deep into competition.

Paneth was playing against Alex Ehrlich, one of the best in the
world, a thoughtful, tall Polish Jew who preferred to play with one
hand in his pocket. Ehrlich wanted to show Montagu the weakness
of his own rules. No stranger to chiselling, Ehrlich had decided to
mirror Paneth's play. The knowledgeable crowd was immediately in
on the joke. The stands 'shook with mirth' as the ball slowly looped
back and forth. The two men barely moved, patting the ball like a
pair of arthritic grandmothers. The first point passed ten minutes,
then twenty. Soon the booing began, but Paneth and Ehrlich played

through the disapproval until the crowd lapsed into silence. Finally, men and women rose and began to leave the building.

Montagu watched the point unfold in disbelief. Later on, his anger would only increase. Men and women who chose to chisel were 'as table tennis players a menace, that must be humiliated, despised, sent to Coventry, driven out of public life, if table tennis is to survive.' Montagu leaned forward and pleaded with the players from the sidelines. He admired Ehrlich, understood what he was trying to do, but couldn't he just speed things up? No, said Ehrlich, he'd 'let his hand drop off before he would hit the ball.'

After the first point reached its thirtieth minute, Ehrlich called for his team-mates to set up a chessboard on a nearby table and started to call out his moves. After forty-five minutes playing the same point, the referee complained of a stiff neck and was replaced. Ehrlich was now sending up ridiculously high balls, tempting Paneth to smash, but back came the patted ball. Ehrlich called for lunch – a cheese baguette – and ate it as he played. Montagu stood, walked out, and sought a quorum of ITTF board members. To their shock, when they returned to the arena, the first point was still being played, two hours after it began. The meeting took place alongside Ehrlich as they discussed how to end the sort of performance the two men were subjecting the tournament to.

There would be a time limit from now on. Twenty minutes of play, timed by a chess clock, then an extra five minutes, and whoever was ahead would win the match. Two hours and thirteen minutes after it began, the point ended in the now empty hall when Ehrlich's soft shot hit the net, paused for a moment, and dropped onto Paneth's side. Ehrlich won the rest of the match in under ten minutes.

The last chiseller to win a world title was a young Austrian woman named Gertrude Pritzi, who would take the ladies' singles the following year in the town of Baden, outside Vienna. She was the victor in a phenomenally dull final and, beaming, stepped up to receive her medal from Montagu. Watching was Bergmann, the men's champion, who witnessed the look of mortification spread across her features as she was roundly booed by her own countrymen.

It was a fascinating moment. Pritzi represented Austria, but would return the next year, 1938, after the Anschluss, to play for

Nazi Germany in a championship of omens and premonitions. Pritzi played against Ruth Aarons, a bubbly, blond American Jew. On the eve of the competition, she'd been approached by a little boy. Aarons thought he was there for an autograph and leaned over. Instead, he raised a palm full of pepper and blew it into her eyes.

At the World Championships there were also two journalists from Japan, 'always smiling, always taking notes,' finally ready to connect the Asian game to the rest of the world. The Japanese had just captured Shanghai, but were now plotting domination not just on the Asian continent but in the World Championships as well. The international game would have to pause for the war on the horizon, but Ivor Montagu would become busier than ever. As he closed the tournament in 1938 with talk of peace for the world, Montagu was about to betray his country.

CHAPTER 8 | **Brothers**

When Montagu went up to Cambridge University, he had been happy to overlap with his favourite sibling, the middle brother, Ewen. At home in Townhill, they had conspired together as kids on homemade fireworks and schemes to create a huge autograph collection. They crashed their bicycles into country hedges and set fire to a car engine that singed their eyelashes.

Ewen had a hound named Lancelot. Ivor had a rabbit named Ferocity. Ewen became a handsome, successful barrister, partial to pin-striped suits. Ivor became thicker around the waist and wore a trench coat and an old beret. The MI5 agents, who had now been following Montagu on and off for fifteen years, wrote increasingly offensive descriptions of him. In 1927 he had been described as 'tall, gentlemanly,' a man who moved in 'curious circles.' By 1940, he was described as 'dirty, of distinctly Jewish appearance,' with a 'hooked nose.' In the words of the Hertfordshire constabulary, he was simply that 'particularly unpleasant Communist.'

The two brothers shared a taste for football that the rest of the family found 'common.' Ivor Montagu had felt a kinship to football ever since he heard that a fan in Russia was called a *Bolelchik* or sufferer. At sixteen, he became president of the Southampton FC Supporters' Club with Ewen as his vice president. They brought a megaphone to the home games and used it to taunt the opposing team's chairmen inside the director's box. But there remained deep differences between the brothers. Ewen was a believer in

37

constitutional democracy, while Ivor still wanted to overthrow the King, patron of English table tennis.

No matter how tense relations had become between Ivor and his relatives, Montagu had always depended on Ewen as a diplomatic bridge; the discreet sounding board for just how far his left-wing activities had upset their mother. In 1941, Ivor had rocked the gilded family boat by accusing a fellow peer, the Duke of Hamilton, of being a Nazi sympathiser. The duke brought legal action against Montagu. The families had tried to arrange a sit-down at a gentlemen's club, but Ivor had refused to meet. MI5 followed the lawsuit closely, tapping not only Montagu's phones but also Lady Swaythling's. The suit was eventually settled, and Montagu was forced into a grudging apology, while his own covert work continued at pace.

The two brothers had different problems at the outbreak of war. Ewen was courted by various branches of government, while Ivor was despised by them all. Since Russia and Great Britain were allied, Ivor was an open supporter of the war effort. He submitted an application for the Royal Air Force (RAF), presumably the service chosen for him by the Soviet Embassy.

To his surprise, his application was accepted. He packed his bags and prepared to leave for St Albans, where he would have direct access to an RAF air base considered vital to the Allied war effort. The error was caught at the last moment. A letter was written in the Home Office: 'We have considerable information about this man, dating back to 1926, and it appears most undesired that he could be allowed to serve in HM forces.' Two weeks later, a letter marked SECRET arrived at the Ministry of Labour, requesting the 'permanent suspension of his Calling Up notice.'

Montagu was not wanted. Next, he tried to install himself in his local invasion committee in Bucks Hill, part of the Home Guard preparing for the possibility of a Nazi attack. Again, to his surprise, he managed to become the leader of his Hertfordshire branch.

Letters began to fly at once. A local captain wrote to his major in February, horrified that a man such as Montagu could 'assume the guise of patriotism, when in fact [he was] fully prepared to attack the well being of this country.' Montagu was removed from his post and offered the comically menial job of assistant food organiser of the Bucks Hill Invasion Committee. Montagu turned it down, citing a need to travel frequently to London. He applied regularly to be sent to Moscow to cover the Russian war effort, but his applications were denied.

By 1941, his brother had one of the top jobs in naval intelligence, which he shared with another uniformed member of the British aristocracy, Lord Cholmondeley. Together, the two men sat on the Twenty Committee, chaired by John Cecil Masterman, a novellist and Oxford don. The British liked their pithy jokes: the committee was named after the Roman numerals XX – a double cross. Though it had 'no real formal written agenda,' its purpose was to turn German agents and then run false information back to their intelligence services.

In very different ways, the Montagu brothers were each going to have 'a good war.' Ivor Montagu's work would necessarily go unrewarded; Ewen Montagu and Cholmondeley were to succeed in a staggering way that would eventually be celebrated. Their masterpiece was called Operation Mincemeat. The idea had originally been suggested by James Bond's creator, Ian Fleming, but it was Ewen Montagu and Cholmondeley who turned one brief line of fiction into fact. The goal was to deceive Hitler into believing that the Allied invasion destined for southern Italy would actually be aimed at Greece.

The two men took the body of a Welsh alcoholic and constructed a painstakingly detailed false identity for the corpse. The cadaver was rechristened William Martin of the Royal Marines, and was provided with underpants from a former member of Lloyd George's cabinet, letters to a fiancée written by Ewen Montagu, and 'wallet litter' that included receipts for an engagement ring and a chiding note from his bank manager at Lloyds. Martin was also attached by the wrist to a leather briefcase, which contained operation bulletins, photographs, and, most important, a letter written from one British general to another. If it sounded authentic, that's because Ewen Montagu had requested that it be written by an actual general. It was a rambling mixture of gossip, the mundane aspects of work, and a vital slip – that the entire Allied invasion fleet would be landing in northern Greece, not Italy.

From Ewen Montagu's point of view, the mission was a race against time. Their dead alcoholic had begun to rot. His body was sped across England by a professional race car driver. In Portsmouth it was packed in a metal canister, covered in blocks of ice, and lowered into a submarine that hurried through the Strait of Gibraltar, past layers of Nazi mines, until it reached the coast of Spain. British intelligence knew that one of Hitler's top spies in that country, the wealthy butterfly collector Adolf Claus, was based in the port of Huelva. If the documents ended up in his hands, it was expected that they would move rapidly through the system all the way to Hitler's desk in Berlin.

When the submarine surfaced two miles from the Spanish coast, William Martin was placed into a launch, motored across the Gulf of Cadiz toward Huelva, and tipped into the ocean. The morning tide would bring him to shore. Either he would be found by one of Huelva's fishermen, or the body would be carried back out into the Atlantic on the evening tide and three months of intricate work would be exposed as an expensive folly. Back in London on 15 April, Winston Churchill was talked through the plan and told that the chances of total success remained slim. 'In that case,' he said, 'we shall have to get the body back and give it another swim.'

Ewen Montagu wasn't the only member of the family working for a secretive group named after a Roman numeral. Ewen had no idea that his brother had been contacted by a member of the GRU, the Soviet Army's vast foreign intelligence service. It had originally been sponsored by Montagu's friend Leon Trotsky and was much larger and much more secretive than the NKVD, with a distinct appetite for military intelligence. Ivor had been asked to form the X Group to gather information vital to the British war effort and report to a contact in the Soviet Embassy, Simon Davidovich Kremer, whose official post was secretary to the Soviet Military Attaché in London. Montagu's code name was INTELLIGENTSIA, and soon he had recruited his old friend and socialist sympathiser JBS Haldane, who would be known by the moniker NOBILITY.

The Soviets had at least four groups working out of England that were directed by the GRU. The first was run by a printer, the second by a Polish woman skilled at recruiting RAF officers 'who had access to the newest developments in airplane constructions,' and the third by a concert pianist with connections to the Air Ministry. But it was Montagu's X Group that showed off Russia's understanding of the British class system. From the beginning, the Soviets relished the prospect of 'his influential relatives.'

At first Montagu did not move fast enough for Kremer. By August, Kremer was tired of pressing Montagu for more action and was leaning toward replacing him. 'I have taken the opportunity of pointing out to the X group that we need a man of different calibre and one who is bolder than INTELLIGENTSIA,' he wrote. A month later, Montagu had been detailed to make contact 'with the British Army colonel picked out for work' but had failed to do so. Kremer concluded that 'I have told the X group via NOBILITY to give us someone else because of this. INTELLIGENTSIA lives in the provinces and it is difficult to contact him.'

Despite his slow start, Montagu had an exceptional autumn, supplying details of the damage caused by the Blitz, British defense capabilities, copies of Haldane's confidential reports, and three particularly important pieces of information. Through Montagu, the Russians learned that the British had discovered how to interrupt Luftwaffe radio signals and that British scientists had perfected delayed-action bombs. Most important, INTELLIGENTSIA had explained 'that a girl working in a government establishment noticed in one document that the British had broken some Soviet code or other.' Thanks to Montagu, Kremer knew that the entire Russian intelligence system might have been compromised. He wrote immediately to Moscow, saying that he had told INTELLIGENTSIA that 'this was a matter of exceptional importance and he should put to the group the question of developing this report.' Montagu would, of course, be a beneficiary of his own work. Any effective breakthrough by his brother's friends in British intelligence would mean he'd be arrested for treason.

| **The End of the Game?**

The international table tennis scene may have died out during the war, but the game persisted in every combat zone. One RAF flyer remembered playing in South Africa, Iraq, Egypt, Uganda, Kenya, Southern and Northern Rhodesia, Ceylon, and Burma. Things were harder at home in England. A single poor-quality ball was so rare that it could be traded for a minimum of three fresh eggs. For a good ball, according to one player, 'generations of unborn chickens must mortgage their output.'

Bizarrely, the game also spread thanks to the Geneva Convention. One of the great fears for prisoners was monumental boredom. To combat that, the Red Cross recommended board games and table tennis sets. Their standard package included '24 balls, 4 bats, 2 nets and a pair of posts.'

Perhaps inspired by British intelligence's close study of Montagu, MI9 designed a table tennis set. The bats had hollowed-out handles hiding silk maps and tiny compasses. These would be sent into camps inside what the Germans called 'love parcels,' separate from the Red Cross's efforts. It was hoped they'd go unnoticed in the plethora of Ping-Pong equipment.

Table tennis's survival might have impressed Montagu, but as a source of propaganda it wasn't useful to him during the war. Montagu had by now written extensively for the Communist organ the *Daily Worker*, a declaration of his open involvement with the Communist Party of Great Britain. Most doubted that a graduate of Westminster College or Cambridge University could actually be anything other than a 'drawing room Communist,' dabbling as an intellectual diversion. Still, John Cecil Masterman leaned across the table in the middle of a meeting of the Twenty Committee and asked a confused Ewen 'how the table tennis was coming along.' Ewen Montagu looked up. 'That's my communist younger brother. He's the progenitor of table tennis, not me.'

If this was supposed to be a provocation, outing a pair of Communists, Masterman was disappointed. Ewen Montagu was a straight arrow. His relations with Ivor were fraternal. They would meet for dinner in London, and Ewen would speak affectionately about him in letters to his wife. 'He is simply enormous, almost all tummy.'

Ewen had special permission from naval intelligence to carry confidential documents back and forth from work in a pannier on his bicycle as long as he always wore 'a shoulder holster and an automatic pistol.' It was breezy presumption for a man who had access to the country's top secrets.

Ivor had confided to Ewen that he was 'really bad on this war,' revealing his involvement with the Comintern, but drew the line at confessing that he was now working for the GRU. But what line had Ewen drawn with his brother? If he truly thought of him as a harmless eccentric, had he amused him with the adventures of William Martin? When they were both dining at their mother's house in Kensington Court, where was his briefcase? Besides, Ivor would have rationalised that even though the two men had started the war on different sides, Russia and England were allies from the moment Hitler had driven his panzers onto Russian soil in June 1941.

MI5 took a more serious approach. The amount of information on Ivor Montagu increased, and his file now ran to hundreds of pages. Neighbours and the local constabulary added to the layered information, spying on everyone from his mother to his adopted daughter on her trips to their local pub, the Rose and Crown. Informers reported that Montagu had access to petrol and that his stepdaughter had boasted of being related to Lady Swaythling. At the bar, chatting casually, she'd told locals that Montagu 'got up at all hours of the night' and had a 'hut built in the garden' where he kept a radio and 'makes a lot of expensive calls.'

A letter arguing for a warrant to search the premises was flatly refused. MI5 remained wary of Montagu's connections. The last time they'd obtained a warrant for him, he'd not only become quickly aware of it, but had written directly to the home secretary to have it quashed, leaning on his cousin Herbert Samuel, a former home secretary himself.

The extent of MI5's knowledge of Montagu's home suggests that agents did gain entrance, whether legally or illegally. They knew who entered and left, how his house was decorated, where his telephones were, the books in his library. They knew how many radios he had and when he listened to them and suspiciously noted that he was 'always very keen to listen to the Foreign News, especially at 20.00 [and] midnight.'

Off the coast of Spain, William Martin's body, still strapped to the briefcase, bobbed up and down on the morning tide close to Punta Umbria, a tiny town a short drive from Huelva. A small boat searching for sardines spotted Martin before noon. Its owner called over neighbouring boats, but no one wanted to touch the rotting, blackened body. Eventually, the fisherman managed to drag William Martin aboard and headed back to the coast with the dead man's legs trailing in the water. On the beach, he hauled the body up into the dunes and placed him in the shade of a pine tree.

The British code breakers at Bletchley Park monitored the German lines nervously as Martin's papers moved slowly around Huelva. Finally, the photographed documents were rushed to German High Command in Berlin, the centre of German military intelligence, and found their way to their intended target, Adolf Hitler, possibly the one individual despised in equal measure by both Montagu brothers.

Hitler sided with German intelligence's conclusion that 'the genuineness of the captured documents is above suspicion.' Almost twenty thousand men, a Panzer division, and numerous torpedo boats were redeployed to the Greek coast. When the Allies landed in Sicily, there were fourteen hundred casualties in the first week instead of the expected ten thousand. Ewen Montagu had helped to start a domino effect that would see Italian dictator Benito Mussolini swinging from the end of a rope within three months. As a direct result, Hitler would call off the offensive in Russia. One brother had inadvertently helped the other.

The End of the Game?

The level of information the Russians received on Operation Mincemeat was extraordinary. It might have come through another source, but could Ewen really have withheld the sheer fun of the adventure from his childhood partner in crime, especially when the ruse had fooled Hitler himself? As the end of the war accelerated, thanks to Ivor Montagu and his fellow agents in England, the Russians were well prepared for the coming Cold War because they were incredibly well informed as to British strategies of deception.

CHAPTER 10 | # The Jewish Question

On the south coast of England, the reigning world table tennis champion, Richard Bergmann, stood as one soldier among 160,000 awaiting D-Day. For the last five years he'd sought refuge as a 'friendly alien,' an Austrian Jew who had been taken in by the English Table Tennis Association under Ivor Montagu's direction. To Bergmann's frustration, the association had done little with him, doling out dribs and drabs of money. The world champion had had to work as a waiter and night porter. Finally, Bergmann had been allowed to join the RAF as a physical training instructor, toiling alongside English county cricketers and Scottish hammer-throwers. Bergmann had also qualified as a signals officer, 'directly responsible for giving information to our front line fighters and bombers as to the strength, positions and types of enemy aircraft likely to be encountered during any specific flight.'

On 3 June 1944, amid the chaos of the invasion preparations, Bergmann was lost on the base, looking for the right building to drop off his application for the job of sports officer. Bergmann opened the wrong door. He saw a large room filled top to bottom with shiny white Ping-Pong balls. He closed the door. Then he opened it again to make sure he wasn't hallucinating. Finally he understood why his table tennis supplies during the last five years had been so grudgingly limited. Ping-Pong balls had been produced exclusively for the RAF to pack into the wings of seagoing aircraft as an inexpensive flotation aid.

Bergmann sped across the English Channel in a landing craft less than a day after the beaches of Normandy were stormed. He carried his table tennis equipment in his backpack. He had burned all his own personal papers before leaving England. Should there be a German counterattack, Austrians like Bergmann would 'unceremoniously be shot out of hand.' Bergmann made it to Berlin intact. There he befriended a German photographer who warmed to the Austrian. He told him he had something he must share because it was acting like 'corrosive acid on his mind.' It was a picture the photographer had taken while working for the German Army. 'The snap showed a dump of human corpses with two uniformed German soldiers smilingly posing in front of it. There were thousands of dead bodies piled up in a ghastly heap.' He gave Bergmann the photograph, and the Austrian turned it over to the military. The dump was eventually found five hundred miles away in eastern Poland.

Pre-war table tennis had been the domain of Central European Jews, who were often smuggled into Aryan sporting clubs under pseudonyms. It was no surprise that many would fail to emerge after 1945. Some were simply recorded as lost, but here and there little pieces of information emerged. Mechlovits, whose correspondence with Montagu had so baffled British intelligence, escaped 'twice from transports to the death camps,' once by leaping from a moving train. Adolf Herskovich, a Yugoslav who had played in front of Montagu at World Championships in Baden, London, and Cairo, ended the war in a concentration camp, having watched his brother being beaten by German soldiers and thrown off a cliff. His father and sister died at Auschwitz.

Alex Ehrlich, the player of the longest point in the history of the game, staggered back into the international table tennis arena. At Auschwitz, he'd survived by foraging during work details. Finding a beehive one day, he'd split it in two, stripped, rolled in the honey, dressed, and walked back into the camp to let his fellow prisoners lick precious calories from his body. Still, his body weight halved. He'd been pulled from a gas chamber by a Hungarian guard who'd seen him play Ping-Pong in the 1930s. When Montagu got the World Championships up and running again in 1948, there stood Ehrlich behind the table, his shirtsleeves rolled up and his numbered tattoo visible on his forearm. Ehrlich would make it to another semi-final before he eased into coaching.

Montagu was back to his busiest. His portly bearing, his family, and his warmth continued to divert suspicion. Of course, everyone knew he was a Communist, but gentlemen of the era were forgiven their eccentric interests. He was like an uncle with an extravagant collection of Victorian pornography. Nobody had ever confused him with a traitor.

And yet, as the war ended, his own family seemed to pull away from him. He would see his mother sporadically until her death in 1965. More mysteriously, he and Ewen kept away from each other. Ewen's children, Jennifer and Jeremy, have only two memories of their uncle in the post-war years: first, the two brothers heading off to see their favourite football team play in Southampton; second, the brothers sharing a car at their grandmother's funeral. Few words were spoken.

As Montagu resumed his travels for the sake of the ITTF in countries behind the Iron Curtain, a team of hundreds was working hard at sites in the United States, the United Kingdom, and Australia, trying to unravel the web of Soviet agents that they suspected now covered the West. The programme devoted to putting names to code names was called Venona.

Montagu had no idea that Venona existed. Even presidents Truman and Roosevelt had been kept in the dark. Started in 1943, Venona lassoed enormous amounts of diplomatic intelligence coming in and out of Soviet embassies around the world. By the time the existence of the Venona programme was leaked to the Soviets in 1945, the Americans had already stored thousands of messages. Incriminating evidence about the agent known as INTELLIGENTSIA sat on the desks of dozens of code breakers; the only problem was that they hadn't yet broken the code.

In August 1945, Montagu flew to Nuremberg and covered the war crimes trial for the *Daily Worker*. He was housed in the Faber Schloss, a grand house built with a fortune gathered from manufacturing pencils. It promised steam heating in all rooms, but Montagu worked in his quarters, always accompanied 'by a small blizzard' that swirled through the windows. The table in the Ping-Pong Room was long gone. At least the rooms had running water, though, according to Montagu, it tasted 'as though it's been strained through a bag that someone had been sick in.' Food was provided by the Americans, and Montagu described it as 'invariably a piece of old leather made out of egg powder.' Montagu suffered through his lodgings at the castle, was sick with diarrhoea, and was then marked with a boil on his nose.

As a Jew, Communist, and aristocrat, Montagu had a unique perspective on the Nuremberg Trials. He sat with his fellow journalists and heard the testimony, felt the scorn, shared the incredulity about the Holocaust.

At the trials, Montagu complained that the only thing to drink was Coca-Cola; he developed a loathing of American journalists, especially the women. 'They are worse than raisin bread,' he told his wife. They charmed men Montagu couldn't charm, were told things they shouldn't have heard, and sat in courtroom seats they shouldn't have sat in. It was obvious which side of the Cold War Montagu would take, despite the increasingly anti-Semitic actions of Stalin's government.

Montagu was always the first British journalist to leap to Stalin's defence. Despite the facts that Stalin had emptied his cabinet of Jews after his pact with Hitler and that the top Yiddish writers were all executed on the same night, Montagu held the Moscow line. The religious rigour of his grandfather's will had been utterly rejected. To a true Communist like Montagu, Judaism and Christianity were just another pair of beams holding up the status quo.

Back in England, it occurred to Montagu that the Cold War would be something different altogether. If the cost of open conflict had brought nations to either defeat or Pyrrhic victories, then it was increasingly obvious that 'hot wars' would be avoided. If, however, the wars remained cold, then intelligence work would be important in the silent battle between cultures. That meant that propagandists like Montagu were more vital than ever. Instead of prisoners, Communism would need converts.

In London in the spring of 1946, after he had returned from Nuremberg, Montagu reconvened the ITTF with the intent of reviving the World Table Tennis Championships as soon as possible and lobbied hard to include Russia in the next tournament, since without the participation of the Union of Soviet Socialist Republics

(USSR), 'no international organisation can feel itself to be really world-embracing.'

As Montagu resumed his table tennis travels, he was followed by MI6. The sport was, as ever, confusing to Britain's representatives tailing Montagu. He was the first person who had passed through post-war Vienna with journalistic credentials who had never approached British Public Relations for help with clearances or transport. By the end of the year, MI6 realised that his entire swing through Eastern Europe 'ran smoothly' because Soviet authorities were taking care of him wherever he went. Thanks to Montagu, British intelligence now believed that England's 'table tennis players had been politically influenced by Russian agents.'

This combination of surfing on Soviet hospitality and evangelising must have seemed like a bright red flag. Surely British intelligence would close in on him? But Montagu wasn't the last Soviet spy in England. All the reports from field agents back to MI6 were addressed to HAR Philby, better known as Kim, the most prized of all Russian moles. Philby had been appointed to the same XX Committee that Ewen Montagu had belonged to during the war. The man leading the hounds in the chase for Ivor was another of the Kremlin's foxes.

An entirely new possibility occurred to Ivor Montagu as the forties concluded. Maybe his father's obsession with the Far East *had* left him a fuller legacy than he'd first thought. Why had Montagu not tried to involve himself with Asia? Why limit himself to the continents of Europe and America? He may have gambled with the Film Society and had limited success. But table tennis was still under his control. Perhaps he should be thinking even more broadly than involving the Soviet Union in the game. Perhaps table tennis might play a part in spreading Communism across Asia.

PART TWO | # The East

| # Table Tennis Bandits

When Edgar Snow left the city of Xi'an, in China's Shaanxi Province, in 1936, the young American journalist had to walk for a week across plateaus and through high mountain passes before he reached the Communist Party's revolutionary base in the north. He was chasing one of the scoops of the century – the first interview with the mysterious Mao Zedong. Most of the country was held by Chiang Kai-shek and his Nationalist Party, who were still seen by the Western world as the surest bet to hold China together against her two great problems: domestic strife and a rising Japan. Chiang had dismissed Mao Zedong as a 'bandit leader,' soon to be enveloped by the Nationalist Party.

Chiang's rosy words were belied by his military orders – Mao was a very real concern to him. By the time Snow left Xi'an, Chiang had already mounted a series of extermination campaigns against Mao's Communists. The survivors had walked for thousands of miles across rivers and mountains in the famed Long March. For the moment, they were contained in the mountainous regions near the town of Bao'an, in Shaanxi Province, trying to present their case to the world. They called for a united front to fight the Japanese, but in truth, they, like Chiang, had their eye on the bigger prize: the uncontested rule of China.

Within two years. schoolboys across the Western world would embrace *Red Star Over China*, the sympathetic book Snow would write about his journey to the Communist enclave, taking it as proof that Mao was a serious contender in China's future. For now, Snow was more concerned with staying alive. He had crossed over Chiang Kai-shek's Nationalist lines without permission. Seven thousand miles from his home in Missouri, Snow, who spoke little Mandarin, trudged into the unknown, having been inoculated against smallpox, typhus, cholera, and the bubonic plague.

When Snow finally appeared at the revolutionary camp, he was greeted by a 'heavily bearded' Zhou Enlai. Behind the beard smiled 'a face so striking that it bordered on the beautiful.' By 1936, Zhou Enlai had openly committed himself to sharing the same fate as the leader of the Chinese Communist Party, Mao Zedong. Mao was the philosopher; Zhou Enlai, the ever-active executioner of reality.

Zhou Enlai had been born into a wealthy family. Like Ivor Montagu, he was pushed into the right schools to serve an empire. Like Montagu, he was to butt heads with father figures, learn several languages before his midtwenties, and develop a lifelong love of Ping-Pong. Zhou Enlai was the most emblematic of all the leaders who would soon emerge to rule China – once from greatness, now from nothing, he would both suffer and inflict suffering. He would become a master of compromise for the sake of whatever Mao saw as progress. The numbers of those who would be sacrificed would be extraordinary.

Zhou Enlai had approved Snow's invitation for a reason. As a young man, thirsty for success, Snow could be influenced. The more access he was given, the better. Snow interviewed more than a hundred commanders, soldiers, and workers and was treated to long sessions with both Mao and Zhou Enlai.

Compared to Chiang Kai-shek, the Communists, Snow realised, were operating on a shoestring. With not a single airplane at their command and many more men than rifles, the Communists were desperate to protect their limited equipment. Their great show for the young American seemed like an illusion. At the bleat of a horn, a thousand camouflaged cavalrymen transformed themselves 'into a vast piece of farmland covered with green foliage.'

The revolutionary base that Snow was visiting was both a troop barracks and home to the Red Army University. Students averaged eight years of fighting experience – and three wounds each. It was 'probably the only seat of "higher learning" whose classrooms were bombproof caves, with chairs and desks of stone and brick, and blackboards and walls of limestone and clay.'

As he walked around the camp that first week, Snow noticed that some of the cadets were playing basketball, lawn tennis, and table tennis by the river. The fact that the Communists were dedicated sportsmen wasn't a coincidence. Sport was an essential part of everyday life because it was already enshrined as Communist policy. Mao's very first published essay wasn't about militarism or Marx, it was about *tiyu*, usually translated as 'physical culture' or sport. The stigma of being 'the sick man of Asia' had haunted all of China's youth. The Japanese triumph over the Russians in 1905 had awakened a sense of possibility of what Asia was capable of, but China's pathetic capitulation to the Japanese in Manchuria in 1931 was evidence of their relative weakness. Mao believed that frailty or strength was a choice that began with the self; he was determined to harden his own body, first through hikes and then through swimming.

It's hard to emphasise how revolutionary this idea was, and how localised. That same year, Montagu's friend the poet WH Auden came to China and noticed at once the split in how sport was thought of. In Guangdong he watched the American and British sailors play football on the docks, 'hairy, meat-pink men with powerful buttocks.' They were watched by 'the slender, wasp-waisted' Chinese, who didn't participate. All sports and all combat were for the labouring classes.

Snow moved slowly through the limited Communist-controlled area. One night, he arrived late at a station called Wu Ch'i Chen. There was no time to prepare quarters for the journalist. Instead, he was put up at a Lenin Club – a communal area for meetings or play, in this case a cave with a dirt floor, whitewashed walls looped with colourful paper chains, and a portrait of Vladimir Lenin. He lit the day's last cigarette and unrolled his bedding on a Ping-Pong table, a metaphorical premonition of the future of Sino-American relations. The man and the sport would be two of Mao's most consistent instruments to express his foreign policy intentions, and both would be used constantly up to and including the dramatic moments of 1971.

Wherever Snow went across Communist-controlled China, he

encountered Ping-Pong. It had arrived in Guangdong shortly after reaching Japan. The British set up a tournament between the ports of Macao, Hong Kong, and Guangdong in 1930. In 1935, it had moved farther up the coast, and a Hong Kong team travelled to Shanghai in 1935 to 'take part in an All-China meet.' It had been played in the usual manner in British and German and American clubs, and then leaked out into the wider community. Snow was amazed that the game had reached revolutionary bases in the centre of the country.

'Many people had been amused to hear about the Reds' passion for the English game of table tennis,' he wrote:

> It was bizarre, somehow but every Lenin Club had at its centre a big Ping-Pong table, usually serving double duty as dining table. The Lenin clubs were turned into mess halls at chow time, but there were always four or five 'bandits' armed with bats, balls, and the net, urging the comrades to hurry it up; they wanted to get on with their game. Each company boasted a Ping-Pong champion, and I was no match for them.

Communism insisted that everything was political – art and film, food, talk, and leisure. Even poker was politicised; every card Snow saw was marked with slogans like 'Down with Japanese Imperialism' and 'Down with the Landlords.' Basketball was taken as an obvious symbol of teamwork. Athletics were overtly political – instead of discuses or shot putts, the soldiers hurled ersatz hand grenades. All foot-races were conducted with pack and rifle. By 1936, perhaps it's fair to say that table tennis was about the only thing on a Red Army base that *wasn't* politicised.

Ping-Pong was the one game that everybody played. Zhou Enlai had been an avid rider until, in 1939, he fell from his horse and shattered his right arm. Part of the prescription for his recovery was table tennis. Zhou Enlai would often play against Mao. Even the legendary Zhu De, the beloved founder of the People's Liberation Army (PLA), played 'a good game of table tennis.'

Zhu De was considered Mao's other half. But whereas Mao was a conniver, a balancer of personal ambition, risk, and revolution,

Zhu De was simply adored. In an age when the Chinese country-side was connected more by rumour than radio, Zhu was seemingly superhuman. Chiang Kai-shek had inadvertently stoked the belief, having printed detailed reports of his death on several occasions. By the late 1930s he was said to fly, see for miles, create dust clouds before a battle, and be immune to bullets. A year before Superman first appeared in the States, readers were introduced by Snow to Zhu De. And like Clark Kent, when he was sitting around the revolutionary base in Yan'an, Zhu De could disappear among his troops and pass for a peasant.

Zhu De had once been the great gamble of a poor family – the favoured son of a landholding peasant who had been pushed through the rigours of Mandarin academia at the beginning of the twentieth century with aspirations to gain a post in the bureaucracy of the fading Qing dynasty. Instead, he had been among China's first revolutionaries and had driven his brothers into the army, only to have them both die in their first week in service. The guilt kept him from his parents. Like many of the Communists who'd come to rule China, he'd shipped himself off to Europe in the middle of the 1920s to escape the brutal crackdowns on the Communist Party. For a while, he had wandered through France and Germany, sitting in museums and attending Beethoven concerts with fellow Ping-Pong enthusiast Zhou Enlai.

When Zhu De returned to China to continue the revolution, he was famed for walking without shoes and sharing his horse with his soldiers. The temptation was to think of him as a basic man, an army man, but he impressed his American biographer, Agnes Smedley, as a deep thinker. In the Communist synthesis between politics and all else in life, he was the first to turn his army into an agent of ideology – wherever his soldiers went, they painted slogans on tree trunks, walls, and cliffs. When he captured a town built around its sewing factory, he'd had his men stitch their own uniforms, including the famous red star on their gray cloth caps. They talked Communism, wrote Communism, and wore Communism. The same red star was posted over the entrance to their Lenin Clubs, where the evening discussions took place around the Ping-Pong table.

Snow was to name his book *Red Star Over China*; one of those rare works whose publication did as much for the subject as for the writer. When Snow was in Shanghai, surrounded by the Japanese in 1938, he gave permission for his book to be translated into Chinese. It was printed and sold from under the counter in areas controlled by Chiang Kai-shek with the innocuous title *Random Notes on a Journey into the West*.

Far East scholar Owen Lattimore described *Red Star*'s effect as 'a fireworks display.' Thanks to Snow, thousands of young Chinese were inspired to head off into Communist-controlled areas. He had created the myth of Mao that Mao would build on: Mao the glorious freedom fighter, eager to drive the Japanese from China, champion of the poor. It was a myth that would take decades to unwind.

Snow's book was read very closely. Those aspiring revolutionaries who decided to make the trek to Communist-controlled areas were taking an enormous risk. Entire families had been executed on suspicion of Communism. Zhu De's wife was beheaded and her head mounted on a pole in Changsha. Mao's own wife and his eldest son were both shot for aiding Communist agents. But what made a good Communist, according to Snow? Suffering, thought, self-restraint. And was there joy to be had? Yes, in comradeship. Communists weren't all solemn. Snow had written of Zhou Enlai dancing and Zhu De playing basketball and table tennis. If table tennis was good enough for Mao, good enough for Zhou Enlai, then it would be good enough for the thousands of youths slowly making their way to the Communist outposts in central China.

Red Star Over China became a huge seller in London; published by the same house as Ivor Montagu's works, it required five reprints in the first month. There followed a string of intrepid foreign journalists, often women, in search of Mao and his Red Army. Among them was Ilona Sues, a Polish-American who was originally in China as Madame Chiang Kai-shek's press secretary during the brief period of the United Front, when Mao's Communists and Chiang's Nationalists were supposedly working together to defeat the Japanese.

One day, to her surprise, she was introduced over lunch to Peng Dehuai, soon to be Mao's minister of defence. By the end of the meal, she had decided to make a 'friendship expedition' to the Communists' Eighth Route Army. Could she bring anything with her that was needed? The Communist Party's chief military strategist asked for paper for their schools, flashlights, batteries, toothbrushes, and toothpaste. 'Any candy?' she offered. 'Cigarettes?' Peng shook his head disapprovingly at these frivolous suggestions. 'No, but if you would bring some Ping-Pong balls, there would be no end of joy.'

Snow's book flourished again a decade later, when Mao declared the birth of the People's Republic of China on 1 October 1949. Japan had withdrawn all troops in the glare of 1945's blinding obliteration of Hiroshima and Nagasaki. The fighting against Chiang Kai-shek's rearguard lingered well into 1950, even after he had retreated to Taiwan.

Ivor Montagu had followed 'the China question' from afar for decades. In August 1937, he had been asked by the Comintern to hold a conference in support of Chinese unification against Japan. But despite his travels, Montagu had never been to the Far East. It was yet another division within the Montagu household.

His mother, who had visited Japan in 1927 and again in 1931, had several letters published by the *Times* in defence of Japan's occupation of China. She strongly objected to journalists using the word 'atrocities' because the numerous Chinese victims of a massacre in Shanghai had included many who 'were soldiers in disguise.' She had pleaded for the British public to pity the Japanese soldiers who had been killed in the Chinese countryside. But she never questioned what the Japanese were doing inside Chinese borders in the first place.

On New Year's Day in 1950, when Londoners were waking up to one more year of drizzle and ration cards, Ivor Montagu sat down to write a letter to the founder of the Red Army, Zhu De, who had been honorary chairman of the Sports Society when Edgar Snow visited. The People's Republic of China was twelve weeks old, and Montagu was determined to build the first cultural bridge between China and international sport.

In 1935 Ping-Pong had ranked twelfth in a list of potential national sports for China, behind jump rope and just ahead of home construction. Basketball was the clear favourite, followed by football. Montagu's timing was exceptional. Preparatory meetings for a nationwide Sports Commission were already under way. 'China must have her own athletes,' said Zhou Enlai to General He Long, who would head the new Ministry of Sports and Physical

Culture. 'Modern technology requires physical fitness.' Ten-minute gymnastic breaks twice a day were ordered for government offices, schools, and factories.

What the Chinese really needed was something that 'would identify sport with the workplace.' It was the same dream Montagu had already had for table tennis, one of the few sports you could play without ever leaving the factory. Ping-Pong was perfect. The celluloid balls were so light that they flew best in windowless rooms without the slightest breath of air. But would the Chinese share his dream?

| # The Trojan Dove

Until the 1950s, Ping-Pong play had been driven forward by idio-syncratic individuals, obsessives with personal plans for world dom-ination. In the background had always been Ivor Montagu, nursing and directing the sport. In 1945, Churchill announced the existence of the Iron Curtain, and in 1950, Montagu held the first World Table Tennis Championships behind that curtain. Montagu's general sec-retary at the ITTF, Roy Evans, innocently wrote that such access 'was regarded with amazement . . . we seem to have been very much in the lead in the countries where Russian influence is supreme.'

Montagu pushed his sport across the globe. His was the first international organisation to let an African and an Asian city host (Cairo in 1939 and Tokyo in 1956). Under Montagu's 'benevolent monarchy' table tennis had the full attention of a government, and not a Western democratic government shackled by institutions of checks and balances. The People's Republic of China (PRC) was top-down Communism, pushing a Soviet template onto China's recent past. Such money, labour, and dedication poured into a small sport have never been equalled.

At first, China behaved like their fellow Communists, who saw sport as politics by other means, distracted by all the variety of options. The East Germans were engineering athletes to compete in every Olympic competition. The Soviet Union was aiming to con-front America in basketball, ice hockey, and track and field. China would look at speed skating, gymnastics, football, swimming, and volleyball. But they would soon come to concentrate very deliberately on the 'little-ball sports,' and the little-ball sport that other Asians were having success with was obviously Ping-Pong.

American diplomats were concerned with the termite theory, a cousin of the domino theory that would draw them into Vietnam: if you didn't keep the termites out of the Western world's institutions, such as the United Nations, they would infiltrate and render them useless. Thanks to Montagu, table tennis was such an unlikely avenue for China's arrival on the international political stage that even in the 1970s, after the rapprochement through Ping-Pong, the extent of its role still wasn't recognised.

The initial outreach to China was made entirely on Montagu's own initiative. He wouldn't confess his overtures to his fellow ITTF members for a full year, until the minutes from a session in Vienna in 1951 revealed that 'correspondence had taken place with China.'

Montagu was eager to bend the rules, if not to break them outright, in order to make the ITTF the first international sporting organisation to welcome Communist China into the fold. He wanted Chinese players in Bombay for the 1952 World Championships, and even after the deadline for application had long since passed, wrote to say that he was open to considering their first letter to him as a fully formed membership application.

To Montagu, it was confusing. Why were the Chinese lagging in accepting his invitation? It was hard to believe that the Chinese, momentarily in lockstep with Soviet Russia, would not have had multiple assurances of Montagu's Communist credentials. The reason had more in common with Groucho Marx than Karl: the Chinese were worried about becoming a member of the one club that actually wanted them. One of the issues was their own skill level. If they simply appeared at a World Championships and were thrashed on the table by the likes of the United States and Great Britain, then how would that reflect on the glory of New China?

Montagu didn't understand that the Chinese were thinking very seriously of table tennis as a possibility to show themselves to the world at their best. According to Sun Tzu, the only battles that should be fought are those that will be won. The desire to participate had to be balanced with the old Chinese adage that 'family shame should not be made known to outsiders.' If they were going to finish last, it would be better to wait before participating. Bombay was passed by, but Japan's taste of victory in the World Championships there was noted with extreme interest.

Montagu and the top ranks of China's Central Committee, all graduates of the now-dissolved Comintern, were well aware of how to send signals publicly to those you wished to deal with privately. In 1951, Montagu sat down to write a long pamphlet published as *East West Sports Relations*.

Montagu presented his true offer to the Chinese. 'Sports relations are well worthwhile in the interests of peace. They constitute an activity which in itself implies friendship and understanding, and above all, they penetrate the barrier to intercourse between nations which those interested in worsening relations seek to maintain.' The tacit message was that table tennis would be a perfect instrument of Communist propaganda, the human face to give Beijing the appearance of warmth no matter how cold or calculating the Chinese government intended to be.

It seemed as if the argument was made, but Montagu closed his pamphlet on the worst possible note. For all his reading on China, he was yet to understand the depth of China's obsession with regaining Taiwan. But Montagu reminded his readers that you didn't need to be a nation to be a member of his organisation. 'Any *de facto* sports body administering a given territory may be accepted and . . . further, where there are more than one such in any country, both must be accepted if they apply.'

To China, this was an outrage. The whole point of its stance, in both sport and politics, was to prove how ridiculous it was that Taiwan should ever be allowed to represent China. In Montagu's version, there was room for both Taiwan and China. To Mao Zedong there was only one China. Taiwan was merely a missing province that would one day click back into place.

The issue for Montagu, and soon enough for Nixon and Kissinger, was what to do about Chiang Kai-shek, ensconced on the island of Taiwan, who stubbornly continued to insist that he represented the mainland despite having been driven from its shores. The international perspective was divided neatly on political lines. The Americans acknowledged Chiang Kai-shek, while Moscow and the Communist Bloc recognised Red China.

Regardless of his false step, Montagu received a visa to travel to China within months of publishing *East West Sports Relations*, even though the Korean War still raged on China's borders. Ostensibly, Montagu was travelling as the British representative of the World Peace Council, a Communist front that attracted a large following in the West.

Montagu had already embroiled himself in the war's propaganda, a move that must have been appreciated by the PRC. The Chinese and North Koreans had accused the United States of conducting germ warfare on Korean battlefields. The outraged *Daily Worker* insisted that one village in the northeast of China 'woke up to find themselves surrounded by large numbers of small rat-like animals called voles' that were suffering from the plague. Eagle-eyed witnesses had seen 'eighteen types of insects' released from American warplanes. Both the International Red Cross and the World Health Organisation dismissed all accusations against the United States, but Montagu was handed samples of these voles and insects at the World Peace Council in Prague and presented them to his old stomping ground, the British Museum. The vole, the museum finally reported, wasn't native to Manchuria. It turned out it was Russian – perhaps a not-so-distant cousin of the voles Montagu had carried back dead from the Caucasus thirty years before. The possibility that the Soviets had provided Russian voles weakened, rather than strengthened, the North Korean case.

Montagu's 1952 visit to China was timed for 1 October, the PRC's third birthday. Buildings in central Beijing were shrouded in bright red banners, and Montagu and some of his fellow delegates were ushered into the VIP section on top of Tiananmen Gate to stand near Mao and Zhou Enlai and the party's Central Committee. The World Peace Council wasn't always so welcome around the world, suspected of being a 'Trojan Dove' where the word 'Peace' was a veneer for 'Communist.' But here in Beijing, council representatives were able to listen to 'the thunder of tanks, guns and bomber aircraft,' a reminder of the Korean War. At night, lanterns illuminated the political slogans that seemed to cover the capital, and fireworks crackled from one side of Beijing to the other.

Montagu had been speaking ceaselessly across England and Europe before his trip to China, but often to drab little gatherings of thirty or forty people, like a provincial book tour. Now the speakers were treated to the biggest crowds of their life: fifty thousand people gathered 'under the golden roof of the Imperial Palace,' all chanting 'Long Live Peace! Long Live Peace!' Montagu heard that 'unemployment has been abolished. . . . Most of the 20 million former idle landlords have land and serve as an additional new labour force.'

Nothing but peace and plenty was reported about New China for ten solid days. Meals were 'as sure as the sunrise.' Back in England, the *Economist* took a more mordant view: 'One would like to hear Mr Ivor Montagu, who has been representing the "World Peace Council" . . . construe the Chinese poem specially composed and circulated for the anniversary, and which contains the interesting line: "We love peace, and smash all our enemies into pieces."'

What the Chinese Communists really wanted from Montagu was advice – not about peace but about Ping-Pong. Montagu was invited to take a short trip to the outskirts of Beijing on 12 October. He would have been impressed by the crowd of seven thousand gathered to watch the All China Table Tennis Championships. During the opening ceremony, the teams, divided by province, paraded before Montagu wearing their various colours. Montagu rose to address the crowd and talked of the possibility of success for China in table tennis, noting 'the exploits of Hong Kong players in Bombay' earlier that year. He concluded his talk with the hope that China would soon be competing with the rest of the world.

Then Montagu sat in the VIP section and watched the best table tennis players in China compete. His report was simple and depressing: 'They weren't much good.' It was what the Chinese had feared; in the usual pattern of twentieth-century Asia, the Japanese had got the jump on them. That year, out of the blue, a Japanese man had just become the first Asian to win the World Championships. It was accepted by the Chinese with a mixture of jealousy and encouragement. If the Japanese could achieve victories in war and now in table tennis, then why couldn't China, fighting the US to a stalemate in Korea, also triumph in sport?

Ivor Montagu preferred the presence of politics in Ping-Pong to be subtle, but the Chinese didn't agree. Instead, the ITTF was one of their earliest forums to lay down the law that they would soon pursue in more formal circumstances around the world. Yan Fumin, in the capacity of China's first ITTF representative, made a solemn statement at the 1953 meeting in Bucharest that the Chinese Table Tennis Association was a national organisation, not a regional one.

This was not a hair-splitting moment in a minor organisation. It presaged the thinking that would dog all countries' interactions with China. Taiwan was the intricate knot that would recur during Ping-Pong diplomacy in 1971. Kissinger and Nixon wouldn't unwind it all at once, but loosen the strings and pass it to the future. Montagu was too wily not to accede to Chinese wishes. After all, this was the dream come true; in a way, he had been thinking too small, trying to nudge Russia into taking table tennis seriously. China was three times the size and wasn't going to drag its feet. Montagu, always thinking like an idealist, always acting like a cynic, acceded from the beginning to Chinese demands. Taiwan would be kept at bay for decades to come. They had every right to join, Montagu would tell the Taiwanese, but only if they accepted the name 'Taiwan Province of the People's Republic of China.' The strategy had been dictated directly to him by Zhou Enlai.

The Chinese knew very well the size of the favour Montagu had done them. 'This was,' said an official, 'a historical opportunity for us. . . . Mr Montagu was a very open minded person.' Open-minded and also an undoubtedly strange man in Chinese eyes. Who else would have insisted on rowing into the middle of the Summer Palace's lake in 1952, then stripping to swim in four feet of murky water? He was followed so closely by solicitous security that 'after twenty yards I gave in miserably and have never had the heart, or the unkindness, to repeat the experiment.'

| # The Rise of Asia

The table tennis table at Tokyo's Tenth High School gym had survived the bombing. There was a hole in the roof, the windows were boarded up, and every morning the table would be covered in a thin layer of white dust blown in through the cracks by passing American jeeps, the rumbling reminders of the lost war. In 1949 the gym was tended to by Ichiro Ogimura, one of the smallest students in the school, who swept it clean every recess. Ogi, as Ogimura would be known for the rest of his life, had no interest in politics for the moment. At seventeen, he cared only for table tennis. He was slowly becoming one of those obsessives whose preoccupation and drive were so intense that they could change the world around them. They pushed against the limits of their current situations and craved change, until, in a flash, it arrived. Ogi's progress would be watched quietly but intently by the highest levels of Chinese government, now trying to build a new foundation for the world's most populous nation. In the long run, it would afford Ogi a unique view of how China worked and become the basis of a friendship between Ogi and China's new premier, Zhou Enlai.

At the end of the war, Ogi was just a spindly, wide-eyed student. He had a good reputation as a baseball pitcher in middle school but he knew he wasn't going to grow much more, and only the taller boys were encouraged to keep playing in high school. If he couldn't be a professional, then what was the point? Instead, he calculated that the new world, dug out of Hiroshima ash, would be one where there would be a time for sport and that table tennis was fated to rise in Asia. It was a large leap of logic to make. He was part of a small group that had petitioned the school principal for a new table tennis table. 'This is a boy's school,' said the principal. 'Table tennis is for girls.'

The sport had arrived in Asia via Japan in 1902, part of that first wave of unregulated Ping-Pong enthusiasm that had emanated from England. A university student had returned to Tokyo from Europe with three Ping-Pong sets. Within a year, at Japan's Fifth National Industrial Exhibition, a sport store showed Ping-Pong equipment that had been manufactured locally. The game grew up in a vacuum. Since there were still no written rules to follow, the Japanese muddled along, playing on a much smaller table and with a lower net than Europeans. As ever, Montagu had a hand in the change, packing his rule book in his parents' cases on their trip to Tokyo in 1927 so that the Japanese could begin to move in step with the international body.

Until the Japanese joined Montagu's ITTF in 1929, there were no prizes for winning tournaments in Japan. Instead, the 'names of the winners are inscribed on a window in the shrine of Emperor Meiji.' There was never a charge to attend a game in Japan, and there was no entrance fee for players. The Ministry of Education paid all expenses. That seemed to lessen its acceptability. As in Europe, it began its life generally disdained. Through sheer persistence, Ogi and his small group of school-mates finally persuaded their principal to buy the table.

They had an unlikely ally in their quest for the acceptance of Ping-Pong: General Douglas MacArthur. He agreed to lend his name to 'The MacArthur Cup' for table tennis in 1947. Out of gratitude, the players drew brightly painted pictures of the general on one side of their paddles instead of the customary wrestlers and glamour girls. Across the sea in China, the American general would soon be known as Mac the Devil and Mac the Madman, thirsting for Asian blood.

The school's new table tennis table was well loved. Ogi and his class-mates heard that polishing the table with the soles of sneakers made the ball bounce better. They bought a bottle of amyl acetate so they could seal the tiny cracks in Ping-Pong balls. Ogi kept a diary, noting the scores of every match he ever played, even in practice. At

the bottom, he wrote, 'You're going to be a genius among geniuses.'
He had lived through Japan's occupation of Manchuria, the expansion of war, air raids, nuclear attack, surrender, and occupation.
'Sport,' he wrote, 'was a kind of salvation.'

In the fall of 1950, a year after Montagu had re-admitted Japan into the ITTF, Ogi found his way to a new table tennis hall that opened in Tokyo, close to the Musashino Hachimangu shrine, where tattoo-covered gangsters would come to dance at festivals. Salarymen stopped by the cypress-wood hall at the end of the day before commuting home. They played beside greengrocers and railwaymen, doctors and schoolchildren. It was part of the classless ambience of which Montagu was still dreaming, though the only place such men were equals in Tokyo was within the club.

Ogi's father had died when he was two. His mother baked bread that he helped sell outside the station at Mikita. He kept some in his pocket and ate as he played. When Ogi paused midgame to pop the bread in his mouth, he didn't chew, but savoured it as he played, like Charlie nibbling at his candy bar long before he enters the chocolate factory. By the time he was eighteen, Ogi was ranked only sixth in Tokyo, which he saw as a severe disappointment. His mother worried constantly about him; she had wanted him to be a diplomat. He only wanted to play table tennis. Eventually, thanks to China, he would become both.

Ogi remained obsessed with becoming the world's best. He had even figured out a way to overcome his natural physical weakness, which he explained to a friend during a brief bout with pneumonia. 'Apparently, all the cells in the human body are replaced with new ones after ten years. Someone who's born strong might have an advantage to start with, but we're all responsible for what our bodies are like in ten years' time.'

Ogi brought a new standard of devotion to the world of Ping-Pong. He ran for an hour each morning, carrying in his right hand a stone he reckoned was the same weight as a table tennis racquet. He jumped from the squatting position for a kilometre and then hit a ball against a wall from five feet. He skipped rope, lifted dumbbells. He went to billiard parlours to study spin. A friend called his self-imposed routine 'torturous . . . terrifying.' Everywhere he went, he carried with him *The Book of Five Rings*, a book on strategy written by Japan's master swordsman. In his mind, he translated the work into table tennis.

Nineteen fifty-two was a year of liberation for Japan. In September, the government signed the San Francisco Peace Treaty, and the American Occupation was over. Almost simultaneously, the worst player in Japan's national table tennis team won the World Championship in Bombay. Ogi watched two players in action, one a symbol of the future and one the past.

Twenty-eight-year-old Hiroji Satoh couldn't have had a shorter moment of fame. For two weeks he was unbeatable; for the rest of the year he barely won a game and then retired from the sport. Satoh looked like a caricature of the salarymen who epitomised Japan's rapid rise in the post-war world. Thin, pale, bucktoothed, and wearing thick black glasses, he wandered the halls of the Bombay Sports Arena staring at the floor, carrying his sacred wooden case.

What was so special, it turned out, wasn't Satoh's speed, strength, or agility, but his racquet. At every game, Satoh would walk onto the court, bow to the audience, place the case down on the table, remove the bat, and humble the best players in the world. The game had been named Ping-Pong for the simple onomatopoeia, but sound was also a way for good players to read the game; you could hear the kind of shot your opponent was making – the sharp crack of a slam, the deeper whoosh of a sliced return. But Satoh had covered his paddle in extremely thick sponge; his shots were silent. Whatever spin his opponent hit at him was multiplied by the sponge and returned. Though Satoh was accused of foul play throughout the tournament, Montagu pointed to the rule book. There were no limitations as to what paddles players could use. You could play with a shoe or your own glasses for all Montagu cared.

Early in the tournament, Satoh came up against the ageing world champion, Richard Bergmann. Unnerved by Satoh's cushioned paddle, Bergmann lost and stormed off the court. In the quarter-finals, it was New York native Marty Reisman's turn to face Satoh. Wearing a pair of sneakers borrowed from Montagu, Reisman soon suffered the same fate as Bergmann. He described the new sponge racquet as a form of silent catapult, absorbing all the energy of the opponent without any sound at all and converting, even increasing the opponent's spin on the way back. 'It hit my racquet in a new way and came off the racquet in a new way.' The loss burned so deeply in Reisman's mind that while the rest of the table tennis world slowly adopted the Asian addiction to sponge, he continued to play with the same hard bat until his death sixty years later, like a sixteenth-century archer who detested the smell of gunpowder.

Satoh's entirely defensive game captured the world title. For a country still reeling from World War II, it was heady stuff. The unmanly game of table tennis was suddenly a way to prove Japan's internationalism and innovation.

Japan swept both the men's and women's titles. Ogi knew that the country's past and its resilience were personified by one of the women's gold medalists, twenty-four-year-old Shizuka Narahara from Hiroshima, a tiny woman five feet tall and weighing ninety-nine pounds.

On 6 August 1945, Narahara had packed her schoolbag and walked to Hiroshima Station. A tram was about to leave, but it was packed. She decided to ride the tram by hanging from the outside. As a freshman at a new high school, she didn't want to be late. Five minutes later, she stepped off the tram, 'when suddenly everything was lit up by a strange greenish flash. Then the houses began to fall around me.'

That was Little Boy, the first uranium-based atomic bomb, dropped from 27,000 feet at the cost of around 100,000 lives. The Hiroshima Station, which Narahara had just left, was levelled; hundreds died inside. But Narahara was doubly lucky. First, she was facing away from the blast. Second, despite wearing the dark school uniform, she'd chosen white underclothes, which almost completely protected her from burns. Her only injuries were on her right arm and the back of her neck. With her 'bullet like forehand' and an understandable absence of fear, she crushed the competition in Bombay.

Later that year, Ogi attended his first All-Japan Championship. He had never faced off against his country's finest, and they had little idea of what to expect from the boy so poor that he travelled with a book of rice ration coupons at the bottom of his bag. Ogi won the tournament against members of the world's best team. He celebrated by drinking his first beer. The dour young man broke into a wide grin and he knew it would last as long as he kept winning.

| Tiny Tornadoes

The Japanese hadn't participated in the 1953 World Championships in Bucharest because their government had refused to let the team travel behind the Iron Curtain. Ogi ramped up his training regime. Now, instead of doing frog jumps for a kilometre, he hopped for four kilometres while carrying a forty-kilogramme dumbbell on his shoulders. He learned to twist his torso so far backward that when he unleashed the bat at the ball, it carried all the momentum possible. But it was financing, not fitness, that was his largest hurdle. A ticket to London cost over a thousand dollars. A salaryman's annual wage in 1953 was $280. The Japanese Table Tennis Association was asking each player to contribute $2,200 to their total expenses, an extraordinary sum for most, and all the more so for Ogi, a mere university student.

He collected it the hard way, cent by cent over three arduous months. Side by side with friends, he begged on the streets of Tokyo for money to send 'Ogimura to London.' Ogimura? They asked. Who's that? He'd explain that *he* was Ogimura, that he was representing the country, that they could win back a title that they hadn't been allowed to defend. Collections dripped in from staff at his university, distant relatives, the College of Art, mayors of local districts. He played matches for donations and spent rush hours soliciting at train stations until he finally had enough for his expenses.

The arduous training regime made him manic. He put a fountain pen lid on the corner of a table and served at it until he could knock it down a hundred times in a row. When he missed, he started again. Then he tried the exercise blindfolded. Before he left for England, he bought a large wrapping cloth from a department store. Ogi was thinking ahead; it was to protect the trophy that Montagu was going to give him.

In 1954, the London that Ogi arrived in did not fit Montagu's utopian vision of brotherhood among all men. It was the bombed-out capital of a country that had won a world war only to realise that its empire was never coming back. There were no economic miracles happening in England; only in Germany and Japan.

Six years of war had been measured in half a million British dead. The only comfort was that the sacrifices had been worth something – an emotion reinforced in hundreds of books and films that regurgitated and reinterpreted the heroism of the war years. High on the list of themes was British stoicism in the face of Japanese cruelty. Stories of British prisoners of war suffering at the hands of Japanese officers during the building of the Burmese Railway had leaked out from the survivors. Six and a half thousand British prisoners had been worked to death laying tracks in the jungle. Ogi arrived in London the same year that the bestseller *Bridge on the River Kwai* was released, rekindling a deep anger against the Japanese.

Ogi was warned. Before he left, he practised his smile. It was a grin, it was a mask of his uncertainty. He was the only member of his squad who was fluent in English, which he had picked up from American schoolkids in Tokyo, then honed when he was allowed to audit a class for translators. He was not only Japan's best shot as champion; he was also its de facto interpreter, the mouthpiece of a nation. On his first day in London, he walked through streets wearing his blazer marked by a Japanese flag. At the first restaurant that Ogi walked into, every customer rose and left. A mother dragged her child away from a full bowl of soup. He watched the steam rise over the empty table. He walked into a barbershop but the barber refused to cut his hair.

The few Japanese in Britain had a simple tactic: they pretended to be Chinese. When Ogi first walked out into the hall in Wembley in front of eight thousand people, it was to a chorus of boos. The British papers couldn't bring themselves to report evenhandedly on the Japanese team. They were accused of snacking on charcoal (it was actually dried seaweed), alleged to be taking drugs, and called Nips, Japs, and Slants. British umpires docked them points when they spoke in Japanese. Their progress was attributed to their 'atomic effort.' During one game, play was halted for forty minutes after a fan pulled out a starter gun and fired, making a Japanese player miss an easy slam.

Ogi tried to concentrate on executing his new strategy, the '51 per cent doctrine.' Instead of heeding his own coaches, who wanted him to probe the opposition for weakness before smashing, Ogi reasoned that every opportunity should be smashed – if you won only 51 per cent of those points, you still won the game. Otherwise a player was waiting for select opportunities that might never arrive. In one of their first matchups, Ogi led the Japanese to victory over the favourites, Hungary. The British press began to soften their tone, though the metaphors they reached for still had a touch of militarism about them. These 'tiny tornadoes' from Japan had 'killer technique.'

Next up was the English team, backed by a fervent crowd and a message of support from Her Majesty the Queen. Ogi beat England's number one in front of a crowd that grew increasingly silent. At the very end of the game, after it was obvious the Japanese would be victorious, the eight thousand sat in absolute silence. Ogi could hear the soft thwack of his sponge paddle as he drove the ball past a former world champion. The newspapers continued their barbed admiration. The 'brainy, superbly fit, ruthlessly efficient terrors of the table' had prevailed. Having won the team event, Ogi made short work of the men's singles.

Ogi stood high on the podium, then bowed to accept the men's trophy. Hell, Ivor Montagu's wife, approached him with the St Bride's Vase, and the cloth caps of London finally broke into applause. Ogi's manager reached into his bag for a Japanese flag for the victor to wave, but Ogi signalled for it to be put away. The diplomat was emerging. He smiled widely as the 'battery of photographers popped flash-bulbs in his eyes.' The *Times* at least appreciated the gesture: 'Let's not regard them with contempt.'

The Japanese would enjoy a victory tour through Europe, never losing a game. Back home, the media wryly wrote that each win came 'much to the astonishment of those who still think that Japan's national sports are cherry-blossom viewing and hara-kiri.'

The crowd that greeted the Japanese team back in Tokyo was the largest the new airport had hosted. Table tennis was no longer a game for girls. Ogimura was celebrated as one of 'the genuine national heroes of post-war Japan.' There was a parade in an open-top car, tours of the country, countless magazine features, thousands of autographs for him to sign. The penniless obsessive had forced a new sport on his 70 million countrymen. Three million registered as players by the end of the year.

The next World Championships, in Holland, were equally difficult for the Japanese. Every day their embassy's flag was pelted with eggs and ketchup. Rocks sailed over the walls. The British weren't the only POWs who had suffered in the Pacific arena. Ogi heard a man hiss at him, 'I'm glad you Japanese were bombed.' His team was booed throughout the tournament, until a game when one of Ogi's team-mates was playing against a one-armed Hungarian. Trying to retrieve a shot near the Japanese bench, the Hungarian stumbled and began to fall. Ogi and his doubles partner managed to break the player's fall and help him back to his feet. Instead of boos, a slow applause gathered.

The next day, for the first time all week, the embassy's flag was free of eggs. On their return to Japan, the prime minister congratulated the team that had 'ended the stone throwing overnight.' If the change in attitude was being watched by the Japanese government, it was also being noted by the Chinese. There was something to Ping-Pong, a strange tone of diplomacy that was allowing the Japanese to reposition the way the rest of the world was looking at them. Of course, no one would have been looking too hard had they not won.

Ogimura's victory was undoubtedly one of grit and ability. Ogi, to graduate from college, produced a short film called *Japanese Table Tennis*. One of the first purchasers of the film, unknown to Ogi at the time, was the Chinese government.

The World Championships of 1956 were in Tokyo. Montagu visited his father's favourite country and wrote that table tennis was a 'contribution of all of us to universal friendship through sport and so, in however modest a degree, to peace among all without exception.' A crowd of ten thousand jammed the stadium. Japanese domination of the sport was now so thorough that all four men's semi-finalists were local. Ogimura managed to keep three gold medals from leaving the country: the men's singles, the mixed doubles, and the Swaythling Cup for the team. The Japanese won the women's singles as well. As the finals ended, the happy 'hysterical crowd' knocked down the partitions between the courts and nearly tore the women's champion 'limb from glistening limb.'

Montagu stopped by the Chinese squad, giving them badges from England. The Chinese team had been watching the Japanese closely. The lesson was obvious. Victory had lent credibility to the claim that table tennis was a 'potent symbol of the country's postwar reconstruction.'

CHAPTER 15 | Reconnaissance

In 1930s China, the murderous tides created by the civil war and the Japanese occupation were strong enough to affect life in the four corners of the nation. Misfortune followed the family of Rong Guotuan, no matter how many times they fled their home in southern China. The tiny town of Zhuhai sat on the far side of the Pearl River Estuary. It was only twenty-five miles from British-controlled Hong Kong.

Hong Kong was a desperate choice for many Cantonese. The need for kowtowing and acceptance of second-class citizenship in return for a family's survival was galling, but it was better than the world of warlords and banditry that had emerged after the collapse of the Chinese Empire in 1911. By 1937, when Rong Guotuan was born, his father had secured a job in Hong Kong working for the British bank of Standard Chartered, a domain of suits and marble vaults. The Rong family's stability shattered when the Japanese seized Hong Kong in 1941, and Rong's father chose to move his family back to his hometown of Zhuhai.

He never recovered his position in the bank after the war. Instead, he tumbled down the social classes until he hit the deck as a cook on a Hong Kong port steamer. One of the few perks was enrollment in the local fisherman's union, which had a clubhouse just big enough to house a small library and a battered Ping-Pong table.

Rong wasn't the healthiest of children. Until the end of his life, he had the look of a quickly constructed scarecrow, a tall, wide-eyed boy with a long face, bony arms, and knock-knees. He found a job with a local fishmonger, but only because 'the fishmonger was operating a table tennis club for gambling purposes and needed an employee who could play for him.' As an eighteen-year-old, just when he should have been developing physically, Rong came down with tuberculosis of the lungs, a common enough disease in the poorer quarters of Hong Kong.

In April 1957, now recovered, Rong was playing for the Hong Kong team when the reigning world champion, Ogimura, arrived for a brief tour of the island. To Rong's own surprise, he beat Ogimura two–zero. When he went back into the locker room, his best friend walked beside him. The friend, Steven Cheung, expected members of the press to pour through the door to interview Rong, but to their mutual embarrassment, there was no interview.

For a moment Rong allowed himself to dream. If he really was as good as Ogimura, then couldn't he win a world championship? Wouldn't that at least bring coaching jobs and sponsorship deals? Ogimura had coached briefly in Sweden and had been well paid. Perhaps a living could be made in table tennis?

Within weeks, Rong found himself part of an all-Chinese Hong Kong squad invited to tour Beijing. Rong shone again, beating all the players the Chinese threw against him. He was issued a strange invitation. Would he have lunch with two of the most important men in China?

It's hard to describe the discrepancy between the Hong Kong guest and his Chinese hosts. The two were marshals, the highest rank established by Mao in 1955 when, 'in a solemn ceremony,' the Great Helmsman had covered the chests of his favoured generals in medals. It was considered a just reward, since they were survivors of the Long March and the top strategists of the civil war. In a nation of 800 million, Rong was being treated to lunch by two of the ten most important men in the country. Why such interest in a tubercular Ping-Pong player?

At the time, Rong's first host, Chen Yi, was not only a marshal but also the country's vice premier and its foreign minister. He'd commanded the Communists during 1948's vast Huaihai campaign, which was credited with breaking the back of Chiang Kai-shek's army, and was in charge of over a million soldiers and militiamen. Alongside Zhou Enlai, he had exiled himself to France in the 1920s to escape Chiang's purge of the Communist Party. He had come a long way from his days as a Parisian dishwasher, a stevedore at the Seine quays, and a worker at a Michelin tire factory. Addicted to strategy in all parts of his life, he may have been a fan of table tennis, but his true passion was Go, the form of Chinese chess where an enemy is never killed, only encircled.

His fellow marshal at the dinner, He Long, was Chen Yi's fellow vice premier. One of the legends of the revolution, He Long had been put in charge of the National Sports Commission. It was another sign of how seriously the Communists were taking their sport, as if General Eisenhower had been asked to run the National Football League or Field Marshal Montgomery were managing the English cricket team.

He Long's political development had come slowly. He had been considered a part-time Robin Hood in the early 1920s, sharing his spoils in peasant villages before roaming off in search of new targets. He was a jovial killer. A Swiss missionary who spent eight months as his prisoner remembered his men hacking landlords to death 'as though they had done nothing more than kill a chicken for dinner.'

To begin with, He Long couldn't even read or write. 'When he gave an order, he wrote the characters of his name on the soldier's left hand. The soldier would go back to his unit, recite the order from memory, then raise his left hand to show He Long's genuine signature.' For all his eccentricities – his gambling, opium smoking, pencil-thin mustache, and preference for travelling by palanquin – He Long had proved himself a man of endurance and courage. Unlike many of his fellows, he continued to be a rule-breaker even after his official conversion to Communism. An American journalist innocently remarked on the bravery of his wife. There was laughter among He Long's soldiers. They started counting the general's wives on their fingers, and needed both hands. 'Pay no attention to them!' He Long begged the journalist. 'All that was before I adopted the new life.' The journalist nodded, but He Long's comment drew 'a howl of derision.'

During that same summer of 1957 when the three men had sat down for lunch, Mao launched the Hundred Flowers Movement. It was supposed to be a period of amnesty during which the government offered to willingly reform itself according to the criticism of its citizens. But the criticism had not been accepted by the government. Had the people gone too far? Or had the campaign always been a ploy by Mao to draw out critics of the Communist Party?

Mao had said that he doubted that more than 5 per cent of Chinese were 'bad.' Privately, Mao told a colleague he imagined there were probably around four thousand reactionaries, yet more than half a million people were 'deported to remote areas to do hard labour,' or worse. Rong Guotuan had heard that Hong Kong's Ping-Pong pioneer, Jiang Yongning, already converted to the Communist cause, was among them. What if Jiang had said something? What if Rong were to say something?

'Mr Rong,' asked He Long, 'would you be willing to return here and work in China?' Rong didn't answer at once. 'Ask for your parents' advice,' continued He Long. 'I don't want some guy in Hong Kong saying we've held you here against your will.'

'Rumours don't worry me,' said Rong. 'I know my father's going to support me.' Outwardly He Long didn't seem to be in any rush for Rong's answer. He leaned over and told him, 'Chinese sports will take at least five years before they reach a world-class level.'

Less than a month later, when the Hong Kong team was announced for the Asian Championships in Manila, Rong was stunned to learn that he hadn't even made the squad. He presumed it was because he worked in a union office suspected of Communist ties. Perhaps his meeting with He Long and Chen Yi had been reported. If he hadn't been picked for the Asian Championships, he knew the odds of being included in Hong Kong's team for the next World Championships were small.

Rong's fear was quelled. A quick trip across the Chinese border to skirmish with the Guangdong Province's team led to a few more victories for Rong, and best of all, Rong discovered that Beijing had sent Jiang Yongning south. He hadn't been arrested, looked happy, and seemed healthy. They met at the New Asia Hotel in Guangzhou, and Jiang encouraged Rong to move to China as soon as possible.

That July, Rong's best friend, Steven Cheung, left for Canada. They met one last time, a pair of penniless young men who knew it was unlikely they'd ever see each other again. An official letter had arrived from Marshal He Long; all that remained was for Rong to travel north. Rong asked Cheung to come to his tiny office in the library, where he gave him his favourite table tennis racquet. Like a true obsessive, Rong's last gift was to show his best friend a new serve he had developed. As he pulled his hand back, it was impossible to tell whether he was putting topspin or backspin on the ball – a breakthrough he'd developed on his own in the union library. Rong admitted he'd have liked to head the same way as Cheung – to North America – but in truth, he didn't have that choice.

Had Rong's ability been in any field other than table tennis, he would have followed Cheung – but he was in a position of unique irony: if Rong wanted to pursue any form of personal glory as a table tennis player, he would have to consider leaving a capitalist system and becoming a citizen of Communist China. If Hong Kong didn't really want him, why not head north? China, he knew from the two marshals, was pouring money into table tennis. Why not at least be appreciated on a strong team?

Most returning Chinese had to undergo a rigorous, nine-month political re-education. Rong's returning contemporaries were met at the train station in Guangdong and escorted to barracks where they would live eight to a room. The majority of returnees were poor young men from Hong Kong or Macao. They were fed rice and vegetables and expected to attend classes six days a week. Meat was a rarity. Before a month was out, many underwent a slow disillusionment. They weren't encouraged to question their teachers, and they soon realised that the teachers were barely thinking for themselves but parroting phrases that they had learned. Obedience was mandatory.

Rong's reception in China could not have been more different. First, he was installed in a large house that used to belong to no less a figure than Chiang Kai-shek. Second, he was appointed a number-one ranker, which ensured access to the best food and housing. He would be paid one hundred yuan a month, compared to forty yuan for a labourer. Not a fortune by any means, but in New China, he had automatic status and appreciation that he believed that he could never have gained in Hong Kong. The government showed great concern for him. At the first sign of a tuberculosis relapse, he was sent from Beijing back to Guangdong and spent six months resting in a sanatorium.

Rong Guotuan was known for his modesty, his hard work, and apparent shyness. But he obviously wasn't feeling so modest when he rejoined the Chinese squad. 'I think I can bring home a World Championship within the next three years,' he said. Rong was wrong; he'd become New China's first-ever gold medalist in any sport within two.

| # The Golden Game

Rong seemed almost schoolboyish at the table in Dortmund, Germany, in long black trousers pulled up to his waist, a pair of new white sneakers, and a red-collared T-shirt. He looked like a throwback to the players of the 1930s and 1940s, while his opponents whisked around the table in their shorts and shirts. Most played fluid versions of the game, but Rong wound his body up early and quickly. Watching him was like watching a spring release with amazing regularity.

Here was the Chinese team, now travelling ten strong with coaches, a much more sophisticated operation than before. Around them was the wonder of post-war Germany. A nation that had wrapped the world in war seemed rebuilt in fifteen short years.

The irony would not have been missed by the officials. America had structured the recovery of both Germany and Japan to balance the twin Communist giants, Russia and China. There were new cars speeding down new autobahns. There was uncensored cinema. There was also East Germany, not very far away. The Chinese team had heard that America was much richer, but West Germany had at least welcomed China. True, the West Germans had treated the Japanese to the best hotel near the stadium and relegated the Chinese to a suburb and given them 'electric cards to take a bus to the stadium every day.' But then, the Japanese were the reigning champions, and China had never won a medal. Not in table tennis – not in any other sport in the world.

Rong's semi-final was against thirty-four-year-old American Dick Miles. Miles was the closed-off, unloved scholar of the game. Back in New York, he kept a bust on his mantelpiece of Beethoven, his fellow maligned genius. Miles had lost a tight first game by a net cord, then battled back to win two in a row in the best out of seven format. But could Rong afford to lose to an American? One of the running dogs of capitalism? What would they say back in Beijing?

Miles recalled it as a purely psychological game, one where both players wanted to be the aggressor. He tried to force Rong to play defence, but the Chinese kept hitting his way out of the corners Miles was trying to put him in. Miles had already claimed two Chinese scalps; there was no mystique about China – not beyond its own borders. 'To be honest,' said Miles's team-mate Marty Reisman, 'we thought they all looked alike.' With just a few more points, Miles could move on to the final. Awaiting the winner was the grand old man of the tournament, the forty-year-old Hungarian bear, Ferenc Sido, who had won the singles back in 1953. Both Rong and Miles fancied their chances against the veteran. The winner was Rong. He beat Miles to a pulp in the last game, with the American winning just eight points.

The final contained all the absurdity and grandeur of the game of table tennis: a packed stadium with two men facing off under a single bright light in the centre of the darkness. It looked like a championship boxing bout, but without the bloodshed. The pair were physical opposites. On one side, Rong Guotuan: tubercular, long and thin, sad-eyed and frail; on the other, Ferenc Sido, Hungary's old pro. His body suggested a wrestler, but his footwork was that of a prima ballerina. You could see that Rong was thinking his way through Sido at high speed, bringing him near to the net with heavily angled shots, making him move his bulk backward with hefty drives. Sido reached up again and again to wipe his forehead.

When Rong won, a huge smile broke out across his face, and you could see the pressure lift from Sido as well. He hadn't seen it coming – no one had dreamed the Chinese would produce a men's champion so soon – but once the match was under way, Sido never came close to a win. He retained the demeanour of a gentleman but waved quickly at the crowd and left the applause to Rong.

At the closing ceremony, Rong Guotuan, China's first champion in any sport, stood to receive his trophy from Ivor Montagu, friend of China. And Montagu had an even bigger prize for China, not just the cup chosen from his grandfather's enormous collection of silver but an invitation that could shift the way China was seen by the international community. How would they like to host the next World Championships in two years?

To China and her National Sports Commission, it was a timely boon. First, it could let them celebrate the achievements of the Great Leap Forward. Second, they could position themselves as an outward and friendly nation, just as the Japanese had done.

An American team would not be travelling to Beijing. It wasn't that the State Department was opposed to attempting *some* form of contact with Communist China – inert ambassadorial-level talks had been going on since 1954 – and it was cautiously considering a Chinese proposal for an exchange of journalists. But these overtures were far from the public eye, and there was no way for American Ping-Pong players to know of or interpret such subtleties. Even though the Chinese were offering to cover a portion of all teams' travel to Beijing, table tennis player Marty Reisman laughed at the idea of applying for a passport to China in 1959. 'What were we going to do? Go and say we wanted to go to China to play Ping-Pong? They would have thought we were fucking insane.' At a time when anything that brushed against Communism could be equated to a lack of patriotism, Reisman understandably believed that 'they'd have put us in a crazy house.'

It was 17 April 1959. Back in Beijing, the news of Rong's victory was greeted jubilantly. Zhou Enlai paused to organise a victory party for Rong held at the Beijing Hotel, usually reserved for the top foreign delegations. Zhou reinforced the work they had done as diplomats. 'I'm the premier, so I can't go everywhere. You're Ping-Pong players – you can go anywhere in the world.' It was Montagu's notion in a nutshell – Ping-Pong could move quietly under the borders and boundaries created by the Communist and capitalist worlds. Rong had done as much as any ambassador to promote China internationally and at home.

Mao congratulated Rong Guotuan personally. He called Ping-Pong China's new 'spiritual nuclear weapon' but was distracted by troubling news from the countryside. In a nation still essentially powered by agriculture, China's true currency was grain, and the numbers were disturbing.

The Great Leap Forward, Mao's plan to industrialise the country rapidly, could only happen if steel was produced. On the party's orders, people had created homemade smelters in villages across China. But Beijing still needed to export grain to garner the cash to continue the Great Leap Forward. On 25 March Mao gave orders that the party had to procure up to one third of the peasants' grain, 'much more than had ever been the case.' At the meeting, Mao announced that 'when there is not enough to eat people starve to death. It is better to let half of the people die so that the other half can eat their fill.' At least that way, the Great Leap Forward could continue at pace.

Still, there was nothing to panic about yet. A year of mild famine was nothing new to China. Propaganda was pumped up to cover the minor blip in China's progress. As Rong raised his trophy, the Chinese press began to defend the Great Leap Forward. 'Foreign friends visiting China keep asking how it was possible to double grain and cotton output . . . the most important factor . . . is the strengthening of the leadership of the Communist Party . . . in other words, the political aspect.'

Now was the time to celebrate the tenth anniversary of the People's Republic of China as well as Rong Guotuan's unexpected victory. Rong Guotuan was 'hailed by the Communist press' for 'bringing glory to the Motherland.' Even the *Daily Mirror* in London, eight thousand miles away, tipped its hat. 'It's easy to mock at the sometimes grandiloquent claims which come from behind the Iron and Bamboo Curtain but there is no gainsaying the fact that these young – in a sporting sense – nations have performed miracles virtually overnight.' A new company was launched. Double Happiness was to produce table tennis balls and equipment in honour of Rong Guotuan's achievement during the PRC's tenth anniversary. 'In three months, Shanghai factories received orders for 21,600,000 balls,' an increase of 700 per cent over the previous year. Ping-Pong was to provide the weakest of smiles in the bleakest of times.

CHAPTER 17 | Setting the Table

After the end of World War II, Ivor Montagu found many ways to make himself useful to the Communist cause. First and foremost, he knew that he had to follow the party line as dictated by Moscow, no matter how much it strained against logic.

As Mao Zedong and Zhou Enlai prepared their final push against Beijing in the summer of 1949, Montagu travelled once more to Moscow, this time as a journalist. With his background in science, he was well suited to the task of writing a series of articles for England's *Daily Worker* on Soviet advances. The main thrust of his visit was to interview the head of the Academy of Sciences, Trofim Lysenko. To the Communist world, Lysenko was the greatest of the peasant scientists, who based their new theories on their childhoods tilling Russian soil. Genetics, to Lysenko, were a scientific dead end; what really counted in agriculture, as in Soviet politics, was ideology. Lysenko's schemes to increase crop yields were promoted by the State not because they were effective but because they reflected Stalin's beliefs.

Weeks before, the *Times* had ridiculed Lysenko as more fraud than scientist and stirred up a vicious debate happily covered by the world's newspapers. According to the *Daily Worker*, the Western press and radio had 'combined to depict him as a monstrous villain.' Even his accusers could not imagine that within the decade, Lysenko was going to aid and abet in one of the century's greatest losses of life. His ideas were going to help kill approximately twice as many people as had died in World War I.

Born a peasant in the Ukraine in the late nineteenth century, Lysenko had managed to persuade an Azerbaijani journalist into running a story in the Russian newspaper *Pravda* about how he had single-handedly vernalised peas so that they could grow in a harsh winter. Never mind that the experiment could not be repeated. Lysenko had already warped his science to reflect Marxist theories. Throughout the 1930s and 1940s, he gradually grew in power in the halls of Soviet academia, until he launched an academic putsch. Inter-departmental fighting is familiar enough in any university, but in Lysenko's time the losers wound up exiled or shot. By 1948, he had secured Stalin's personal assurance that those who believed in Mendelian genetics would be considered reactionary. They lost their jobs, their homes, and their lives. Lysenko gained three chauffeured cars, a beautiful dacha on the outskirts of Moscow, and his own theme tune, which was played by a brass band before speeches.

Lysenko claimed that nearly all Western scientific thought was limiting, if not useless. He ordered millions of trees planted in Siberia in an attempt to warm the climate in Russia's south. More dangerous was his political belief that seeds were like good Communists: the more you planted close together, the more likely they were to help one another in brotherly spirit. Mao had read these stories in his revolutionary base in Yan'an and adored them. They would lie at the centre of China's agricultural policy during the Great Leap Forward.

Once the extent of Lysenko's power was known in Moscow, the predictable happened: surviving Soviet scientists started producing work to support Lysenko's theories. Lysenko continued to work on his crops. He wasn't too worried about statistics – he preferred questionnaires filled out by farmers.

Lysenko's rise made horrific and perfect sense. His results and conclusions were all viewed through a prism of Marxism. Even when there were contradictions, they could be marched far enough to the left to fit Stalin's world. Though Lysenko had heretically admitted that men might not be born equal, he believed that the human race could be controlled and pushed toward the 'desired requirements,' an idea that was 'of immense political and social significance to the regime.'

On his return to Moscow, Montagu was not travelling alone. He was accompanied by JD Bernal, one of England's finest scientists and a renowned Communist sympathiser. Wherever they went with Lysenko, they travelled quickly, bypassing Moscow traffic with special passes. Stalin had appointed Lysenko chairman of one of the two houses of the Soviet Parliament in addition to his role as president of the Academy of Agricultural Sciences of the Soviet Union – could Montagu or Bernal possibly speak against him?

Montagu's handwriting was so small and spidery that he could cover a single sheet of paper in two thousand words. Reading his writing required two aspirin and a magnifying glass. When he first shook Lysenko's hand, he was impressed by its coarseness and imagined that the man could 'handle grain as though utterly fitted to do so.' His eyes 'were deep set' and he wore 'a frequent smile of mischievousness and complicity,' along with a pair of sandals. There was a portrait of Charles Darwin in his disorganised office. Montagu took an immediate liking to him. Bernal was not so convinced. He asked Lysenko a series of probing questions about genetics. Lysenko's catchall answer was, 'I never said and never thought I knew everything. Nobody does.'

There were few such moments of doubt for Montagu, who was sympathetic to Lysenko's frustrations with the barrage of criticism from the West. 'There are none so deaf as those who don't hear,' said Montagu. Lysenko laughed aloud, and Montagu jotted down in his notes, 'This tickles Lysenko who repeats it with relish and approval.'

How could Lysenko have achieved some of his results? Could wheat really change its genetic structure so quickly that it could be grown in deepest Siberia, surviving ferocious long winters? Wouldn't that save the world from famine? No one would ever starve again. Bernal and Montagu failed to pop Lysenko's bubble. They returned to England, and Montagu wrote an aggressive defence of Lysenko's methods.

During the mid-1950s, Mao was eager to implement Lysenko's ideas. Soviet scientists were sent across China giving lectures and spreading the 'Law of the Life of Species,' where Lysenko's cooperative seeds meshed with Mao's deep belief in class struggle. Those Chinese who still believed in genetics were 'enthusiastically persecuted.' When blights did occur, they were attributed to environmental factors. In 1958, China's fate was sealed. Mao 'personally drew up an eight point Lysenkoist blueprint for all Chinese agriculture.' Montagu, one of the few Westerners to visit Lysenko who had a background in both science and journalism, had missed an opportunity to puncture the myth.

Montagu would reappear twice in China during the worst of the coming famine. As it began, he offered China the opportunity to host its first large sporting event of any kind: the 1961 World Table Tennis Championships. Ping-Pong would become more political than ever. All propaganda had been funnelled down to the two weeks of April 1961. So much was at stake. First, China would have to host the World Championships, complete with foreign players, teams, and journalists, without the truth of the Great Famine slipping out. Second, China would have to win. This was not a victory that could be achieved through illusion or massaging of numbers. There would be real friends and enemies present, including Ogimura and the Japanese. They would all have to be beaten.

In 1961, the year when the last of the bodies slumped to the ground, when villagers had no more energy to bury their dead, when the death toll had long since passed into millions, Montagu would return to China. It was the year when Ping-Pong's first Communist passed the torch of politics and sport directly into the hands of the Chinese.

CHAPTER 18 | # The End of Brotherhood

It was a brisk spring day, which in Beijing meant warm winds and a mouthful of Mongolian grit. The vastness of Tiananmen Square was filled by a huge crowd celebrating May Day with a parade in honour of Mao's Great Leap Forward. The famine had already begun to grip the country and was slowly heading toward the cities, but that morning all eyes were on Beijing. For the tenth anniversary of the People's Republic of China, the whole city gleamed with optimism. 'Workers marched with the staffs of factories proudly displaying charts and models of their latest products and production successes.' As they reached the figures of Mao and Zhou Enlai, they released balloons in the shape of dragons and phoenixes, balloons carrying flower baskets. 'The sky was a weaving mass of colour.'

The *Daily Worker* poetically described how doves were released into the air to swoop with Beijing's birds between the red balloons. The doves had little company. Less than a year before, the Campaign against the Four Pests had helped launch the Great Leap Forward. Sparrows were designated thieves of the people's grain. Millions of loyal citizens had run through the streets and over rooftops, waving jackets and bedsheets to prevent any bird from finding a place to rest. Hours later, thousands of birds simply dropped dead from the sky. The insect population exploded. Soon 'caterpillars wrapped the foliage in great nets of silver strands, a lovely lethal sight,' which quickly killed most trees in Beijing. It was merely a premonition of the madness to come.

The Great Leap Forward had been a busy time in the capital, the centrepiece of a nationwide effort to compete openly with the world's greatest powers. It was supposed to rocket China into an industrial age in five short years. Targets were set for steel production (Great Britain would be surpassed) and wheat yields would rise fivefold (to equal the output of Canada and the United States combined). A few faithful journalists were shown evidence. 'One province alone,' wrote journalist Anna Louise Strong, an old friend of Montagu's, 'now produces more wheat than the entire of America.' But what was a cake without icing? In 1957, in order to celebrate the tenth anniversary of his revolution, Mao had unleashed a sweeping programme of construction, planning one daunting edifice for each year of his revolutionary decade.

Among the buildings that were to be completed by the tenth anniversary that October were the Workers' Stadium, the Great Hall of the People, and the Beijing Railroad Station. All were designed by Russian and Chinese architects working together to meld a form of Stalinist architecture with Chinese characteristics. The message to the individual was clear: You are small and you cannot survive alone, so join us and enter as part of the community. It was an enormous diversion of funds and labour – the railway station had two million men working on it at a cost of 60 million yuan and was completed in an extraordinary seven months. One additional undertaking had just been approved by Zhou Enlai: the Chinese were about to start building the largest Ping-Pong stadium in the world. It would be the only large-scale structure based on Western designs.

On 1 May 1959, three and a half thousand miles away, similar celebrations were occurring in Moscow. 'Brilliant sunshine broke through to flood Red Square' just as Premier Nikita Khrushchev led the Soviet government up the steps to the 'top of the Lenin-Stalin mausoleum.' It was a big day for Khrushchev. He was being awarded the Soviet equivalent of a Nobel, the Lenin Peace Prize. Another man had been awarded the same prize that day: Ivor Montagu, the son of a baron, Hitchcock's film producer, the founder of modern Ping-Pong.

Montagu was lauded across the USSR, and his biography ran in every Communist organ in the world. He was named one of the world's 'outstanding fighters for peace,' and it was noted that he'd made 'considerable contribution to the consolidation of peace and cooperation among nations.' Most extraordinary of all was the boldness of the next line. Despite having been born 'into an aristocratic family,' 'the life of this man is a vivid example of a progressive representative of the Western *intelligentsia* finding his real calling in joint struggle with the masses of the people.' Montagu was being congratulated using the code name INTELLIGENTSIA assigned to him by the GRU. The message was clear, at least to Montagu. He had received the Lenin Peace Prize as much for his work as a spy as for his role as a propagandist for the Communist Party.

In Beijing, the Chinese also drank to his health. They had been selected to host the World Championships of table tennis. If industry and agriculture were to be the meat and bones of the Great Leap Forward, then sport was New China's muscle tone.

By the time Zhou Enlai had accepted Montagu's offer for China to host the 1961 World Championships, it was already obvious to the premier that the remainder of 1959 and 1960 would be difficult years. The realisation that the Great Leap Forward would not be great and that the leap might actually be backward made the coming tournament even more important than Zhou Enlai had previously imagined.

That 1 October, with Tiananmen packed once more for the official celebrations of the tenth anniversary of the People's Republic, ITTF President Montagu and General Secretary Roy Evans were among the VIPs attending the event. Evans wrote that 'for about four hours we watched this incredible [display] march past, symbolising all of Chinese life,' while they sipped on green tea and the potent fermented sorghum called Maotai. Montagu busied himself organising the coming World Championships, but Evans was confused that they were attached to a group called Friends of China, another of Montagu's left-wing organisations back in London. They spent their time in Beijing being 'carted around in "big black Russian cars [that] were always at our disposal,"' looking at the plans and site where the world's greatest Ping-Pong stadium was about to rise. By 3 October, Montagu had reached Moscow to pick up his peace prize in person and bowed to receive his gold medal. After a 'warm speech' congratulating Montagu, the Englishman was allowed to speak. 'The forces of war had been shaken and weakened. Peace will not be handed out on a plate,' said Montagu, 'it had to be won.'

There would be difficulties ahead for Russia and China. Mao had drawn a line in the sand between the Russians and the Chinese. China may once have publicly accepted the role of 'younger brother' to Moscow, but neither believed it anymore. Tiananmen Square itself was a symbol of the growing divide. The Russian advisers had recommended an expanded Tiananmen fit inside the nine hectares of Red Square. Mao had pointedly signed off on forty-four hectares.

Khrushchev was, to Mao, a reactionary who waffled over providing China with nuclear technology and skewered Stalin's legacy in the wake of his death. Mao had never liked Stalin. Stalin had backed Chiang Kai-shek for a while in the civil war. He had called Mao a 'margarine Marxist.' In Korea, Stalin had promised Mao's troops air cover and then left tens of thousands of Chinese infantry open to bombing runs by American planes. Mao's favoured son was among the dead. Yet, despite all this, Stalin was the granite bust alongside which Mao was chiselling his own image.

Khrushchev's reconsideration of Stalin's past could encourage Mao's successors to reinterpret his own legacy. This alone was more than enough reason to distrust Khrushchev. Besides, Khrushchev had dared to visit America, attending a white-tie dinner at President Eisenhower's White House. What sort of brazen revisionism was this? Mao chose to humiliate the Russian premier, who, he believed, wanted 'to control China's seacoasts.' Inviting Khrushchev to swim with him in his private pool in the leadership compound of Zhongnanhai, Mao lectured the Russian as he swept through his laps. Khrushchev, who had never learned to swim, floated impotently in a rubber ring, watched by his bodyguards.

In July 1960, the Russians were thrown out of China overnight. The declarations in the Russian press from the fall of 1959 seemed ridiculous eight months later. 'We treasure this friendship like the apple of our eye,' proclaimed the *Moscow News* of the harmony between China and Russia. 'This friendship will live for centuries.' From that moment on, the Moscow newspapers held their silence on China; the word was rarely written. The enormous International Congress of Orientalists that took place in Moscow that same summer was notable for the fact that Nigerian speakers were drafted to cover for the absent Chinese.

The tension had been bubbling for years. In April 1955, Zhou Enlai's 'vigorous advocacy of anti-colonialism won a warm reception' at a conference in Indonesia and had led many in the Third World to believe that China could beat a new path between the two great rivals of the Cold War. Moscow insisted that the Kremlin remain at the centre of socialist and Communist thought. In Communist China, the land of no coincidences, Zhou Enlai's performance was celebrated six years later to the day, during the table tennis tournament.

What the Russians *had* left behind as they packed their bags in 1960 was an effective recruiting system for all sports. Promising youngsters would be spotted by primary school coaches. They would be streamed into local sport schools, which in turn would feed city teams. They would provide teams to compete at the provincial level and from there, the national team coach would cherry-pick the best players. Once again, a Chinese spin was put on a Russian framework and directed at table tennis.

| Preparation

CHAPTER 19

In September 1960, with only six months to go before the tournament, 108 of the best male and female table tennis players gathered for winter training. This was far from an arbitrary number. Every child in China knew the book *The Water Margin*, an epic version of Robin Hood, though altogether angrier; it described a revolt of 108 men who had risen against corrupt emperors. They were the so-called brigands who fought to protect the people. Heads flew from shoulders; guts lined mountain roads.

The most famous tale in *The Water Margin* concerned the emperor's garden, where every perfect blade of grass, every beautiful flower was revealed to have come at the cost of the lives of his own subjects. The ruler's magnificence was measured in the suffering of his people. Never was there a clearer metaphor for what the National Sports Commission was up to with their table tennis programme during the century's greatest famine.

Teenagers from around the country were uprooted and sent, proudly, to one of three areas concentrating on Ping-Pong: Shanghai, Guangdong, or Beijing, where He Long had been busy building a training area by Dragon Lake with no windows on the windward side to disturb the players. Their isolation would be total.

They were the cream skimmed from the top of sponsored table tennis tournaments across the nation. In Shanghai alone, three hundred thousand people had played. Beijing, Nanking, Chungking, Xi'an, Wuhan, and Harbin all held tournaments. Had Montagu been able to float slowly over China, he would have seen an absurd realisation of his dream: millions of Ping-Pong balls popping back and forth in dormitories, factories, classrooms, and dining rooms.

The oldest school in China, founded in 141 BC, now contained half a dozen Ping-Pong tables. In one hospital, three hundred of the four hundred workers entered the competition, including the head nurse and the director. Reporters and newspapermen 'took on the dual propaganda role of competing in as well as covering the events, while leading citizens such as Communist Party secretaries, college presidents and industrial managers either played themselves or acted as referees.'

The best of the best, the 108, were assigned to a seven-story dormitory inside a huge complex near the Temple of Heaven. From the rooms at the top you could see the gold and purple temple roof, one of the few spots of colour in Beijing outside the red party slogans. Built with the help of the Soviets, the sport complex was designed to house a nation's elite athletes. There was a football pitch, indoor and outdoor running tracks, an Olympic-sized pool, an arena, a huge weights room, and, of course, the specially designed training room for Ping-Pong players. Just yards away were offices for the sports press, as well as the National Sports Administration Centre, staff dorms, even a garage for the cars and buses the athletes and officials might need.

The nation's best athletes ate together in a huge dining hall the size of two basketball courts. Athletes would keep their own bowls and utensils on checkered shelves against the wall next to the entrance. They'd pick up their rations at the far end – half a bowl of milk, a sweet cake, rice porridge, and wheat flour buns with as many pickled vegetables as they wanted. That was just for breakfast. Other meals included at least two dishes with meat in them, as well as a bottle of yogurt. When they were finished, every athlete was expected to wash his or her bowl and place it back near the door again.

Those selected to be part of the 108 were dedicated to the state. Han Zhicheng had left home in 1959 when he was seventeen. He didn't see his family again until 1962. This, he said, was typical. 'We weren't encouraged to go back home for spring festival. We were supposed to be a model for the people.' As the slogan went, 'Mother and Father are good, but Chairman Mao is great.'

For most, any fear of being away from home was overcome by the relative luxury of the facilities. There were no rich people in China anymore. These were young men and women who had carved their own bats, built their own tables from sawhorses and doors, or drawn them with chalk on cement. Bamboo poles had been used as nets. When shoes had worn thin, they had been taped up. Now, at the party's expense, worn shoes were replaced, there were choices of bats, the balls were shiny and whole. 'The new life,' remembered one player, 'was glorious.'

There were tiny signs of how much weight table tennis was suddenly expected to bear. He Long had announced that it was a vital component of how 'he wanted to use sport to raise the spirit of the people.' There were no other sporting options. By 1958, China had withdrawn from both the International Olympic Committee (IOC) and the Fédération Internationale de Football Association (FIFA). There were only two other sports kept alive in the period of the Great Leap Forward: volleyball and speed skating. It was hard to imagine the northern sport of speed skating finding support among the highest-level leaders, all born in central provinces. Men's volleyball was still dominated by those with enormously developed physiques. Not even the National Sports Commission expected the Great Leap Forward to have produced such specimens yet.

The head coach for the men's table tennis squad was a man named Fu Qifang. Fu, who, like Rong Guotuan, was from Hong Kong, looked like an inverted version of their world champion, a solid Cantonese verging on chubby. Unlike Rong, who was familiar with some tenets of Communism through his father's union activities, Fu was strictly apolitical. He was an athlete in the American mold who played hard, drank hard, and preferred two women to one. On a good night, he was easily capable of downing ten bottles of beer.

Back in the early 1950s, Marty Reisman, one of the best players America ever produced, spent years out in Asia for the simple reason that if you played table tennis, that was where the money was. On the table, the thin American was known as the Needle, but off the courts, in English suits and Italian shoes, he looked as elegant as a fountain pen.

Table tennis matches between Fu and Reisman brought out the biggest gamblers in Hong Kong. The two men would face off against each other in Southorn Playground, attracting crowds of more than four thousand. 'Fu was like me,' said Reisman, 'a showman.' They would combine to draw out the matches, filled with flying bodies and Reisman's trademark shots accompanied by 360-degree pirouettes. Fu, already carrying extra weight, was made to sweat for his points in the soupy heat of one Hong Kong July. Run back and forth by Reisman, Fu collapsed on the floor and lay there panting. The crowd began to boo. Reisman walked around and helped Fu back to his feet. The Hong Kong native won the game, but Reisman took the match and the money.

Back then, the Chinese were already watching Fu. At the Bombay World Championships in the pivotal year of 1952, when the Japanese Satoh dispatched all comers with his magic racquet, Fu had been part of the team from the tiny rock of Hong Kong that had won the bronze medal. Montagu's rules meant that Hong Kong, despite being a British Crown colony, was allowed to enter an entirely Chinese team.

In Bombay, Fu had been on familiar territory. Fu was not alone among table tennis players in having 'no other apparent source of income' than his paddle and living 'close to abject poverty.' Practice halls, even at the World Championships, had become both gambling dens and trading posts. In the post-war world, rationing systems were in effect in most of the countries that had been touched by the conflict, and luxuries were hard to come by. Back then, explained Reisman, 'Everyone came to trade, a sort of unofficial smuggling. The Czechs would arrive with linens, the French with cognac and perfumes.' Players 'would pull out wads of two, three, four hundred dollars,' not always easy to get hold of.

Underneath Montagu's nose, the tournament had metamorphosed into the sort of black-market capitalism that had taken root in the streets of Central Europe and Fu's Hong Kong. There were two sets of laws, one to obey in the presence of officials and another when the players were left alone in the practice hall.

Earning money in table tennis wasn't illegal according to Montagu's rules, but it was suspicious. Players were required to have all their matches approved by their national associations, a rule imposed from on high by a man who had a lifelong income provided by his father. Montagu had essentially gamed the sport so that it could prosper only in countries where the governments were willing to throw their support behind Ping-Pong. It was a gap the Chinese were now hoping to exploit. Individuals who tried to make a killing were often suspended or dragged down in red tape. Or, like Fu, they could lose heavily at the tables and fall into debt.

Fu's situation was even more complicated than his friend and rival Marty Reisman knew. A bigamist, Fu was struggling to maintain two families in Hong Kong without any other source of income but his paddle and speed around the table. His debts had become enormous. In 1954 his precarious existence was seized on by the Communists. Come to Beijing and coach in China, offered Marshal He Long. Choose one wife, he was told, one of your families, and we will take care of the rest. For all the inflexibility and terror meted out in the first years of the Communist regime, the Chinese could prove disarmingly accepting of foibles when something they truly wanted was at stake. Fu was given the astronomical sum of 200 yuan a month, 500 per cent more than other players, though it was divided between his two families. He Long had come to call this 'The Buy Policy' – just a little bit of capitalism to strengthen the Communist cause.

There were plenty of players but few coaches. Fu couldn't train all the players, so he recruited coaches from within the 108. Liang Youneng had attended university, where he'd studied railway construction, hoping to contribute to China's push to criss-cross its vastness with the veins of railway tracks. His Ping-Pong career, he believed, was temporary. But the National Sports Commission saw his learning as a reason to think he might be a good coach, and he found himself as Fu Qifang's second-in-command.

It was that sort of mixture of grassroots improvisation and the proletariat that made the game feel Chinese, despite its rumoured roots in the British Army. The name was easily translatable: Ping-Pong became ping pang. The two Chinese characters are mirror images of each other. 'Whoever came up with the words was a poet,' explained China scholar Robert Oxnam:

> The ping is a cannon shot. The pang is a bang. Then, if you over-
> lay the characters one over another, you get the word for soldier. It

100

has diplomacy embedded in its characters, but it's a military diplomacy. If you go back to Sun Tzu and the *Art of War*, it's the intimate knowledge of your opponent that allows you to win, not superior strength.

Ping pang suited China perfectly.

Zhou Enlai knew that for the moment, China was far from a position of military strength. In truth, it couldn't even feed its own people. Now was the time for subtle advance, a time to disguise failures and magnify successes so that China could be positioned as a leader of the Third World. But in order to display its credentials, China would have to win the tournament.

There had been political matches before. At the Utrecht World Championships in 1956, China had to play against Japan. China was also drawn in a group with South Korea and the United States of America – China's two opponents in the recently concluded Korean War. 'We were so nervous,' remembered a male player, Zhuang Jiafu. He kept calm and won a close match against the South Koreans, then won all three of his games against the Americans, too.

Even without a medal, the trip was seen as a heady success. The imperialist Americans and the reactionary Koreans had been vanquished. At the airport on the team's return, Marshal He Long singled out Zhuang Jiafu. His salary was raised to level one, the highest of the men's team. The elder statesmen also embraced the team's rise. Mao, Zhou Enlai, and Zhu De had all attended the National Workers' Sports Meeting just a few months earlier. But that was a private success. Hosting and then winning a World Championships would be the true test of Ping-Pong as powerful propaganda.

CHAPTER 20 | **Sacrifice**

What was unfolding across China during the Great Leap Forward was not natural. The burgeoning famine was a homemade concoction of ideology and science, mismanagement and cruelty with the brunt borne by those farthest away from the centre of Communism, in terms of both power and geography. As cities faltered, more and more grain was requisitioned from the countryside, until barely a grain of rice could be found outside state granaries.

Weather patterns had nothing to do with the famine. One intellectual, imprisoned in a labour camp in the Great Northern Wilderness, remembered 1960 as a 'bumper harvest of corn, rice, wheat and soybeans.' Without outside interferences, the prisoners acting as farmers had managed to thrive in terrible conditions – until their crops were requisitioned for the nearest city and the prisoners given food substitutes: ground corn cobs and husks. The men were reduced to nothing but 'muddy rags and a ghastly pallor.'

How to pay for Beijing's rash of buildings and the world's largest table tennis stadium? How to pay for the projected success of the Chinese Communist Party? By exporting grain. At the beginning of the famine, the amount of grain exported actually went up. China would continue to pay off debts to the Russians in grain, continue to ship food to Third World brethren as a sign of their largesse. Historian Jasper Becker called the resulting famine 'deliberate murder on a mass scale.'

In Russia, the first five-year plan had been carried out at a time when the peasants were relatively wealthy. In China in the late 1950s, the majority of the country was living barely above the level of sustenance. Even a small increase in the amount of grain requisitioned would push the countryside into starvation. There was no escape – unless, of course, you were a Ping-Pong player.

The Chinese were a nation of smallholders, but now all land belonged to the state. It cost the individual farmer more to grow the grain than the government was willing to pay for it. There were no other buyers, thanks to collectivisation. On the farms, nothing, from animals to utensils, belonged to the farmers anymore. The only people left with incentives were the Communist cadres who were supposed to be delivering record-breaking yields to the state granaries.

Failure to achieve one's quota was a political catastrophe – a demotion in rank within the Communist Party meant a cut in rations. Lies were invented and sustained at every level across the country. Magazines and newspapers heralded the advances. 'How bold the peasants have been in their close-planting experiment – bolder than any scientist would have imagined,' boasted one government publication. Another improvisation was 'deep planting' of rice, which required workers to stand up to their waists in water. Chairman Mao's doctor, sitting beside him on the train as they steamed from Beijing into the countryside, looked out at the fields of peasants wading through the rice plants. Instead of a 'technological advance,' he saw an 'open invitation to gynecological infections.'

The orders came down directly from Mao. 'Grain should be taken before the farmers could eat it.' If violence had to be employed, so be it. 'There is something ideologically wrong with you if you are afraid of coercion.' The Chinese government believes that there had been 17 million 'excess deaths' by the spring of 1961, when Montagu returned to Beijing. Western experts, such as Frank Dikötter, place the number at 45 million.

Once a human body is driven to starvation, it makes calculations of its own; there was certainly no energy left to enter the fields, no matter the threats made by ever more angry cadres. Villagers shirking work or stealing food were drowned, frozen, burned, and otherwise tortured. By the time the World Championships started, between two and three million had died directly as a result of violence.

The starving were prevented from leaving their villages by the *hukou* system, a form of internal passport that required a government-issued stamp for travel. It was instituted in 1958, and without a *hukou* a worker couldn't receive food coupons in the city or a communal share in the countryside. Within the villages, as within the cities, access to food was a matter of political loyalty – except for Ping-Pong players, who were fed three times a day, whether they were Communist Party members or not.

In the countryside, labourers stood in line at the communal canteen and awaited the ladle. Nothing was more closely watched than the level of that ladle; it wasn't a question of pettiness but a matter of life and death. The politically disaffected, those who had written letters complaining of food shortages or ill treatment by the cadres, could be killed slowly, ounce by ounce. The ranks of the Communist Party were to swell during the famine, going from 12.5 to 17.4 million in the space of three years. This wasn't a political awakening but a desperate strategy to gain access to food.

If the *hukou* system prevented villagers from travelling to spread news of the famine, their lack of energy ensured that the few who did travel didn't get far. Most died in their villages. The last to die, in the spring of 1961, were left unburied; in many villages there was no one left to dig. Amid such weakness, disease flourished – polio, meningitis, hepatitis, and malaria rates all soared. Beijing was one of the few places where, to some degree, the misery was kept at bay. If the nation was to survive, then the capital must be maintained as the exception.

The summer after Rong Guotuan's victory, a strong coalition emerged against Mao at a conference the Chairman was attending in Lushan, pressing him to change course. Peng, the minister of defence, wrote a letter pleading with Mao: 'the people urgently demand a change of the present condition.' He had visited the countryside and witnessed the repellent mixture of starving children and boastful cadres. His letter directly contradicted the Chairman's own stance. 'Putting politics in command,' wrote Peng, 'is no substitute for economic principles, much less for concrete measures in economic work.'

For two days, Mao was silent, brooding over the letter of a man he had once glorified in poetry. Then the Chairman took the stage, letter in hand, and eviscerated his minister of defence. Criticism of Mao was now equated with criticism of the party – there was no longer any difference. Mao compared himself to Marx and Lenin, both of whom had also made mistakes. To criticise the Great Leap Forward for economic reasons such as the grain quota of a province was a rightist, bourgeois idea.

Mao threatened to split the party in two, go back to the countryside, and lead another revolution of peasants. Peng was abandoned by his allies and immediately relieved of his position. There was much that could have been done. Exports of grain could have been cut and immediately distributed to the worst-hit areas, but the loss of face for China in the international arena was considered an even greater cost.

The minister of defence, who came so close to saving millions of lives, sat down in silence. Anyone attached to Peng would find himself at the wrong end of Mao's plotting. In the system of Chinese infighting, a man's underlings and support systems would be picked off first, before he was attacked. Little did the nascent Ping-Pong team realise that in the decade to come, it would end up as the focus of a vast campaign of vengeance. Mao's favourite movie that year, as his doctor reported, was Gary Cooper's *High Noon*.

| **Nourishing the Team**

For the moment, the concerns of the National Sports Commission were immediate. Chief among them was how to keep the Ping-Pong team well fed. He Long realised that the ministry had a secret weapon to fight hunger – the international shooting team. They were sent into Inner Mongolia, a dozen hours' drive from Beijing, in order to hunt yellow goats. Once they had plenty of goat meat to barter, they soon found a plentiful source of eggs.

Living conditions were simple. The team moved into a one-story house near the practice hall with no indoor plumbing and 'a roof that leaked when it rained,' but their food was first-class. They had milk, pork in a can, and fresh eggs every day. The players were presented with their training uniforms and socks and shoes. 'When you wore through a pair of shoes, you just went and got a new pair.'

The schedule for the 108 was punishing, yet nothing compared to the pain and death being meted out across China. They were divided into four teams: men's, women's, a mixed team, and a youth team. All would rise at 6am. It didn't matter how cold it was; they would be turned out into the courtyard or the playground and begin a series of exercises and weight training, then go for a morning run. Breakfast was at 8.30, followed by three hours of table tennis, a large lunch, and a nap; three more hours of table tennis from 3pm to 6pm, then dinner and a mixture of training and meetings in the evening. There was very little free time. Perhaps they'd see a war movie once a month, but despite their generous salaries, there was little to buy. Often, table tennis films would be screened – hard-to-obtain footage of Ogimura and the Japanese as well as of the Hungarian squad, the players who were considered the main threat to the Chinese drive for a world title. They watched the films at normal speed, then studied them in slow motion.

Han Zhicheng was a practice player. His job was to study the film, then, when the foreign teams arrived in Beijing, try to watch them practice. He would run back to the practice hall and imitate their technique for the best players in the Chinese squad. 'What you have to understand,' he says, 'is that we were united. It was a total team game. We were fighting for the glory of our unit.' The word *unit* can also be used in the army, or a factory – but the idea is a strong one: unit first. Individual actions don't count unless they are part of the whole. Any success achieved by individuals belongs to the entire team.

Patriotism wouldn't be mentioned in the actual competition, but in the practice halls it was a common subject. Though Zhou Enlai would try to defuse the mounting tension in the country, the players knew that they were bearing a heavy responsibility. News of the famine had filtered down to them. It was hard to read letters written with controlled desperation, then look at a can of meat or a plate of vegetables without making the mental calculation that you owed your countrymen everything.

The biggest problem for the players wasn't the physical pressures but the psychological stress. 'Some players were very nervous, and they couldn't shake it. They had to be replaced by those who could stay calm.' Officials more accustomed to setting policy and attending banquets now stood at the back of the practice hall, scooping up stray balls. Their jobs, too, were on the line. Rejected players or demoted officials could find themselves on a train back to their hometown. In the winter of 1960, returning home could be a death sentence.

Zhou Enlai had a country to run. He squeezed the most out of his days by keeping to a particular schedule, working late into the night and accepting no meetings before 11am. His visits to the Ping-Pong team would usually happen around midnight, when the players would have to tumble out of bed to present themselves to the premier. Foreign Affairs Minister Marshal Chen Yi was another visitor who hoped to break the tension, but more likely added to it. 'If you lose a game,' he told them, 'I'll invite you to dinner. If you win, I promise I won't.' It was an uncomfortable joke; giving a dinner for a loser in China was a signal of banishment, rather like a last meal on death row. Everything seemed to increase the pressure, never more so than when Chairman Mao stopped by to 'offer encouragement' during training.

Nothing was left to chance. The team's training schedule was advertised to attract spectators, so they could learn to play before a full house. In a time when there was little in the way of entertainment, the stadium was packed. Inside, the crowd would be controlled by the PA system. 'Now applaud for your Chinese team!' Clapping. Then ordered silence. Then clapping again. Afterward the players would linger outside the stadium. All 108 stayed to answer any questions on table tennis the crowd might have.

Despite the bubble that the chosen lived inside, they weren't impervious to the increasing desperation among their relatives. Many had some idea of the famine because it had crept right to the heart of China's greatest city. At the theatre, a visiting doctor remembered that all around her 'men and women were falling asleep in their seats. Tired and cold.' At dinner, she was chastised by her waiter for leaving a few grains of rice in her bowl.

'In villages a few miles outside Beijing, most peasants were grotesquely swelled by edema and were dying in sizeable numbers.' Inside Beijing, things were better, but you didn't have to walk far to see those suffering from edema, which, by the time the Ping-Pong tournament started, 'affected roughly ten per cent of [Beijing's] population.' Stores were empty, except for salesmen sitting passively in front of empty shelves. People roamed without hope, with 'their heads well within their shoulders and scarcely lifting their feet, [they] went from store to store.'

The Foreign Ministry apartments were heated for no more than two hours a day. Even in Zhou Enlai's house, the rationing had begun to bite, as his wife served tea made from nettles. The letters that arrived inside the training grounds were specific enough to worry some players deeply. But what could they do? By now you couldn't send food out to the countryside, and 'There was no point sending money home. There was nothing left to buy.' Yet the World

Championships programme then heading to the printers called Beijing 'a scene of booming prosperity.'

Fu wandered through the practice hall with his pen, pausing beside tables to watch the practising players; he 'wrote everything down in a notebook.' His brilliance was that he was creating flexibility within a very taut system. While the rest of China was trying to pump out cadres that dressed and spoke and thought the same, Fu was trying to create a varied arsenal to launch at the Japanese and Hungarians. He would need expert servers, spinners, blockers, drivers, shake-hand players, penholders. He would then be able to deploy these weapons at will.

Things weren't going well for the women's team. Officials at the National Sports Commission were worried that the Japanese ladies still held the edge. China's best hope was the veteran Qiu Zhonghui, a tiny, bespectacled woman, the daughter of a high school teacher. She had spent the first years of her life watching other people play Ping-Pong at high school until someone had picked her up, put her on a stool at one end of the table, and placed a racquet in her hand. A student held her by the waist as she leaned side to side. As a tiny child, her performance was a schoolyard novelty act, but as soon as she could see over the tabletop, it became harder and harder to beat her.

Qiu was raised in Changsha, where Mao had begun his political career. She wanted to be a volleyball player and made the high school team despite her size, but 'frankly, my teachers pushed me toward Ping-Pong.' Back in 1953 the Hunan Sports Commission had selected her as one of four people from the entire province sent to Beijing. Even though two of her companions were men over thirty years old, the commission entrusted her with the travel money, which she sewed into the hem of her coat. It had an almost religious quality for her. 'It wasn't mine,' she said. 'To me, it was the sweat and the blood of peasants.' The bus journey to Beijing took seven days. Qiu chose the cheapest hotels and restaurants, got the tiny squad to Beijing just in time for their table tennis examination, and returned to Changsha with half the money left, a fact that amazed the provincial officials. A month later a letter arrived. She had been chosen as the alternate for the national team.

In 1955, she had toured Auschwitz after the World Youth Festival

109

in Poland. A year later, she'd travelled to Japan, where she first met Ivor Montagu. 'He brought us these special brooches,' she said, and doted on the Communist Chinese players. In 1959, when Rong won the gold, her own bronze medal had been overshadowed. Now she was China's best hope for victory.

She was experiencing pressure she had never felt before. What if the Japanese women had improved since 1959? How could Chinese women say they were holding up half the sky if the Chinese men won everything and the women went home empty-handed?

He Long ordered a special practice for the women's team, packed with noisy spectators. Qiu awaited her opposition at the table. In walked the ugliest women Qiu had ever seen, speaking loudly in falsetto voices. For a moment she was confused, until she finally grasped that it was the men's practice players in drag. 'We laughed and laughed. Honestly, no one could play. We were laughing too hard.'

The audience played its part. When the women finally triumphed over the men's practice squad, the audience rose, roaring approval, and hats went flying into the air.

The Ping-Pong team had become symbolic of the utopian state China should be, and yet it was obvious that the rest of the country was failing, and in the most dramatic way. Marshal He Long arrived at the practice hall one afternoon and called a halt to their session. He would usually sit, because his feet were so scarred from wearing straw sandals during the Long March. That day, he stood before the men's team. 'Listen,' he said. 'Playing Ping-Pong is like fighting a battle. If you are afraid of death, you will die. You have to control that fear. Conquer it and you won't die out there.'

The players nodded in understanding. 'Let me tell you another story,' said the marshal. He paused for effect, brought his hands to his mouth, and removed his teeth. He continued, now lisping through his gums:

Once I was in a cavalry charge in battle. We had to charge forward, and I was on the first horse. I was shot in the mouth – all these teeth were shattered. But if I hadn't been sitting up firmly in my seat, that shot would have passed six inches higher and gone right through the centre of my brain.

'We were really encouraged by this speech,' remembered a player. 'We just weren't afraid anymore.' The constant attention from the highest levels had made the team feel both cherished by and indebted to the nation. Thanks to Coach Fu, there was also a high level of confidence in their own ability. And then, overnight, it fell apart.

| # Ping-Pong Espionage

The Chinese had already done an extraordinary amount of home-work, especially concerning the Japanese. 'The most studied of all was Ogimura,' said Coach Liang Youneng, who remembered an incident in 1962 when a Japanese player passed through Beijing on tour and came up against 'himself,' a second-ranked Chinese prac-tice player whose sole job had been to imitate his style. 'He was amazed,' laughed the coach, 'and also jealous,' because not even Japan had such resources.

Now, just seven days before the tournament was due to begin, the Chinese received disturbing news. The National Sports Com-mission had had an article from a Japanese magazine translated. 'It was a very boastful article, talking about how Japan was the best team in the world' and how this 'supremacy would be kept thanks to a new secret spin that their players had developed for their serves.'

Ping-Pong can be reduced to basics, as with Ogimura's 51 per cent doctrine, where an all-out offensive attack needed to succeed only just over half the time. The serve was key to the 'three-ball attack.' Effective service would leave the opponent scrambling just to return it. A weak return, one that cleared the net a touch too high or was hit too softly, could immediately be punished. If the Japa-nese really had developed a new serve, then the Chinese would be at a huge disadvantage. In 1959, games had often come down to two or three points, and an unreturnable serve could give the Japanese the win. Politically, it would send the wrong message: the Great Leap Forward wasn't truly great.

What could be done in a week? It was a matter of the highest importance. The National Sports Commission believed it had one last shot. Table tennis, like war, was now an extension of Chinese politics, and Zhuang Jiafu was asked to be China's first Ping-Pong spy.

Zhuang grew up in Punyu, an impoverished town outside Guangzhou. No one in Punyu could afford a table tennis table. When Zhuang's parents left early in the day to sell fruit, their children took the front door off its hinges and used it as a playing surface. Zhuang's physical education instructor encouraged him to join the city team, where he excelled. When India sent a touring team to Guangzhou, Zhuang, now a postal worker, was the only player who won his game. His reward was a thirty-six-hour train ride to Tianjin to play against the best players in China. Having come so far, the postman had become a vital part of the national squad.

On He Long's orders, Zhuang travelled to Hong Kong, that outpost of British imperialism, to spy on the Japanese. He didn't want his wife, a member of China's basketball team, to worry about him, so he told her he was going to Shanghai. Zhuang took a prop plane from Beijing to Wuhan, then flew to Changsha, where he was grounded by heavy rains. As a postman, he had memorised train schedules across China and knew he had to make the next train south or else lose a vital day. He requisitioned a local car and sped across Changsha to the railroad station. Arriving in Guangzhou at six in the morning, he took a taxi to the local sports commission. The commission's director rolled out of bed and joined him on the last leg, a short train trip to Shenzhen. There the director handed him over to Mr X, a Chinese intelligence agent based in Hong Kong.

The first rule was that once Zhuang and Mr X were in Hong Kong, they could not be seen together in public. They would walk apart and pretend not to know each other. The second rule was always to wear sunglasses in public. The third rule was to keep calm at the border crossing, no matter how tense the situation became. There were three different checkpoints between China and Hong Kong. Zhuang was told that Mr X would take care of any surprises.

Zhuang felt rising panic. He was on a mission for the Chinese government on behalf of table tennis, and yet, if he was arrested, he had no proper documentation. The best he could hope for was immediate deportation from Hong Kong; the worst would be his arrest and trial as a Communist agitator.

At the first checkpoint for entry into Hong Kong was a uniformed Englishman with a policeman at his elbow to deal with translation issues. 'Why are you here?' asked the Englishman.

'Visiting student,' said Zhuang as instructed. From the corner of his eye, he could see Mr X several people behind him in line.

'Student identification, please.'

He pulled his card from his pocket, and as he did so, realised that it had been issued by the Beijing police bureau. The Hong Kong policeman stepped forward and looked it over. 'This one's come all the way from Beijing – the fucking capital of Communism.' It was the moment when Zhuang's legs began to tremble. Mr X appeared at his elbow. 'This guy,' he told the Hong Kong policemen in Cantonese, 'his cousin is that travel agent in Shenzhen. That son of a bitch should have given him a bribe for you, but you know, he's just the cousin.'

Zhuang pretended not to know what was being said. He was amazed at Mr X's relaxed manner and felt as if he were watching someone else pass through the motions. 'It was exactly like being in a spy movie,' he remembered. They were waved through. Mr X gave Zhuang his train ticket into Hong Kong and whispered the name of their station. Zhuang, he instructed, was not to sit anywhere near him.

When he left the station, Zhuang began to walk through the Hong Kong streets. Mr X passed on the other side and, after a few minutes, disappeared into an apartment building. Zhuang followed, walking up several floors. He would be staying in Mr X's house, and there he would address Mr X as Uncle; Mr X lived with his wife, his son, and their servant. Only the wife knew who Zhuang really was. After an awkward family breakfast the next morning, Zhuang headed toward the stadium trailing Mr X.

Before they left, Mr X presented him with two tickets to the table tennis match – one cheap, one expensive. He was instructed to use the cheap one to enter the stadium among the crowd and then the expensive one to sit close to the action. Their biggest fear was that Zhuang would be recognised. He had played against a few of the Hong Kong players in previous tours. He had even faced off against Ogimura in the World Championships. Mr X checked Zhuang's sunglasses and handed him an early edition of a Cantonese newspaper to hide behind.

They arrived at Queen Elizabeth Stadium half an hour before the matches were due to begin. Zhuang took his seat in the second row with his heart racing; he peeked out from behind the newspaper. The first match was supposed to be close – Hong Kong's finest chopper against one of Japan's top spinners. Within minutes, the Japanese had taken a ten-to-zero lead. Zhuang could see that the experienced Hong Kong player just couldn't read the serve; the ball was flying to the 'left, to the right, up and down, no two returns were alike.'

The Hong Kong audience had little patience. They started to stand and boo. Shouts rained down on their own athletes. 'You shouldn't even be a player! Go back home!' Zhuang looked about him. It was hard to imagine this kind of dissent taking place in Beijing. 'Go back to the farm! Go back to shovelling pig shit!' The next victim trotted up to the table and was again easily dispatched by his Japanese opponent. Yet, by the time the third game took place, Zhuang had a revelation. The Japanese could only capitalise on this kind of spin if the opposing player was kept away from the table. The spin could be counterbalanced if you stood your ground.

Zhuang didn't know it, but he wasn't the only spy in the crowd. The Chinese had also sent a photographer with a specially adapted camera. He stood in the front row alongside the sportswriters, taking a series of high-speed photographs of the Japanese serves.

After the match, Zhuang disappeared into the crowd, making his way back across the border toward Guangzhou to catch his plane north. Running late, he sprinted up the steps and, thoroughly relieved, ducked through the doorway. To his horror, he looked down the aisle of the tiny plane. It contained the entire Japanese table tennis team. They were on their way to the capital a few days ahead of the tournament. His rival Ogimura stood up, gave a short bow, and greeted him.

'It's lovely to see you,' said Ogimura. 'Are you on your way to the championships?'

'Yes, yes, yes,' said Zhuang, quickly inventing a story that he had been visiting relatives in Guangdong.

After a silent five-hour flight feigning sleep, Zhuang went directly to the training centre. His room-mate, Rong Guotuan, and the two young prodigies, Zhuang Zedong and Li Furong, were waiting for him, along with the responsible officials. They listened to his report and set a strategy in place. 'Don't be afraid to lose a point or two, but keep them close to the table with short shots, spread the ball left and right, but don't let them put too much spin on the ball. When you have a chance, hit hard and hit long.' It remained to be seen if knowledge could be translated into victory, but at least Zhuang had given them hope again.

| **Cheery Martial Music**

The authorities must have been worried by the prospect of so many visitors descending on China at once. That January, just weeks before the first foreigners landed, one province alone had seen five hundred cases of train robbery, as peasants made desperate attempts to find food.

Most of the foreigners came to China through Hong Kong, an itinerary that the government could not control. It meant that their first taste of China would be Guangdong. 'It was an incredibly depressing place' stacked with dilapidated buildings, remembered Alan Tomlinson, New Zealand's top player. On the loudspeakers, cheery martial music played. It was the first piece of propaganda the group would hear. The fragile image projected by the Communist Party of a healthy, vibrant China was already very close to cracking. For their first meal, the championship participants were offered 'an absolute book' of a menu to choose from. It didn't matter what they ordered, they all received the same fish.

If China's image was going to survive two weeks with dozens of foreigners wandering around Beijing, the organisers had to ensure several things: first, that the foreign contingent did not wander far; second, that they didn't speak Mandarin; and third, that they were always accompanied by translators chosen for their political allegiance and energy. 'There was no chance you could be allowed out of their sight,' remembered Tomlinson.

The outside world, knowing nothing of the intensity of China's preparation, still considered the Japanese favourites. The Hungarians were also considered extremely strong, since the team contained wild-haired Zoltan Berczik, the current European champion. The Chinese were thought to have a good shot at third place.

Ushered onto buses at the Peace Hotel, which housed every single player, coach, and journalist, they moved along Chang'an Avenue, one of those intimidating Beijing thoroughfares wider than an American highway. The heads of delegations followed in chauffeur-driven black cars. Thousands of Beijing cyclists parted before them like sardines swerving to avoid a pod of dolphins. Many of the players were struck by the strange combination of busyness and silence; seeing so few cars and hearing so little honking made them feel as if they were passing through a silent film. 'To hear any noise,' wrote a British journalist, 'is as rare as seeing a Chinese blonde.'

The team buses pulled up in front of the brand-new Workers' Gymnasium for the first practice session. The players stared at the building with a sudden sense of déjà vu. It was an identical copy of the building where the players had last seen one another in 1959, as if the Westfalen stadium in Dortmund, Germany, had spent the last two years being dragged slowly east.

At a time when China could not afford to import grain or wheat, the building was a costly marvel. There were treatment rooms, TV and radio facilities, buffets, and clubrooms. The entire stadium was linked by loudspeakers. Specialists from the Chinese Academy of Sciences had ensured that the 'velocity of movement of air' was kept far below Montagu's recommended limits so that nothing could disturb the true flight of the little white ball. Within seconds, heavy curtains could blanket daylight. With no wind and no light, the stadium was the perfect metaphor for the country's claustrophobic isolation.

The approach to the building was marked by 'statues of athletes of various sport events in different poses.' A German journalist staring at the stadium turned to an English counterpart and confessed, 'I must admit the copy is better than the original.'

When the New Zealand player Alan Tomlinson stepped from his bus on a tour that took table tennis players out of Beijing to the countryside, there was a strange request from the guide in charge of the foreigners. If they were not hungry and did not finish their boxed lunches, could they please return any leftovers to the bus. 'Don't throw anything away,' he was told, 'just leave it in the box, and the staff or somebody will eat it.'

It was one of the few tiny glimpses of the famine that the players noticed, and then only in retrospect. Tomlinson remembered the look a waiter gave one of their female players who returned her food untouched and a third player who asked if the waiter could find him some tomatoes for breakfast the next day.

Montagu had personally arranged visas for three of Britain's best sports journalists. It was a calculated risk, but China had two advantages. First, the visas were for a specific amount of time and no travel was allowed before or after the tournament. Second, no one had experience in China; no one knew enough to realise that the police had forbidden the publication of death notices or that 'mourning bands' were forbidden among Beijingers.

As hunger closed in on the capital, people had begun to improvise. Children tipped sticks with glue and hunted for cicadas to eat or tied strings to the legs of female dragonflies, walked the edge of ponds, and ate the males that came to mate. The bitter joke was that the only thing with two legs that couldn't be eaten was an airplane. The only thing with four legs considered unpalatable was a bench.

People scoured the small patches of green in search of plants and weeds to add to their thin soups. But city dwellers often lacked country knowledge. In a single week in Beijing, there were 160 deaths from the digestion of cocklebur plants, a long, agonising process leading to convulsions and death. Qiu Zhonghui, China's number-one hope in the women's singles, remembered being given permission to leave the training grounds after weeks of work. She was stunned by the emptiness that had descended on Beijing's streets. Finally, she spotted someone. It was a woman, perhaps in her thirties, who was digging up weeds from the side of the road. She'd never seen such a thing and approached her to watch. 'What are you looking at?' snarled the woman.

'What are you doing?' asked Qiu.

'What planet are you from?' The woman kept digging for weeds in silence, then looked up and whispered, 'The whole country's starving. I'm making soup.'

| # The Chance to Shine

Finally, the opening ceremony began. 'It was like Cirque du Soleil but it was in 1961, it was unbelievable. I'd never seen anything like it,' remembered New Zealand player Murray Dunn. 'It was that spectacular and it went on for an hour or two . . . a mass display of gymnastics and dancing and tumbling.' Zhou Enlai was spotted sitting on the rostrum next to Ivor Montagu, 'who looked like the cat who ate the canary,' undoubtedly 'the man of the moment.'

While he'd already dined with the premier and Mao's wife, Jiang Qing, Montagu had done his best to ignore all overtures from Britain's Beijing Liaison Office, reluctantly attending a single tea with the English team. The head of the liaison office dismissed Montagu. 'He struck me as being something of a drawing-room Communist and I doubt whether he had talks of any importance with the Chinese.'

Montagu had also been welcomed the night before at a vast banquet by He Long, whose remarks were in lockstep with Montagu's own view of sport. Table tennis players, said He Long, were about to make 'due contribution to the strengthening of the solidarity of the peoples of all countries and to the defence of world peace.' No one was there to simply entertain.

When the games finally got under way, there was no holding back the crowd's enthusiasm. The Chinese team, prepped, fed, and polished, was hungry for victory. Playing a first round match against the Cubans, their fellow Communists, the Chinese players began ruthlessly: twenty-one–zero, twenty-one–one, twenty-one–zero. The

Chinese public had waited so long for their Ping-Pong Spring that they bellowed constant approval of the rout. Halfway through the game, a message came over the loudspeakers. Be careful, it advised, your reaction could be misconceived as inhospitable. Could you please begin to cheer both teams evenly?

'Had they done that in Europe, the audience would have got even worse.' But this was China. 'All the cheering stopped; it changed completely.' The Cubans won a grand total of four points in the remaining games. The crowd applauded each of them.

The journalists wandered the halls of the stadium in between games, marvelling at the contrast of its modernity compared to the 'lowly, grey tiled resting places' in Beijing 'where seven million lay their heads.' Every single reporter noted how 'desperately proud' China was of 'her new role.' 'There is no austerity in the stadium. The restaurants are doing booming business with Chinese champagne, which tastes rather like bubbly brandy . . . you can eat anything from bird's nest soup to shark fins and Peking ducks.' The Ping-Pong stadium was the emperor's garden, a tiny isolated bubble of bounty in the middle of a country shocked into silence.

The first time the New Zealanders played, Murray Dunn looked up into the stands and was amazed at the uniformity of it all. Staring at the chanting crowd of twenty thousand, he realised that 'everybody, and I mean everybody, wore . . . blue denim.' Everyone had the same short hair. 'It was hard to tell the difference between a man and a woman, quite frankly.' The reporter from the *Express* went further. The women reminded him 'of British Railway engine drivers.'

Unbelievably, as Dunn finished off his game and headed past the wooden barricades that separated the tables from the stands, he heard his name called from the crowd. It was a Kiwi accent. 'G'day Murray!' He looked up into the blue sea and scoured the faces. A hand waved. Almost unrecognisable under his blue denim cap was an old friend from school, 'a bright fellow' named York Young, the New Zealand son of Chinese immigrants. He had returned after the revolution, one of thousands of optimists who had wanted to help in the Great Leap Forward. Young rushed down to meet Dunn beside the barricades, but immediately his interpreter pushed forward until she was between the two men. She took Young by the arm and 'grilled him for ten minutes' then pulled Dunn aside 'to make sure the stories coincided.'

With the interpreter now standing between the school friends, Dunn didn't know what to say. 'I said something silly like "we'll have to have a coffee."' Young just looked at Dunn and said, 'We can't talk again. We're not going to be allowed to talk again.' He turned and merged sadly back into the blue-clad crowd. Another small opportunity for open conversation had been lost. 'That was the last I ever heard of him,' said Dunn.

Thanks to Montagu's willful ignorance, the Chinese had pushed the laws of the game to the limits. The host country was legally allowed to invite extra players into the tournament. The Polish were the largest travelling contingent, with eleven players. The Chinese had seventy. Their strength was extraordinary, and the inevitable soon happened in the singles competitions: Chinese were drawn against Chinese. The players would then further bend the rules by playing their games slowly, waiting to see who would win the game that would provide their next competitor. There was no direct translation in China for the British sense of fair play that went hand in hand with sport. Sports were political, they were simply serving one aim: victory for Communism. Depending on which type of player was best matched, the other Chinese player would throw the game.

In case there were any doubts as to the politics of the sport, the biggest news of the decade was announced to the Chinese public not in the *People's Daily* but in the middle of the Workers' Gymnasium. All the lights were turned up; the New Zealanders' big match was suddenly brought to a halt. A huge victory for Communism was announced. Russia's Yuri Gagarin had orbited the earth and returned. A Communist was the first man in the history of the world to leave the planet. The Soviet team was brought out to take a bow. Russia's top young star, Gennady Averin, made a sweet speech: 'Even though Major Gagarin in his spaceship *Vostok* has not won a table tennis title, his name is known all over the world.' Laughter swept the stadium. The New Zealand squad, standing to one side alongside their proud translator, tapped her on her shoulder. 'When are we going to have our table back?' they asked.

In the men's team competition, the Swaythling Cup, it soon

became obvious that the gold medal clash was going to be the grudge match that the Chinese team had prepared for: Japan against China. It was Japan's chance to create history. Victory would mean they were the only team in the world that had won six straight championships. All the Chinese efforts to use the tournament as a propaganda push could suddenly be transformed into an alternate world view. Japan could emerge as the nation that dominated Asia, even when playing in the capital of the old enemy.

Rong Guotuan faltered when victory seemed close for the men's team. The noise in the stadium grew for every point Rong Guotuan won, but the points he lost were greeted with shrill, desperate screams. Rong Guotuan, the world champion, looked distinctly worried. To the consternation of the crowd, he couldn't find a way back. The Japanese won, forcing another game.

For the Chinese, with their world champion beaten, the stadium's hopes would be carried by a local teenager, a handsome, bowlegged boy named Zhuang Zedong. He had been born in a mazelike Beijing *hutong*, or alley. Without money for a table, he'd hit balls against a wall in his own home. His mother didn't worry about it until he grew strong enough to break his first window with a Ping-Pong ball. From then on, she'd encourage her Tiger Cub to run to school an hour early to hit before class.

Zhuang was utterly fearless, with the same height and the same extraordinarily developed legs as Ogimura, but seven years younger. He walked out to face the Japanese to a home crowd's vigorous applause, a mixture of encouragement and appalling expectation.

Of all the countries in the world that harboured deep-seated resentments against Japan, none had as much reason as China, which had suffered fifteen years of brutal occupation. The Rape of Nanking alone had seen three hundred thousand casualties. Photographs of the humiliated dead – the rows of Chinese heads lining the city streets and the women impaled on bamboo poles – were seared into the Chinese collective memory. The government said the 1961 World Championships were friendly, but the crowd of twenty thousand Chinese was frantic for victory. Team-mate Xu Yinsheng remembered looking up into the stands just before the game against Japan started and being amazed at the number of old faces that stared back. 'These were people who didn't know a thing about table tennis. What they understood was that this was a grudge match.'

It must have been deeply discomforting to Zhou Enlai. He had made a special effort to greet the Japanese players personally – not because he believed in overextending the hand of peace, but as a signal to Tokyo. China had no fleet worth speaking of and was desperate to begin to charter as many Japanese ships as possible to import food.

Ogi and Zhuang Zedong were tied at two to two. Montagu sat in the stands next to the Chinese premier. The stadium, now crammed past capacity, was 'a sweat pit.' Ogi waved his hand in the air, calling a temporary stop to play, unable to think in the clamour. The whole stadium was shaking with so much noise that the Japanese coach complained to the officials. Another plea went out across the 'big brother loud-speaker' but this time the noise didn't abate. Ogi opted to continue. 'When Japan scored a point there were moans and a long wailing cry of Ay-yah.' But Ogimura didn't score many more points against Zhuang Zedong, the hometown teenager. He was utterly humiliated.

The fastest man in table tennis, so sharp that the Chinese had nicknamed him The Brain, looked like he was wearing stone trainers. Zhuang knew that 'every shot against the Japanese players was revenge for the Chinese [who had suffered the Japanese invasion].'

The final game ended twenty-one–thirteen to Zhuang Zedong. The Japanese team then folded, allowing Rong Guotuan quickly to dispose of his last opponent. When the final point was over, the whole stadium rose. 'Hats and scarves and gloves were thrown into the air.' It was a freezing, windy April day, but not a soul cared. 'It was genuine happiness.' 'China was champion of the world. This arena broke apart like a huge Ming bowl, done in pastel shades. The normal fixed smile of the Chinese shone like a new moon as they cheered, clapped and danced and the team hugged and kissed like English football players.'

Somewhere in the control room, a technician flashed the stadium's lights on and off, on and off, as the Chinese players stood in a row applauding their fans. The stadium shook. 'China! China! China!' The chant rang hardest inside the stadium, then out the doors and through the gathering crowd. It could be heard echoing around every radio set in Beijing.

After the stadium emptied, the workers walked through the empty stands in silence. They filled bag after bag with the hats, scarves, and gloves that, in a time of so few personal possessions, had been thrown freely in the air. Throughout the night, the city reverberated to the banging of drums and the crack and whine of fireworks. The scenes were repeated as Qiu Zhonghui won the women's singles and then again as Zhuang beat his young rival Li Furong in the men's final. The only moment the applause was equalled was when Chairman Mao was spotted inside the stadium. 'He got a huge reception,' remembered a player. 'Everyone stood up to clap in his honour, including Mao himself.'

In order to obscure the harshness of the crowd's reaction in the final, the only team Zhou Enlai hosted a goodbye party for were the Japanese, most likely thinking of his shipping needs. Before departing, the ITTF delegates met one more time, and President Montagu was 're-elected without any other nominations.' He'd stood and congratulated 'China's fledglings' such as Zhuang Zedong, who had showed 'themselves to be daring, willing to learn, modest in victory and undaunted in defeat' – although they hadn't needed to be undaunted in defeat. At long last, China had seen nothing but success.

| **Fallout**

From any sporting standard, the Beijing World Championships were a stunning accomplishment. Normally an international sporting event such as the Olympics is aimed as a show of strength to the rest of the world. The 1961 World Championships were even more important as a domestic statement because they implied that the sacrifices made had been worth it. The Great Leap Forward had driven the country to the edge of yet another rift, but the lie had held: progress was being made. There were many, like the head of the British Mission, who shrugged off the World Championships as 'a not entirely negligible fillip to the regime.' That was missing the bigger point. Propaganda is often about hiding, not making news. The death of somewhere between 17 and 45 million Chinese remained an internal secret.

Not even the depth of the split between Russia and China had been revealed. Though it was well known even to midrankers in the party, the crowd had betrayed little to foreign journalists except a very predictable prejudice. England's Ian Harrison had been the darling of Beijing on 5 April when he came up against Ogimura and, against all expectations, took the Japanese to five games and won. His victory caused 'the great roar of China.' Yet, the following day, when Ian Harrison beat a Russian player, 'you could have heard a lotus blossom drop.' 'There was no room for doubt where the Chinese spectators' sympathies lay – and it certainly wasn't with England.' This suited Zhou Enlai perfectly. While China continued to find its path to independence, it was far better to be thought to be standing under Russia's nuclear umbrella. It helped show China's dealings with the West from a position of strength.

There were a few grievances in the foreign presses, but from a propaganda standpoint, the tournament had been a heady success. Even those who shed their roles as thankful guests to criticise the hosts were looking in the wrong direction. There were complaints about the airplanes, the quality of the food, and that the country was made up of '650 million blue ants.' To their horror, the British journalists had explored an entire commune and failed to find a single pub.

Those who did travel farther did so with the permission of the Chinese and cheerfully parroted government statistics. A *Daily Worker* journalist declared that 300 per cent increases on national target figures 'seem to be well within the area of possibility.' Edgar Snow, who had slept on a Ping-Pong table in China thirty years before, was back again and saw no indications of famine anywhere he went. But the novellist and doctor Han Suyin had seen signs of beriberi throughout Beijing; 'the swollen faces were obvious.' She couldn't bring herself to write about it for another nineteen years. It was a question of saving face. At a time when 'the whole world seemed to rise with glee to threaten China,' she considered it her duty to start 'lying through my teeth (with a smile) to the diplomats and the newsmen who probed.' All was good in the world; all was good in China.

As far as Cold War score-keeping was concerned, the spring of 1961 continued an excellent run of results for the red team. Within a week of the end of the tournament, it was clear that Fidel Castro had successfully repelled the Bay of Pigs invasion of Cuba. Zhou Enlai lent his support in speaking out against 'The United States imperialists [who] have no scruples in shattering world peace and in dragging their people into war.' Gagarin still dominated the news, and then, on 23 April, the French Army revolted in Algeria, yet another indication of colonial powers faltering.

There were very few signs that journalists had discovered anything at all about the famine in China. One Japanese photographer, who had followed his team beyond Beijing in the wake of the World Championships, did note that:

Almost all the people in their fifties and above that I saw in the cities and the countryside were depressed. I tried to have talks with some of them but they were reluctant to answer my questions for fear of something. They seem resigned to their fates under a regime they did not understand.

Members of the British Foreign Service in Hong Kong were among the few who suspected a mass famine in China. The freight trains bringing produce into Hong Kong from the mainland were marked with their province of origin. The British weighed every pig and chicken, noting their frail state against past plumpness. They suspected the death toll must be huge. But what good was empirical data against a well-publicised interview? The same week the players left China, Viscount Montgomery spoke to the *Sydney Morning Herald*. He talked of his own visit to China months before, calling Mao 'a genuine democrat,' insisting that 'China is closely allied to Russia,' and concluding that 'life is much better now than under the emperors [because] at least they have enough to eat.' Zhou Enlai couldn't have written a better defence himself.

With the Beijing World Championships, the Chinese learned that Ping-Pong was a palatable digestive – Communism seemed softer, just as Montagu had predicted. Friends had indeed been made, and this was certainly a factor when the time would come for 1971's Ping-Pong diplomacy.

The other events of 1961 would have repercussions on China's doorstep. President Kennedy had also learned something that spring. The Bay of Pigs fiasco had sent a worrying signal that America was capable of pathetic disorganisation. Worse was to come. With Cuba now having proof of aggressive American intentions, Castro would goad Russia into supplying the Caribbean island with nuclear missiles. Within the year, the world would be poised on the edge of nuclear war. After the threat had passed, America flexed her muscles and escalated her role in Vietnam, tripling the number of American advisers in 1961 and then again in 1962. For China, it was enough to make the United States the number-one enemy. The Chinese feared that a US-sponsored victory in Vietnam would leave them surrounded on all sides – by the United States, Taiwan, India, Japan, and the Soviet Union. The silence between China and America was becoming very loud.

CHAPTER 26 | Heroes of the Nation

For the victorious Chinese players, these were heady times. Not only had the men won the Swaythling Cup, but Zhuang Zedong had beaten his own team-mate Li Furong to win the singles title. Qiu Zhonghui had taken the women's title.

More important, the famine had lifted, and the players could begin to enjoy themselves without having to equivocate between their success and the state of the nation. Thanks to Rong Guotuan, Ping-Pong had achieved real popularity in 1959, but now, in the summer of 1961, it became a full-blown craze. Crowds gathered around stone tables in the parks. Wherever you walked, you could see Ping-Pong bats 'kept down the back of people's trousers.' In the streets of Beijing, students shuffled to school making short punches through the air with imaginary racquets.

Zhuang Xieling, one of the members of the victorious men's team, remembered leaving his apartment in a gleaming white shirt. By the time he returned home, the shirt was covered with handprints and finger stains. Everyone thought it was good luck to touch the world champion. Qiu said she was lucky 'to have a plain face.' In public she wore a scarf to mask her appearance. 'Rong was too distinctive looking,' she said, and had to wander through the city in a face mask.

The table tennis players, whose victories had been followed by millions, had become celebrities, but they were Communist celebrities, in many ways created and nurtured by the state. All the players knew that they weren't simply Chinese; they were representatives of the Communist Party whether they were party members or not.

The players received pay raises, but these amounted to a handful of dollars a month, significant, but a pittance in comparison with modern wages. They were also famed for remaining humble, signing 'table tennis player' beneath their autographs as if they still had to explain who they were.

The players became a reflection of Zhou Enlai's and Chen Yi's foreign policy. In 1962, they were sent, with Rong Guotuan as their captain, to tour Guinea, Mali, Ghana, the United Arab Republic, and Sudan for two months, part of Zhou Enlai's burgeoning strategy to forge a bloc of developing countries independent of the United States and the Soviet Union. Since the PRC was still not recognised by the UN, sports visits were one of the only ways Zhou Enlai saw to help foster diplomatic relations. In Ghana, the one match the Chinese lost was against the chairman of its Table Tennis Federation, who also happened to be the minister of defence.

Members of Fu's squad were now both world champions and diplomats, polished by the International Cooperation Department of the National Sports Commission, where they were coached in table manners and propriety. Nevertheless, things didn't always go smoothly. At a banquet at the World Championships in Yugoslavia in 1965, they were faced with chicken legs and knives and forks. One player cut down heavily into the bone; the plate 'was propelled into the air' and neatly caught by another player across the table.

Players who travelled to represent China were given a huge three-hundred-yuan allowance, but it had to stretch over three years. Tailors would cut them bespoke Mao suits. They were measured for shirts and shoes. When they returned to Beijing, the Mao suits would have to be returned for others to use, unless the players had saved up enough money to buy their suit at a discount. Even the shirts weren't always full shirts. Sometimes they were just cotton patches that could be easily detached, washed, and dried. Abroad, players received twenty yuan each in pocket money – again, a lot of money to them, though it was no more than what Jimmy Greaves might add as a tip to a post-game meal.

The Chinese approach to diplomacy wasn't always welcome. In the summer of 1966, four Chinese table tennis players were arrested in Tunisia. They'd come over to teach the sport, 'but used every opportunity to enlighten young Tunisians on the thoughts of Chairman Mao Tse Tung.' Finally, a player watched by Tunisian authorities was intercepted, interrogated by police, and returned to the Chinese embassy. Diplomatic relations were immediately suspended.

The most famous players of the new generation were Zhuang Zedong and Li Furong. They had been doubles partners at fifteen years old. At first glance, they seemed like good friends. They were photogenic, and Li Furong was known as the Handsome Bomber. Together they led Chinese domination of the next two World Championships, with the squad providing nearly all of the semi-finalists. In three consecutive championships, Zhuang Zedong and Li Furong faced off across the table in the men's final.

Individual gold, it was now decided by the Chinese government, should reflect each player's efforts for the team. Zhuang won his first medal over Li in 1961 because he had secured the vital victory over Ogi. That gold was a reward ordered from above. In 1963, Zhuang won more victories for the team than any other player and was allowed to beat Li in the gold medal game again. Yet when Li starred for the Chinese squad in 1965, winning more games than all of his team-mates, he was directed to lose to Zhuang in the final. At the last moment, it had been decided that it reflected better on China to have Zhuang win three golds in a row. Zhuang benefited, and Li bowed his head to Montagu to accept the silver yet again. It would have been of small consolation to Li that he was the crowd favourite and that his ovation always overwhelmed Zhuang's. The squad gave him the teasing honorific of 'younger brother.'

During championships, the travelling table tennis players were now pampered by China's embassies and their chefs as if they were diplomats. It became 'almost routine for the Chinese to descend on world tourneys with a contingent of forty or more – by far the largest – that included players, newsmen, photographers, delegates, propagandising interpreters, masseurs, cooks and even laundrymen.'

The players of the table tennis team became national heroes, second only to Mao's warrior statesmen who had founded New China. The squad met with these otherwise elusive government leaders twice a week and every day during important national holidays.

Both He Long and Zhou Enlai hosted dinners in their houses for top players. It was a distillation of Montagu's dreams. The only guests at the dinners were Ping-Pong players and officials from the Foreign Ministry. In front of strangers, Zhou would often hide the crooked arm that he had broken back in Yan'an, but with the table tennis team he felt comfortable enough to exhibit it.

To visit with the premier was always considered like 'a visit to one's own family, so simple, with no protocol of any kind.' The only extravagance in his home was the number of books on the shelves. In the living room, there were no antiques or curios, just worn sofas, rattan chairs, and a cheap carpet. Players who excused themselves to the bathroom had to walk through the premier's bedroom and would catch a glimpse of the two 'small wooden twin beds, old blankets, no carpet on the floor, a wash basin, a desk with a lamp.'

Qiu Zhonghui remembered the moment when she first stepped foot in Zhou Enlai's kitchen. The premier stood beside Qiu with his sleeves rolled up, 'making these special little meatballs. They're called the lion's head.' Privately, the table tennis team called Zhou Enlai 'the good premier.'

At He Long's house, they'd gather around the table, and the moustachioed general would pour drinks for them all. With Qiu, he'd use terms of affection normally reserved for a daughter or a niece.

In the summers, when they weren't representing China abroad, the teams would travel to Beihaide, where the Communist Party elite summered on the wide beaches of the Bohai Sea. Originally developed by the British, Beihaide was lined by plum trees and close to both forests that could be scoured for mushrooms and its famous shallow waters that holidaymakers waded into to escape the heat. All the leaders gathered on the beaches, including Chairman Mao and his wife, Jiang Qing. Mao never got over the embarrassment that his wife's 'right foot had six toes.' She 'kept her feet covered with rubber shoes even when she waded into the ocean.' It was she, as much as anyone, who would ultimately determine the fate of the Ping-Pong squad.

At night the team was invited to dances with the top officials, the same dances Mao had been hosting for the Communist elite for more than thirty years. Zhou Enlai always attended with the two other stalwarts, Chen Yi and He Long. He glided along, preferring the waltz. He Long, with his scarred feet, could only sit and watch. Zhu De 'danced alone in place, tranquilly waddling to one side like a bear, right foot, left foot.' Even dancing could be dangerous. Zhou was once accused of favouring a turn to the right. When Mao arrived to shuffle stiffly around the dance floor with women thirty or forty years his junior, Zhou would retire for the night.

Table tennis was very much the precursor to China's latest sporting policy. Zhou Enlai's political aspirations for China lay behind the Games of the New Emerging Forces (GANEFO), an alternative Olympics that would be hosted first by Indonesia in 1963 in direct opposition to the IOC. If table tennis had been used as a wedge to create a fresh space between Russian and American sporting and political dominance, then the GANEFO was supposed to widen it. Fifty-one countries sent two thousand five hundred athletes into Jakarta. China would dominate, a perfect promotion of Beijing as 'the leader of world revolution' against imperialism. Among the most lauded of the athletes was a North Vietnamese sharpshooter 'already famous for his part in downing many US pirate planes,' who went on to win gold in the 50-metre pistol competition.

In the 1960s, Ping-Pong was fast becoming the quickest way to read China's political intentions in the greater world. The team moved around the globe like the phantom hand of Zhou Enlai, kind to those they were instructed to be kind to, turning their backs on others, refusing to play against some countries altogether. Considering that not all of America's China watchers believed in the Sino-Soviet split, they would have been better off watching Ivor Montagu than dissecting the Chinese media. In 1965, a furious argument between a Russian and Chinese player erupted during the World Championships over a service from a Chinese player that the top-ranked Russian deemed illegal. Insults were traded, accusations were made, and Montagu himself came to play peacemaker. Western news coverage, of which there was little, presumed the episode stemmed from a personality clash, but in the Chinese squad, there was no such thing.

The incident was the perfect reflection of China's growing disdain for the Soviet Union. The Kremlin may have regarded itself as the centre of the Communist world, but to Mao and Zhou they were now revisionists with imperialist tendencies. In fact, Russia was quickly becoming as repellent to China as America itself. Thanks to the successful nuclear test of 1964, pointedly conducted during the Tokyo Olympics, China was feeling worthy of independence. There were few, and none of them vocal, who would see the larger picture; China was quickly backing itself into a solitary corner with barely a friend in the world.

CHAPTER 27 | **Spreading the Gospel**

Before Ogimura, the deposed world champion, left Beijing in 1961, he gave an interview to Radio Peking chastising the Chinese players for their lack of sportsmanship. They had pushed the rules to their limits, consulted coaches in the middle of games, saturated the competition with their own players, played for time. Ogimura crashed out early in the men's singles and flew back to Tokyo, confused. Japanese domination had ended in a flash, but how on earth had the Chinese ripped the sport of table tennis from Japanese hands?

Ogi was about to find out the answers to all of his questions. In the spring of 1962, an invitation arrived in Tokyo. Would Mr Ichiro Ogimura care to return to Beijing to make a personal visit to the Chinese premier, Zhou Enlai? Ogi knew that Zhou Enlai 'was known for his fanatical love of table tennis' and had heard the rumour that the Chinese premier always carried two briefcases. One was said to be filled with official documents, the second 'with papers and books on his favourite sport.' Back in Yan'an, he'd been told that Mao and Zhou had played table tennis through Chiang Kai-shek's bombing raids inside one of the roomier caves that made up their wartime capital.

The government compound of Zhongnanhai neighboured the Forbidden City, part of the same system of man-made lakes, garden paths, guesthouses, and vermillion walls that had housed six hundred years of emperors. The one thing that Ichiro Ogimura would have noticed as he walked through the compound was a gleaming

135

table tennis table in the wide corridor that led to Mao Zedong's door.

That afternoon, Ogi lunched with Zhou Enlai in his home. They sat together, sipping soup. Finally, Ogi could stand it no longer. 'Why am I here?' he asked. Zhou smiled and answered with a question. 'Do you know that Chinese women practiced the art of foot binding?' Ogi admitted he knew of the practice.

Zhou said, 'In the end, foot binding makes girls physically frail, and children born of women whose feet have been bound also have poor physiques. This custom created a vicious circle for our people.' Table tennis was a way out. It could be played anywhere in China, at any time, by anyone, explained Zhou. 'There's another reason which is embarrassing for us.'

Ogi nodded and waited for the premier to continue. 'Ever since the Opium Wars, we have suffered many humiliating experiences. We reasoned that sport is a way to wipe away the sense of inferiority created by these humiliations.' Wasn't that what Ogi had done for Japan?, asked the premier. And physically, what was the difference between Chinese and Japanese? 'That's why I want you, Mr Ogimura, to use your experience and ability to convey the wonder of Table Tennis to the people of this country.'

It was strange enough to be greeted and treated so well by the premier of the world's most populous country, but Ogi was truly puzzled when they went together to visit the Chinese national team. The premier talked not just of Ping-Pong but of politics with the team.

Ogi looked around and saw that the room was piled to the ceiling with books and documents about table tennis, 'most of them relating to Japan.' They had films of him dating back to 1956. They had bought a copy of his graduation project from Nihon University, a short film called *Japanese Table Tennis*. They had been studying him for years without his knowledge. Ogi was stunned.

Zhuang Zedong came up to shake his hand, one world champion to another. No partisan crowds, just a pair of obsessives. 'You know,' said Zhuang, 'your film was the perfect textbook for us.' In the film, Ogi had rallied with Tanaka, another Japanese world champion. 'Watching the two of you practice made us realise that you don't just swing a table tennis racquet with your arms, you hit the ball with your feet.' Zhuang explained that five years earlier, when he was just a student, he had heard that National Sports Commission officials were going to have a screening of Ogi's film. He tried to sneak in and was stopped by a doorman. He had bowed and scraped 'and fallen to his knees and eventually he'd let me in. Once I saw that film, you became my mentor, Mr Ogimura.' It was a strange revelation. Without ever meeting, Ogi had helped a young pretender develop a game specifically aimed at defeating the Japanese.

By the time of Ogi's return to Japan, he had travelled throughout China, coaching everyone from farmers to schoolchildren. Back in Tokyo, he despaired for Japan. A place now existed where coaches thought 'about table tennis twenty-four hours a day.' Promising players had eight hours a day at the tables. He even liked the lexicon that the Chinese had developed around the game. The service was now called a launch, the first chance to attack. The Japanese had been too soft in adopting the English word for service.

A year later, just after his thirtieth birthday, Ogimura captained the Japanese team against China in Prague in the 1963 World Championships. The Japanese were humiliated five–one. In the men's singles, six out of eight of the men's quarter-finalists and all the semi-finalists were Chinese. The same two players, Zhuang Zedong and Li Furong, would contest the final again, and it was Ogimura's own accidental progeny, Zhuang Zedong, who would win.

China's love for table tennis still bemused Westerners, including those in Beijing at the British Mission. One Foreign Office memo from 9 June 1964, quoted an editorial that claimed the Chinese team's success was 'due to the fact that they have raised high the great banner of Mao Tse-tung's thought.' The British diplomat explained to his London colleague, 'Lest you should think they used Volume One of Mao's Works instead of a bat,' that the Chinese players had actually developed their table tennis technique 'in accordance with the party policy to "let a Hundred Flowers Bloom."' The letter concluded, 'Flowers sometimes bloom in strange places in China.'

In the spring of 1964, the National Sports Commission was worried that the Chinese women would fail to take gold in the approaching World Championships in Yugoslavia. Xu Yinsheng, the top men's double player, partner of Zhuang Zedong, was asked to give a speech to the women's team. 'I never thought anyone would write it down,' he said. The speech was typed up and sent to He Long. He made a few notes in the margins and sent it on to Chairman Mao. Mao added a few notes of his own, including the comment that he had 'not read anything so good for years. What he talks about is a ball game; what we can learn from it are theory, politics, economy, culture, and military affairs. If we do not learn from the young "generals," we shall be doomed.'

Chairman Mao, the great believer in continuous revolution, student of Marx and Lenin, the man who had driven China back to unity, was transfixed by the words of a Ping-Pong player. The sixteen-page tract, entitled *On How to Play Table Tennis*, was sent to the highest officials in every province. Within a week, the entire speech was reprinted in the *People's Daily*. Millions of copies were distributed and carefully digested. 'Mao made everyone read Xu Yinsheng,' a retired official explained. 'And I mean *everyone*.'

The essay was, in retrospect, one of the very earliest signs of what was to come during the Cultural Revolution. 'To rely entirely on the team leader or coach does not necessarily make for a good game,' Xu wrote. If you just accepted a coach's regimen as perfect, and never challenged it, then the coach would stagnate and foreign competition would catch up. 'Have the guts to speak out and state your views,' Xu urged. 'If politics are not in command, you cannot play a good game.' Xu had made the connection between politics and Ping-Pong more explicit than ever. 'We should realise that small though a table tennis ball is in size, its implications are great.'

Just because he had written the greatest political tract of the year didn't mean Xu Yinsheng could avoid the coming typhoon. By endorsing Xu's point of view, Mao was at his most cunning. The essay made two points. One, that Mao himself was above criticism. His thoughts alone could bring victory. If that was true, then it put Mao in a unique position. He could unleash chaos and, as a living god, stand above it, knowing he could descend to restore order once his enemies had fallen.

Secondly, Xu had made plain that elders should be open to criticism by the generation below, no matter their standing. This key point to the Cultural Revolution didn't spring from the lips of China's best doubles player, but it's clear that what Xu said fit in with Mao's plan. The established belief – that the first shot was fired by Mao eight months later in 1965, through his wife's critique of a play that allegedly compared the Chairman to a corrupt emperor – seems wrong. Table tennis as a sport was already central to Chinese culture, and culture was already political. Xu's words were clear, Mao's support was obvious, and the message was threatening: let the old men tremble, because a new revolution was coming.

Mao's fellow Long Marchers, such heroes of the revolution as Peng Dehuai, Chen Yi, Liu Shaoqi, and even Zhou Enlai, all of whom had dared to doubt the success of the Great Leap Forward and had sought to steer China slowly away from Mao's ideas, were about to pay the price. Only He Long stood between the players and the whirlpool of political violence.

The athletes didn't know that He Long, their protector, had once been handed an assignment by Mao to investigate Peng, the former minister of defence who had confronted Mao in Lushan. Instead of producing a report that criticised Peng, He Long had justified Peng's actions and dwelled on the failures of the Great Leap Forward. Peng would be one of the first victims of the Cultural Revolution. He Long would not be far behind, and without him, who would protect the nation's sportsmen?

The table tennis team believed they had no reason to worry. They had won glory for China again and again. Their consistency was staggering. At the beginning of 1966, Fu Qifang's squad was perhaps the only thing produced in China that was truly competitive at an international level. The gold medals they brought back to Beijing had turned into a biennial victory parade. After their third victory in a row in 1965, a huge party had been held inside the leadership compound of Zhongnanhai. The players drank and chatted with the country's top politicians. In the middle of the room on a table sat the Montagu's family heirloom, the Swaythling Cup, alongside all the other table tennis trophies. The presence of so much silver seemed to suggest a shimmering future. And then Mao flipped China on its head.

CHAPTER 28 | # The Grinding Halt

If the Great Leap Forward still echoed through China like distant thunder, then the Cultural Revolution arrived like a bolt of lightning to show that the storm hadn't passed. The next ten years of life in China played out against the Great Leap Forward. Before, it had been easy for Mao to divide the country, always drawing new lines in the sand and accusing groups of being rightists, reactionaries, or counter-revolutionaries. Mao would declare his position and watch China shuffle into line with him.

In order to consolidate power, Mao's new strategy would gamble everything on an incredibly divisive campaign. Now he spoke only in muddy aphorisms, letting both sides claim that they were trying to act in his name. On one side was the old guard, symbolised by pragmatic Zhou Enlai; on the other, the younger radicals, headed by the Chairman's own wife, Jiang Qing. Mao insisted that revisionists were hiding in every level of leadership. They ought to be removed through violent class struggle.

He would float above, a god who refused to intervene, covertly directing both sides while keeping them in a state of constant tension. It was like watching a man walk two dogs who despised each other, one a tamed Doberman and the other an energetic pit bull eager to bite on command. Back when he had confronted Peng at Lushan, Mao had said, 'If others attack me, I always strike back. Others attack me, I attack them later.' Now the time had come.

The Chinese people were inured to the relentless campaigns of the

140

Communist Party. If your family was lucky enough to avoid scrutiny, then most campaigns were little more than arbitrary privations. In 1964, houseplants and flowers were condemned as bourgeois affectations. Perhaps the Cultural Revolution would be similar. Roads were renamed, which was confusing but hardly life changing. The British Mission now found itself on Anti-Imperialist Road. The Russian ambassador resided on Anti-Revisionism Road. And on those roads, the cars were now encouraged to forge ahead at red lights, the colour of the revolution. Cars should also move forward on the left. Only the lightness of traffic kept the city from grinding to a halt.

The men who had built New China found themselves unexpectedly on the defensive. Suddenly, their revolutionary character was cast in doubt. Mao, to their surprise, announced that the party was being threatened from the inside by a creeping bourgeois mentality. What was really needed, he suggested, was a burst of revolutionary zeal to weed such elements from the party and secure the future of China. The only thing the Cultural Revolution secured was Mao's position. What it risked was the unity and sanity of a nation. In order to reverse the order of logic in China, Mao chose the most credulous section of the population: the students.

The young had inherited rather than fought for the revolution. They had been born into a Communist state and learned that the time of revolution had passed them by, and with it, the chance for real achievement. Yet suddenly, the father of the nation was telling them otherwise. It wasn't too late. Revolution, according to Mao, was continuous.

Best of all, the young were to be directed against authority figures, just as Xu Yinsheng, the Ping-Pong player, had written. They could test the length of the leash against their own teachers. In schools, ten-year-olds picked up brooms and planks of wood and beat their teachers. The fortunate teachers were humiliated by being made to stand in bathrooms, cleaning the stalls with slogans tied around their necks. The unlucky were beaten with clubs embedded with nails and died in schoolyards. Humiliation could also kill slowly. The suicide rate rocketed in both Shanghai and Beijing. The statistics for the summer of 1966 showed a rise of more than 800 per cent over the previous year.

The table tennis players thought little about the Cultural Revolution when it began. After all, those who had been with the national squad for a while knew that Ping-Pong players weren't part of every-day society. Any political examination of the players had supposedly been made before they had entered the elite programme, 'because the purpose of the training is not only to produce champion sportsmen but to help develop a generation of young builders of communism.'

These days, players vacationed with party leaders, they danced with their wives, they ate the best food in China, because they *were* the best of China. If the horrors of the Great Leap Forward hadn't touched them, why would the Cultural Revolution?

During the first outburst, the table tennis team wasn't even in Beijing but in the north of Sweden, in a tiny town of twenty thousand people, conducting yet another goodwill tour. When the team returned, not a soul was there to greet them at the airport. Before they left the terminal, Xu Yinsheng, so celebrated the year before, was arrested. When the players reached their dorm rooms, they had been emptied. No washbasin, no quilt – even their carpets had been taken. One player wandered down to the kitchen and found it closed. 'Don't worry,' said one of his team-mates, a practice player who had stayed behind. 'Every restaurant's opened its doors. Everything's free.'

Across the country, schools were creating their own Red Guard units to practice Mao's latest revolution. With food and travel for the Red Guards suddenly declared free by Chairman Mao, the limits of the *hukou* were lifted. A whole generation of people who had been tethered to their birthplace was released. Railway stations across the country filled with Red Guards making their way to the capital. The rumours had already begun. Chairman Mao was willing to meet the Red Guards. He would shake their hands and thank them for their revolutionary attitudes.

Proof of their loyalty to the Chairman manifested itself in the violence against authority figures, from teachers and parents to factory foremen, from traditional 'class enemies' to previously lauded elderly cadres. The initial burst of bloodshed was encouraged by Mao and his wife, Jiang Qing. The truth was that rather than practicing revolution, this was a generation reduced to imitating it. They wore uniforms without joining the army, then deliberately suffered entirely avoidable hardships by trying to replicate the Long March. Thousands turned their noses up at the free trains toward Beijing. They were going to walk to the capital to celebrate their living god. Instead of boots, many wore straw sandals like He Long. They marched through the countryside 'at the forced pace of an army at war.'

When the Red Guards arrived in Beijing, it would have been anti-revolutionary to deny them a thing. They had already been blessed by Mao. They needed food, housing, and things to do. When Xi Enting, the game's latest prodigy, reported to the National Sports Commission one day, he couldn't believe his eyes. The entire complex had been taken over by the Red Guards. He walked into the practice hall and found Red Guards sleeping on the table tennis tables, under the tables, in the corridors, their battered travel bags pushed up against walls.

The previous version of reality was being replaced. Ogimura, still a frequent visitor to China, found himself in Beijing in the first weeks of the Cultural Revolution in the summer of 1966, on tour with a small Japanese squad. Walking through the streets, he saw something he had never witnessed before, 'a man in a three-cornered hat being marched down a main road with his hands tied behind his back, followed by a mob ringing bells and banging drums.' He walked close enough to learn that this was the manager of a local factory. The pack marching behind him was made up of his own workers.

That afternoon, Ogi walked past a school and saw a new white statue in the schoolyard – but it was moving. It was the principal, his blue suit completely covered in the 'phlegm and saliva' of his students. In his favourite record store, Ogi found 'all the records by classic European composers had been smashed on the floor.' They were part of the 'Four Olds' that Mao declared due for destruction. Old culture, old habits, old customs, and old ideas. Everything from statues to buildings, books to paintings was busted and broken. Many storefronts had been completely covered by photographs of Mao, the one infallible image.

Cyclists now taped the Chairman's quotations to their handlebars. The trees in the streets they rode through were covered in Mao photographs. When they travelled, they found the trains equipped with a loudspeaker in every carriage, spewing endless praise for the great leader. Even the hillsides of China had been carved with Maoist slogans thirty feet high.

At least table tennis lent an air of stability. In the first competitive match in Beijing, Ogi pitted his touring Japanese squad against the superior Chinese. He could feel the atmosphere in the gymnasium change as soon as the Japanese won several points in a row. A local woman with a megaphone started shouting, 'In times of difficulty we must not lose sight of our achievements!' The three thousand spectators watched her. 'We must see the bright future!' yelled the woman at the top of her lungs. Suddenly the crowd seemed to respond as one. 'We must see the bright future!' When someone with such revolutionary fervour stood up, explained a spectator, you had to go along with it.

Ogi looked over at the Chinese bench. Fu Qifang glanced at Ogi and then 'immediately averted his gaze and stared at the floor.' By now, Fu must have suspected how he was viewed from outside the team; he wasn't the coach who had led his team to a series of gold medals but an authority figure surrounded by young men and women who might move against him at any moment.

The Japanese tour continued south toward Guangdong. They found the same Mao posters coating the streets, the same Mao quotations strung above the stadiums. When the Chinese women practiced playing, 'they tied Mao slogans to their table tennis nets.' The ball was thwacked back and forth over the Chairman's sacred words.

The Japanese team's final night in China included a goodbye dinner; the two coaches, Fu Qifang and Ogi, were seated next to each other. At the end of the meal, Ogi leaned toward Fu and asked him in English, 'What do you think of the Cultural Revolution?'

Fu looked around him. 'The ideals are wonderful,' he said. 'I'm getting too old. I'm worried I won't be able to keep up with this.' Ogi nodded. The talk was innocent enough. But Fu leaned in again toward him. 'You and I are good friends united by table tennis, are we not?'

'Yes.'

'Someday, there may be a time when I can help you.'

'Yes, I may need your help one day,' said Ogi.

'Likewise.' Fu leaned closer. 'You may be able to help me now.' At that point, the officials returned to the table. Unable to speak any more to Fu, Ogi sat silently thinking about the stories he'd heard of bodies washing up in Hong Kong as the desperate swam for their lives. The next time Ogi would hear of Coach Fu, Fu would be dead.

| # Under Pressure

Mao was the centre of the Cultural Revolution. The capital filled with 'the mock soldiers' dressed in green uniforms, who spent their days buoyed by a sense of revolution, finally partaking in the stories of their parents. Tiananmen Square filled within hours every time a rumour spread that Mao might soon be present. His eight actual appearances were greeted with the same hysteria that the West reserved for the Beatles. Twelve million Red Guards passed through Beijing by the end of the year, all in search of the Chairman's blessing.

Fainting teenage girls were carried out of the throngs; boys screamed their adoration as the Chairman rode through the square on the back of a jeep, one hand trailing over the side touching the hands and heads of hundreds of Red Guards. Soldiers wept as the Chairman passed.

During an athletic meet in the Workers' Stadium, the encroaching lunacy lent every event a manic shine. Weightlifters consulted Mao's works before raising their bars, high jumpers held up the *Little Red Book* of Mao's aphorisms after successful leaps. Red Guards were allowed to run back and forth across the stadium, handing out written slogans to encourage athletes ahead of their races.

The division in China's national table tennis squad was at first simple. The most famous of the players were in the 'conservative group.' Veterans such as Rong Guotuan and Fu Qifang, now both coaches, and top players, such as Zhuang Zedong and Li Furong, were obviously closer to the officials. They were friendly with Zhou Enlai, He Long, and Chen Yi. They were, or so they thought, standing in the shade of strong trees.

On the other side of the Ping-Pong split, in what was called the Heaven Group, were the younger players and the practice players – those who had not yet been given a chance or those who would never be given a chance, who had faithfully spent their lives imitating the style of foreign players, using up their bodies in service to their country without recognition. Some of the younger players simply felt bad for their elders. Xu Yinsheng, whose essay had been read by all of China, was locked alone in a room. Xi Enting, one of his protégés, would be allowed to visit, smuggling in love letters from Xu's girlfriend as well as a pair of scissors to give his mentor a haircut.

Another of the youngest – and the most promising – was Liang Geliang. He was fairly typical in that he had a lot of admiration for players like Zhuang Zedong, but at seventeen he felt a natural affinity with the youthful Red Guards.

One day, Liang Geliang heard that the Red Guards were going to raid Zhuang Zedong's home. What could they find in the home of the finest table tennis player in the world? 'I followed the Red Guards down the street,' he remembered. But instead of acting with the Red Guards, Liang hung back. How could he betray Zhuang? Two years earlier, when he was just fifteen years old, Zhuang had helped him. Liang had been of what they called 'perfect revolutionary character,' or what we might call dirt-poor. He grew up in the mountains of Jiangsu, the shoeless child of a deaf seamstress. The first newsreel he had ever seen was of China's 1961 victory in the World Table Tennis Championships. The first time he ever wore shoes was after he had been sent north to Beijing to become a national team member. He shivered so much in training that the coach had bought him a hat and gloves out of his own pocket.

In the winter of 1964, he received a letter from his mother. The local doctor had diagnosed her with cancer. Zhuang Zedong, the top Ping-Pong player in the world, offered him help. With Liang balanced on the handlebars of Zhuang's bicycle, the two players pedalled around Beijing until they found a doctor willing to prescribe a radical treatment, pills that were a mixture of mercury and arsenic. Eighteen months later, she seemed to have made a complete recovery. How could Liang take part in any action against 'a truly openhearted person'?

Dozens of Red Guards forced themselves into Zhuang's house. They went through every shelf and every drawer, and sat in small groups intently reading his letters. In a time when even a word could be used against you, Liang was right to worry on Zhuang's behalf. Anything that represented the Four Olds could be destroyed or, worse still, used to prove that you had been running down the capitalist road to a bourgeois life. Calligraphy was shredded, antiques broken, letters and family photographs torn up. Liang looked on in horror. 'They emptied the place, took everything away.'

Back in the table tennis halls, another division could be seen. In the conservative group, a new line was drawn between the reckless and those who feared retribution. Practicing table tennis had been banned. The national sport was in danger, but the most daring waited until the Red Guards had left for the day, then kicked their clothes off tables, cleared their belongings out of the way, and continued to play. They locked doors that had been ordered kept open and batted the ball back and forth.

When the Red Guards returned, the players hid their racquets and sat beside them. Together, along with the rest of Beijing, they busied themselves writing 'big character posters.' These large pieces of paper were posted in public places to praise Mao, denounce a stranger, defend an ally. They'd been used since imperial times, but now they were being produced in their millions. The remainder of the time, the squad studied Mao's essay *The Problems of Strategy in China's Revolutionary War*. Mao's thoughts could win them more victories – yet they could only prove it if they were allowed to play.

The team had hoped that once the Red Guards began to drift out of Beijing, there would still be enough time to travel to Sweden for the 1967 World Table Tennis Championships. Their first champion, Rong Guotuan, sat down with some of the more established players and wrote a letter to the National Sports Commission. Its receipt wasn't acknowledged, but there was pointed interest in who had written it. Even though the numbers of Red Guards were finally dwindling in the city, this didn't mean that the Cultural Revolution was concluding.

CHAPTER 30 | House of Cards

In China, the weakest position both in imperial days and under the Communists was to be alone without a patron, vulnerable to either side. The table tennis squad was still protected by the men who had used it as an extension of politics and international relations. But one by one, their positions were weakened. He Long, who had never liked Mao's wife, Jiang Qing, now faced retribution. In front of a meeting of twenty thousand supporters that month in Beijing, Jiang called He Long a traitor. He Long appealed directly to Mao. 'There's never been any trouble about you,' said the Chairman to his face, knowing full well that He Long had refused to condemn Mao's enemy Peng when he'd been placed in charge of investigating him. Still, He Long's friend Zhou Enlai preferred to act cautiously. He found a safe house in the hills north of Beijing and discreetly moved He Long and his family there during the cover of a winter night.

Jiang successfully chipped away at her husband's support of He Long. Dozens of Red Guards rushed to He Long's apartment, and the police were ordered to let them pass. His safe was discovered and 'more than 1,000 confidential documents' were seized.

Within days, He Long's hideout was discovered. At the age of sixty-nine and diabetic, He was sent to 'struggle sessions,' a form of punishment the Chinese had adopted from Soviet Russia where the accused would submit to a public self-criticism often accompanied by violence. He Long was 'beaten regularly, being first wrapped in

148

a blanket so that the welts would not show.' Insulin was withheld, and he received glucose injections instead, 'a sure process of medical murder.' During the height of the summer, he and his wife were pent up in their courtyard house without water and given a total of three cents a day to buy their food. The older guards would hum revolutionary songs over the walls so that He Long would know he was not forgotten. For two years, he would remain under house arrest, finally dying in June 1969 as a result of his untreated diabetes.

Chen Yi, He Long's fellow marshal and Ping-Pong enthusiast, also suffered. Despite being foreign minister, he was dragged to struggle sessions with a dunce cap on his head. On orders from Jiang Qing, ten thousand Red Guards chanted Chen's name every night from their encampment near the leadership compound.

Chen Yi did not go quietly. Some days he would walk up to the gate, shouting back at the mob that it was made up of 'ignorant children,' 'wahwah' babies who still wore slit pants. He said to them, 'If you want to go make revolution, why don't you go and fight in Vietnam?'

Again and again, Chen was called into struggle sessions, ordered to give an account of his political missteps, screamed at and humiliated. He would go straight from struggle sessions to his house, wash, change his clothes, and head out to diplomatic receptions. On other nights, before finally heading to bed, his old friend Zhou Enlai would approach the gates and try to reason quietly with the Red Guards in Chen's defence.

Chen Yi was not merely one of Zhou Enlai's oldest friends; Zhou had also entrusted Chen with his adopted daughter, who worked for the marshal in the Foreign Ministry. Speaking immaculate Russian, she had translated for Mao. Arrested as an underling of Chen, she was ordered to turn on her boss. Despite all of Zhou's efforts, he couldn't find where she was being held. The first news he had of her was eight months later when he learned she had died in jail. He demanded an inquest and received the following reply: 'Dealt with as counter-revolutionary. Cremated. Ashes not kept.' If Jiang Qing was behind the death, as all of Beijing suspected, then the message was clear: she was aiming to topple Zhou Enlai.

Zhou Enlai was China's number three. To be sitting in the seat of heir apparent was traditionally a dangerous place. Liu Shaoqi,

Mao's second-in-command and formal head of state, had already been arrested. He had been guilty of criticising Mao after the failure of the Great Leap Forward and was now undergoing intense struggle sessions, humiliated in front of tens of thousands of Red Guards. His wife suffered at his side, a string of Ping-Pong balls around her neck to mock her for having worn pearls on a state visit. The necklace was a personal touch from Mao's wife, Jiang Qing. Liu would die 'covered in his own vomit and diarrhoea,' rotting slowly alone, just as He Long had done.

If Mao was worried about the maintenance of power and his legacy, Jiang Qing was concerned with positioning herself as the Chairman's heir. Even Zhou Enlai was not immune. By May 1967, Mao's wife had stirred up an old story, accusing him of 'anti-Communist sentiment.' On 17 August 1967, while trying to defend Chen Yi, he suffered a minor heart attack. By the time he had recovered, the Foreign Ministry had been seized and the British Mission burned to the ground.

The Russian Embassy was under siege as well. Soviet diplomats were attacked by Red Guards, who rolled their cars over and forced them to crawl under posters of Chairman Mao. Ten thousand Red Guards were rumoured to have defecated inside the embassy grounds.

Jiang Qing worked alongside three other rising stars of the radical elite. Together they were known as the Gang of Four, setting fires at a pace that outdid Zhou Enlai's ability to put them out. How to choose who to defend? Zhou had failed his only child. He had successfully defended Chen Yi's life, if not his position. And what had he been able to do for He Long, one of his oldest comrades? Every afternoon for years, He Long had visited Zhou, putting out his pipe before entering the premier's house. They had shared a small glass of mao-tai together, and Zhou Enlai had stretched his bad arm out, playing table tennis while He Long looked on.

All across the country, the two sides claiming to act in Mao's name exploded into direct conflict. Jiang Qing told the Red Guards that if they needed to criticise and replace members of the army, then so be it. Barracks were looted of weapons, and pitched battles were fought in Beijing and Shanghai. From the players' perspective, it seemed as though the concerns of the nation were now so large that they were no more than a forgotten cog. Perhaps even without a protector, they might still escape unharmed.

In schools and factories across China conflict was the rule, not the exception. Situations escalated from poster battles to beatings, to gunfights up and down streets. The marshals were furious that Mao had encouraged discord. A group had been rumoured to have confronted him, led by an ageing Zhu De banging his cane against the floor. Soon even Zhu De's name appeared on big character posters calling him the Black General who had dared to declare himself the founder of the Red Army. The message was clear: only Mao was above the fray.

At the end of 1968 would come the relief of the Down to the Countryside campaign, where the army would regain the upper hand against the young mobs as Mao ordered millions of students out to be re-educated by the peasants. On Mao's orders, the army entered every institution in China in an attempt to restore a semblance of order. But Jiang Qing had prepared yet another campaign, Clean Up the Class Ranks. This time it would devastate the table tennis team.

The entire sports system was suddenly accused of being 'full of spies, traitors and capitalist roaders.' Table tennis was a convenient target. Everything foreign remained under suspicion, and one of the easiest attributes to identify was a Hong Kong childhood. The table tennis team was accused of being a hotbed of spies. Schoolchildren dragged their Ping-Pong tables outside and smashed them into splinters. The struggle sessions against the players started at once and grew in intensity. The first to undergo interrogation were the three heroes of China's original Ping-Pong glory: Jiang Yongning, the pioneer who had come across from Hong Kong in 1953, Fu Qifang, the finest coach in the world, and Rong Guotuan, the first person to have won China a gold medal.

As ever, the pincers exerted political pressure as they crushed their way toward their true targets. Zheng Mingzhi, one of the best players on the women's team, was made to stand up in a small-scale struggle meeting. 'I said, "I'm a player. It's my duty to try and win glory for China." I told them I didn't think I'd done anything wrong.' This was incorrect; it showed an impurity of thought. What she was guilty of, what most Chinese Ping-Pong players were still

guilty of, was 'trophyism.' To believe that the purpose of sport was to obtain trophies was 'revisionist thinking.' Players like Zheng, though not detained, were forced to stay in their dorm rooms and were given only one book to read, *The Complete Works of Chairman Mao*. They studied it for a few days, were checked on constantly, were expected to be reading it both day and night, and then they were called again to another struggle meeting. Detailed notes were taken for their files to help interrogators offer judgement on their political progression.

The entire squad's sanity was under attack. Orders to parade might arrive at one in the morning, and the players would rush into their clothes. In the dead of night, the finest players in China would find themselves shivering along dark avenues. Xi Enting marched alongside his team-mates through Beijing's streets shouting the words of Chairman Mao. Even worse for Xi, because he was the strongest of all the players, he'd have the responsibility of dragging around a heavy cart covered in big character posters aimed at either praising Chairman Mao or denouncing someone new. They also carried players' confessions, often a mixture of self-critique and sharp accusation. 'Every now and then we'd be ordered to stop,' said Xi. 'They'd make us do this "Be Loyal to Chairman Mao" dance.' Then Xi would pick up the handles of the heavy cart and drag it down another avenue.

CHAPTER 31 | Death to the Doubters

As Xi Enting walked at midnight, chanting the songs, moving his feet in steps faithful to Chairman Mao, he mostly thought of how his best years as an athlete were passing him by. 'I felt like a piece of bamboo that somebody kept cutting back every time it started to grow.' In Stockholm, at the World Championships the previous summer, a huge poster of Xi had been hung from the girders of the stadium, but the Chinese team never arrived.

It was now declared that any player who had ever won a medal at the World Championships would have to come forward for criticism. The fact that Xi hadn't been able to go to Sweden the previous year was, for a brief moment, a benediction. 'The more honour you'd brought to the nation the more you were criticised, because you were considered favoured.'

It was an inevitability that death was coming to the squad. Why not? It had come to all ranks, to the cities and the countryside. By now, more than a million people had died in the upheaval. Criticism in the Cultural Revolution was fantastically inconsistent, mostly because few knew who was giving the orders. Who could protect you? Who could you turn to? Some were dragged up for criticism just once; some would suffer again and again. Some would be tortured, some incarcerated, some driven to suicide, and some beaten to death. It meant that when your name appeared on a big character poster and you were called to enter the crucible, you had no idea what the limits of your persecution would be. Players would

153

pause in front of the posters, analysing them, trying to recognise calligraphy.

If success was a crime, then Zhuang Zedong was the guiltiest of all. Covered in glory and gold, he was the most famous young man in China. Frequently, his name would appear on the posters, and he would follow his persecutors through the doors to attend struggle sessions. As the insults and accusations were hurled, Zhuang was ordered to bend forward. It was a position called 'the airplane' that would become one of the symbols of the Cultural Revolution. The accused were force to squat down and throw their arms up behind them with their heads held high into 'something like the position of a swimmer about to do a racing dive. It stiffens the back and every time you try to straighten, you get punched in the stomach and your head is forced back again.'

Conversations Zhuang barely remembered were turned against him. In Japan for a match years before, a guide had taken the Chinese to the coast and told the team that it was the closest point to Taiwan. 'So near?' Zhuang had asked. The conversation was used as proof that Zhuang wanted to join his sister who lived in Taiwan. After all, they rebuked him, wasn't his grandfather once known as the king of the Shanghai landlords? Shouldn't Zhuang confess that he was aching 'to collude with the enemy to commit treason'? Half of his hair was shaved off so that he had 'yin-yang head,' a walking admission of guilt.

When Zhuang returned to the dormitories at the end of the day, he would give his team-mates tips about what to expect and how to handle it. When you're in the truck, you've got to sit this way. When they put you on the stage, 'you keep your head down, your legs relaxed, and you try to relax your neck.' Xi Enting, one of his room-mates that year, watched him walk in from a struggle session, sit at the table, down an enormous plate of food, and then retire to their room. By the time Xi joined him, Zhuang 'was snoring away.'

Not everyone could deal with the inquisitions as easily as Zhuang Zedong. Across Beijing and Shanghai the suicide rates remained high. The Ping-Pong spy, Zhuang Jiafu, who had been so instrumental in China's victory over the Japanese in 1961, was detained for one month. He was accused of espionage, of having visited Hong Kong for nefarious reasons. Any affiliation with Hong Kong whatsoever often led to horrific torture. One man accused merely of having a relative in the British colony was 'hung over a tree branch with his ten fingers tightly fastened by flaxen threads . . . his fingers lengthened, bit by bit, until they were doubly long.'

Zhuang Jiafu's story as a Ping-Pong spy was pored over. 'I thought of suicide. Yes, I did. But I thought it would look more like an admission of guilt.' Suicide, like murder, was a political crime for party members. The notion would be absurd but for how detailed the millions of individual files being compiled were and how the actions of a grandparent could still limit the progress of a grandchild. Every perceived crime had a genuine echo. But how could people not think of suicide when some of the tortures were so cruel? There was 'duck swims on dry land,' when victims had the skin on the soles of their feet removed by an iron brush, and 'smoking anus,' when the accused was made to sit on lit cigarettes.

Fu Qifang, easily the most successful coach in the history of the game, was next in line. Struggle session after struggle session ensued. Beaten by team-mates, 'humiliated and slapped by younger players,' he waited until the table tennis team left for morning exercises on 16 April, and then hanged himself from a curtain rod. The fleeting optimism he had felt sitting at Ogimura's side the year before had long since gone.

The next to die was the first to have arrived. Back in 1953, Jiang Yongning had been the Ping-Pong pioneer, the first Hong Kong-ese to have trusted He Long and Chen Yi and returned to China to help their struggling table tennis team. In Jiang's room, investigators had found a photograph of him as a child, dressed up in a shirt 'emblazoned with a Japanese flag.' No context was necessary. The Red Guards didn't pause to remember that Hong Kong had been taken over by the Japanese in 1941, or that as a five-year-old, Jiang wouldn't have known the differences between any two flags. Besides, he was famed among team-mates for poring over newspapers, a habit now labelled 'intelligence gathering.' This was a clear sign that he had spied for Japan. On 16 May, he was found hanged in his fourth-floor dormitory.

At seven in the morning on 20 June, Qiu Zhonghui was still lying in bed. She was now coaching the women's team alongside Rong Guotuan. The two had engineered victory in the 1965 women's team championship, the Corbillon Cup, finally dethroning Japan. When a halt had been called to the table tennis programme, Qiu had been coordinating with the scientific institute over developing a robotic table tennis arm. For months now, she had been trying to step quietly through the minefield of the Cultural Revolution. It had been a hard time for her, since her husband's parents had once been ambassadors to that revisionist hotbed, the Soviet Union. She'd been asked by officials to divorce him, but had stood resolute, insisting that neither of them was political. For a year she had been waiting for his release. Though she was only thirty-five, her hair had suddenly turned gray. She rolled over in bed and thought she'd get a few more minutes of sleep, but then she heard a voice screaming. Qiu sat up and listened closely.

'Rong Guotuan is dying, he's dying! Rong Guotuan is dying!'

She rushed out and ran toward the voice; she found Rong 'lying on the ground, covered in a cloth.' Qiu was told that Rong had been cut down from a tree, that he must have hanged himself the night before. 'My first reaction was, "Impossible." It couldn't be true. He would never do a thing like that.' She knew he had become pensive, no longer laughing and joking around, but they 'were in the same group who didn't support the destruction of things – he wasn't actually tortured by the people.'

Before a crowd could gather, Qiu pulled back the cloth that covered Rong Guotuan, her friend and team-mate for a decade. 'I checked his neck, and there were no marks. There was no bruising. No bloodshot eyes and no tongue sticking out.' To Qiu, the story that was released that week – that Rong had decided to take his own life rather than be subjected to yet another humiliating struggle session – seemed false. She never saw the note later discovered in his pocket that purportedly said, 'I am not a spy. Please do not suspect me. I have let you down. I treasure my reputation more than my own life.'

There was more than enough reason for a beating. He had been the one who had dared suggest the squad compete in Sweden. He not only possessed a property, his talent, but had been responsible for China's first gold. In the inverted world of the Cultural Revolution, he was a repeat offender – a man who always wished to compete, who thought in terms of medals, who had travelled in foreign countries and lived in Hong Kong.

Twice, Qiu Zhonghui approached officials in the National Sports Commission with her concerns about Rong Guotuan's death. Any investigation that might have been considered was discouraged by Rong's wife. She had their daughter to think of. What good would come of proving that he had been murdered by Red Guards? The more common reaction belonged to Zhuang Zedong. 'At the time,' he remembered:

I felt miserable because I was close friends with those who were tortured to death. But on the other hand I had complete trust in Chairman Mao. It was him who started this campaign and I feel my belief in Chairman Mao is bigger than my feeling towards my friends.

Zhuang was thousands of miles away from the aging Ivor Montagu, but the sentiment was identical. Once you bow before a system, the faith must be kept, even if the system is no longer faithful to its original incarnation. Both men had contorted themselves to adhere to their party line. Friends? Well, what were friends compared to the desires of a Stalin or a Mao, men who were always rewriting the verses of their own Bibles?

In the 1950s, Montagu travelled to Prague on table tennis business. There he learned that his old friend Otto Katz had been arrested. Like Montagu, Katz had been born a Jew and forfeited his faith in the name of Communism. As a Comintern agent, he had been credited with everything from Trotsky's murder to pushing the Czechoslovak foreign minister out of a window. Nothing mattered now that the state had turned on him. During his interrogation, a Czechoslovak security officer had told him, 'We'll bury you and your filthy race ten yards deep.'

Montagu called Katz at his apartment, as he always did when in Prague, to ask him to lunch. His shaken wife answered and mumbled that Otto was travelling. The next day, Montagu was approached by an employee of the Ministry of Information, who told him that Katz had been jailed. Back in London, Montagu was taped speaking of his fear that his friend of twenty years had been 'scrubbed.' He was premature but correct. Katz was hanged weeks later. Montagu never even paused in his outspoken support for Stalin.

In 1963, the year when Zhuang Zedong shook Montagu's hand and accepted his second World Championship, the Czechoslovak government issued a statement absolving Otto Katz 'on all points of indictment.' It noted 'the inhuman methods of interrogation and the use of drugs on the prisoners.' That same year, the Venona programme finally uncovered Montagu's greatest secret: that he was a Soviet agent. Back when Montagu was spying, treason had been a hanging offense. The last man caught spying had received a sentence of forty-two years, the longest ever handed down at the Old Bailey law courts. Would Montagu flee to the East, like three of the Cambridge spies?

He gave no sign of moving, because MI5 gave no sign of arresting him. To bring Montagu to trial, MI5 would have had to disclose the success of the Venona programme at a time when it was considered better to let the Russians think their codes remained unbroken. Besides, Montagu's unveiling would have been a deep embarrassment to his prominent family, the government, and the monarchy.

Instead, British intelligence would have to watch Montagu move back and forth across the Iron Curtain. He led British delegates to World Peace Council meetings in Moscow. Even from afar, it was obvious Montagu was still trusted by the Russians. When a 'bearded and sandalled' group of British delegates decided to march against the bomb in both London and Moscow, it was through Montagu that they were warned that a demonstration in Moscow would be considered 'a breach of hospitality' by the Kremlin and that they would be immediately deported. Despite such ringing reminders of Montagu's past influence, MI5 decided to leave him alone.

When he finally retired from his position in the ITTF in 1968, a German magazine suggested that the sport of table tennis be renamed Montagu, 'because the game with the little white ball which has spanned the whole world is really the work of one man.'

Zhuang Zedong may have been a true believer but, unlike Montagu, he wasn't in control of anything. And with Moscow remaining a hotbed of revisionism, there was nowhere for a Chinese Communist to flee to unless they dared to lose their faith and then risk their lives in escape. Zhuang never stopped to consider either possibility. He gambled on riding out the revolution.

| **Down to the Country**

Had there been any proof against the three dead members of the Chinese table tennis team? No. And there wasn't any evidence against the former world champion Zhuang Zedong either, but his name began appearing on the dreaded big character posters again. 'Let's drag out Zhuang Zedong,' they declared. 'He's a hardcore Bourgeois loyalist.' His young wife, a pianist, was also in trouble. She was guilty of relying on one of the Four Olds, the piano, symbol of Western bourgeois affectation.

Zhuang probably knew what was coming. One of his squad members pulled him aside and explained that his position was untenable. 'It's time to join one group and fight back, to be a rebel.' Zhuang would be a big prize for Jiang Qing's leftists, a world champion who 'could influence many people.' Called back to the struggle sessions, Zhuang ended up signing a big character poster accusing He Long of 'promoting revisionist policy ideals within the independent realm of table tennis.' It also stated that Zhuang believed he had been 'both mentally and physically injured and ruined over the preceding eight years on the table tennis team.'

Zhuang Zedong's big character poster would have echoes for decades to come and carried with it a bitter stain that he never escaped. Worst of all, it didn't stop criticism of him. Soon, he was called 'a fake rebel.' When officials were dragged up onto the stage in front of thousands, Zhuang was forced alongside them, bent over into the airplane position. By the end of the summer of 1968, the newlywed Zhuang was thrown in jail, his wife quarantined in their home, his new father-in-law imprisoned. Interrogators tried to turn wife against husband, father against daughter. Zhuang was occasionally 'beaten with sticks and displayed in front of the public.' A Red Guard held up his right hand in the air and threatened to cut it off – the right hand that had brought three gold medals to China; the right hand grasped and shaken by Ivor Montagu, now raised in front of thousands baying for blood.

Zhuang Zedong had written on that damning character poster that he 'wanted to revolt, he wanted to rebel, and he wanted to be a people's servant.' But he was not about to become a people's servant, he was about to become the servant, or perhaps even the lover, of Mao's wife. His new position couldn't have been more tenuous. The back-alley gossip said that now when Jiang Qing called on the phone, Zhuang Zedong's 'knees would shake.' Still, his salvation from prison after four long months wasn't by her hands. He owed his survival to Ping-Pong's greatest supporter, Zhou Enlai, Jiang's mortal enemy.

In 1969, in a move that some interpreted as the final stroke against He Long, who was still dying slowly from diabetes, almost 90 per cent of the National Sports Commission was exiled from Beijing. They ended up in Shanxi in a farming community at one of the notorious 7 May Cadre Schools designed for re-education through compulsory labour. Almost five hundred players and officials travelled slowly by train to the middle of nowhere. Shanxi was considered one of the harshest assignments for those 'going down to the countryside' to learn from the peasants. Athletics, where they existed, continued to be as military as they were political. Girls were still being trained in the art of the grenade toss.

Photographers followed the exiled athletes to take stunning shots of the world's best table tennis players dressed as peasants with bales of freshly cut wheat over their shoulders. Players built aqueducts, dug in the fields, wielded pickaxes and shovels, helped with the harvest. In truth, they depended almost entirely on nearby towns and communes for their food. In return, the players were expected to entertain the peasants, slamming the ball back and forth on a shoddy table retrieved from a farmhouse. They wove a table tennis net from straw and leaves. Entertainment was now the only acceptable role for sports. Nobody kept score, nobody lost, and nobody won; table tennis simply served the people.

Life was dull, but not easy. One player remembered getting sunstroke while harvesting wheat. She crawled to the shade of a tree, where she 'was caught by a commissar comrade who ordered her to take out the *Little Red Book*, *Quotations from Chairman Mao*, and read the admonition, "Be resolute; fear no sacrifice and surmount every difficulty to win victory."' Once she read that, he said, she'd recover unaided. 'Instead, she vomited at his feet.'

The 1969 World Championships in Munich came and went. There was no Rong Guotuan to dare to gather a petition to suggest they defend their titles. There may have been no one that naïve left in all of China. The news slowly filtered all the way to Shanxi that the Japanese had won the Swaythling Cup again. How could this have happened? How could a team that was the centrepiece of Chinese sporting achievement, ambassadors to the Third World, victors over imperialists and revisionists, have met such a fate?

If they could have sat with Zhou Enlai, he would have counselled patience. Though it seemed as if he'd abandoned the table tennis team, he had no such intention. The premier, having finally managed to send China's ambassadors back out into the world, had something even more stunning in mind – not so much a resurrection as a transfiguration. The table tennis team would help pull off the single greatest foreign policy feat of the century, realigning the world's largest country, China, with the strongest, the United States.

PART THREE | # East Meets West

| # The World at War

The Cultural Revolution wasn't the only revolution in the world during the 1960s. Thousands of miles away, the United States was having its own generational spasm. China watchers in the United States were comparatively starved for information, relying on translations of state newspapers and radio broadcasts, or interviews with travellers from other nations willing to talk to their consulate in Hong Kong. In China, government agencies had America's entire free press to digest. What to make of the open talk of sex? Of drugs? There were tens of thousands gathering in a field near the village of Woodstock in New York State, listening to music powered by electric guitars. Black Americans were taking to the streets, burning down parts of America's greatest cities in protest against racial injustice. President Kennedy, his brother, and Martin Luther King Jr, the country's greatest civil rights champion, had all been shot dead by US citizens. By the end of the decade, antiwar protests against US involvement in Vietnam were weekly events. Was this a coming revolution?

Thanks to new satellite television technology, in the West you could watch the world writhe in real time. Protesters were beaten on live television not just in the United States, but in Japan and during the Russian invasion of Czechoslovakia, when dozens of tanks made a blunt statement in the streets of Prague about the liberalisation of Soviet satellite states. Alarmed by Russian mobilisation, Beijing decided to restart low-level talks with the United States in the interests of 'peaceful coexistence.'

Russia and China shared a border almost three thousand miles long, a boundary that was of increasing worry to both Mao and Zhou Enlai. The Ussuri River, which separated the two countries in China's northwest and the Siberian Far East, was demarcated in a strange manner. Usually, river islands belonged to the country they were closest to, yet in the 1900 Treaty of Beijing, Zhenbao Island (Damansky Island to the Russians), a half step from the Chinese bank of the river, had been granted to Russia.

By 1969, the behaviour of both armies guarding that desolate spot was increasingly unrestrained. Between the snowstorms that often blanketed the region, patrols would shout insults across the frozen river. The Chinese would drop their pants and moon the Soviet troops. The Russians would hold up photographs of Mao to accept the homage. In late January of that year, the local Russian commander noticed that Chinese troops had dared to step onto Damansky Island. He ordered troop carriers out over the thick ice to confront them. With both sides refusing to retreat, the situation turned into a brawl. Noses were broken, and tensions escalated.

On 2 March, the Russians noticed another incursion on Damansky Island. Again they piled into their troop carriers, drove across the frozen river, and with their rifles slung over their shoulders, approached a line of unarmed Chinese soldiers. That first line stepped to one side. Behind them lay a second line of soldiers who aimed their weapons and fired. The Soviet officer in charge of the border post fell immediately.

It was a calculated attack. The Chinese had reserves with heavy machine guns on the high ground behind them. After two hours of fighting, a handful of Soviets managed to pull back, leaving behind thirty dead and fourteen wounded.

In Beijing, demonstrations were immediately called to condemn the 'Soviet aggression.' The following day, in Moscow, a huge march culminated with 'the smashing of windows and throwing ink bottles at the Chinese embassy.' Back in Washington, the news was being slowly digested for what it was – final proof of the depth of the division between the Soviets and the Chinese. When the Soviet ambassador approached Henry Kissinger, President Nixon's national security adviser, to lay before him evidence of China's actions, Kissinger argued that it was of no concern to the United

States. The ambassador disagreed, saying that 'China was everyone's problem.' The extent of Soviet agitation was now obvious.

What was Mao up to? There was precedent for provocation. In 1958, Mao had bombarded some of the tiny islands off the Taiwan coastline as a 'challenge to Khrushchev's bid to reduce tensions between the Soviet Union and the United States.' It had been a statement that Mao wanted China to be part of a triangular relationship, not a territory to be divided between Cold Warriors.

The 1969 border conflict fascinated Kissinger. Though approaching China had been on Nixon's mind since 1967, Kissinger's efforts to begin 'exploring rapprochement with the Chinese' only started in February 1969. As he now studied satellite photographs to try to determine the seriousness of the situation, the Russians approached various Washington players to see how they would respond to an attack on Beijing's nuclear capabilities. Nixon and Kissinger thought there might be an immense opportunity at hand; it seemed the Soviets and Chinese now feared each other more than they feared America.

What would Nixon do with the moment when the monolith of Communism shattered? The easier option would be to strike a deal with Moscow: the United States would green-light a Soviet nuclear attack on China if the Soviets agreed to stop arming the North Vietnamese. Yet the Soviets were reluctant to withdraw their support from Vietnam, and Nixon worried that a Russian nuclear offensive would leave the Soviet Union as the central power across all of Asia. Ultimately, a deal was never brokered.

Mao was pursuing a high-risk strategy against Russia. To underline the intensity of the crisis, cities across China began digging elaborate nuclear fallout shelters. Within the year, Zhou Enlai believed 'that the whole of China could be underground within five minutes.' It was a wise precaution. The Soviet defence minister continued to lobby for 'massive nuclear strikes on Chinese cities.' But then what? Invade a country of 800 million people? Many Russians believed the most likely outcome was a limited nuclear attack on Chinese military installations. The air between the two countries froze. 'So withering is Russia's hostility' toward Beijing, one commentator wrote, that in Moscow, Chinese 'diplomats seldom venture outside the forbidding fastness of their embassy.'

By late 1969, Nixon and Kissinger began looking very closely for a path to Beijing. The intentions were pure realpolitik. Mao had the ear of the North Vietnamese, and if the Russians wouldn't hasten to the peace table, then China was the only other player with influence in Hanoi. Nixon would be standing for re-election in 1972. Vietnam and a declining relationship with Russia had ground down Johnson's presidency, but an olive branch to China could turn the world on its head. Kissinger strategised that rapprochement with China would show Nixon to be a man capable of imagination, cauterise the bloody wound of Vietnam, and bring isolated China back into the international arena. Above all, it would worry Moscow into much warmer behaviour.

But what would the Chinese have to gain from the relationship? For Mao and very few others, the Cultural Revolution had been a worthwhile gamble. Those who had sought to challenge him in the past had been dismissed, imprisoned, or murdered. But efficient bureaucratic centres, such as the Foreign Ministry, had suffered hugely in the culling. With so many experienced diplomats banished to the countryside, could China find a way out of such a tight corner?

In August 1969, Mao had told his doctor a riddle. 'We have the Soviet Union to the north and the west, India to the south, and Japan to the east. If all our enemies were to unite . . . what do you think we should do?' A day later, Mao revealed the solution. 'Beyond Japan is the United States. Didn't our ancestors counsel negotiating with faraway countries while fighting with those that are near?' Mao said that he 'liked to deal with rightists' like Nixon. 'They say what they really think.' The doctor was aghast at the implications.

Mao and Zhou Enlai turned for advice to the very man Jiang Qing had so berated at the beginning of the Cultural Revolution, one of table tennis's greatest friends, Marshal Chen Yi. Together with three other marshals, he was asked to convene secretly and give his opinion on China's foreign policy options. Chen concluded that a nuclear attack by Russia was, for the moment, unlikely and noted that Nixon had been making quiet overtures to China. If communication with America was going to be re-established, better that it should be done through new channels with no preconditions rather than falling back into the torpor of low-level diplomatic talks.

There had indeed been talks going on for fifteen years, with 134 meetings between the United States and the Chinese taking place in Warsaw. They were notable, according to Kissinger, in that 'they represented the longest continual talks that could not point to a single important achievement.' The rooms they were conducted in were so compromised electronically that it was said that passing taxis could tune in. Chen and Kissinger had reached the same conclusion independently. A new channel would have to be opened up. But could the situation bear the wait?

With a million Soviet troops now on the border, Mao ordered two hydrogen bomb tests near the Russian frontier, designed to carry radioactive fallout over the Soviet positions. This extraordinary display was immediately followed by an offer to the Soviets to reopen negotiations.

America took the opportunity to play a signal move of its own, temporarily withdrawing vessels from the Taiwan Straits as a sign of goodwill. For a moment, it seemed there might be a dialogue, suggested by both sides during what would turn out to be the last Warsaw talks. Instead, Nixon launched the invasion of Cambodia in May, and the Chinese promptly cancelled the planned session. At Kent State, four students were killed by the National Guard while protesting the first foray into Cambodia, and the Nixon administration began to quake. More than thirty thousand young American men had already lost their lives in Vietnamese jungles. The longer the war bled on, the more damage it did to the government.

What Washington had failed to calculate was that behind the seeming monolith of the Chinese Communist Party, there was strong opposition to any détente with America. Mao's number two, General Lin Biao, an ally of Jiang Qing, was advocating easing difficulties with the Soviet Union instead.

The cancellation of the Warsaw talks turned out to be an opportunity. With the State Department out of the picture, Kissinger was freed to look for a secret back channel. After attempting to send a message to Beijing through both French and Romanian connections, Nixon mentioned to visiting Pakistani president Yahya Khan that he hoped to communicate with Beijing that fall.

On 8 December 1970, the Pakistani ambassador arrived at the White House carrying a handwritten note from Zhou Enlai.

Winston Lord, then Kissinger's special assistant, explained, 'the ambassador would come in to Kissinger's office and he would give us a handwritten note from Zhou Enlai and we would take it to the President and draft a response and go back to the Chinese.' The Americans didn't use official stationery. The Chinese didn't even use a typewriter. Envelopes were sealed, then placed in another envelope. There were no cables sent, just letters moving very slowly via diplomatic pouch from one continent to another. Kissinger and Nixon agreed to keep the State Department in the dark, anxious there should be no leaks. It looked as though they'd made a breakthrough. There would be no preconditions to sending a high-level American diplomat to China – perhaps Kissinger himself.

During 1970 a slow-motion flirtation began. When Nixon used the words 'People's Republic' for the first time in an official speech, it was noted in Beijing. China lifted a restriction on American oil companies. Passport restrictions on Americans planning to travel to China were eased. In a wide-ranging interview in Beijing on 17 December 1970, Mao hinted to his old friend Edgar Snow that he might be willing to deal directly with Nixon; he made sure the state press ran pictures of them standing together.

Mao and Zhou were sure that Snow 'must be working for the CIA' and would quickly pass along the information to Washington. Snow would be backed up by photographs that showed him standing with the Chinese leadership. Mao and Zhou were far from the mark. Snow had had his lengthy, opaque article based on his interview with Mao rejected by the *New York Times*, and the White House wanted nothing to do with him. 'We thought he was a Communist propagandist,' explained Kissinger, 'and we didn't pay any attention to him.' *Life* finally agreed to print the interview but month after month slipped by without publication.

Having missed that signal, 1971 brought deep unease to the White House. The last communication of any kind was in late January, when Kissinger fired off a note to Beijing repeating his earlier willingness to meet. Now, as Kissinger said, 'there was nothing to do but wait.' He surrounded himself with China books and scholars, ordering papers in preparation for what he prayed was inevitable: Sino-American détente.

The continuing silence shook the Americans deeply. 'We hadn't heard anything for several months,' explained Winston Lord. Could it have anything to do with the new military campaign to cut Ho Chi Minh's supply route in the panhandle of Laos? They scoured Beijing's *People's Daily* every morning, reading little into anti-American speeches since it was obvious that the real opprobrium was still reserved for Moscow. But why the silence? Were the Chinese serious or not?

The only mention of table tennis in the translated Chinese press that year could hardly have been more anti-American. A Vietnamese Ping-Pong team had arrived in Beijing that November 'fresh from the battlefront,' where they had been entertaining Vietcong troops. While the United States shipped entertainment directly from Los Angeles and New York to the troops in Vietnam, the Vietnamese Ping-Pong players were forced to wade across 'rivers, penetrate heavy forests and often risk their lives to pass through enemy raided areas.' When they finally reached the front lines, they made table tennis tables out of shell cases and played their exhibition match in an 'enlarged section of the trench to give themselves a bit more room.'

During one exhibition, they were interrupted by a coordinated raid from American forces. 'They saw US planes screaming down toward them. They scattered and took aim. As bullets spat from their guns, one plane burst into black smoke and plummeted to the earth, then another.' After the two planes had been brought down, the Ping-Pong players helped the soldiers shoot down eleven American GIs. For this superb display outside of the World Championships, in Beijing they were given the honorary title 'Intrepid Fighters against the US Aggressors.'

The Chinese were told all about these paddle-wielding heroes. It was the finest distillation of the teachings of Chairman Mao, a stirring display of how greatness in sport could serve the defence of a nation. That same month, the American troops were being entertained by Bob Hope.

The American methods of signaling China had been military and economic: withdrawal of the fleet from the Taiwan Strait, the lifting of sanctions, tiny increases in trade. Mao's messages to the Soviet Union were bloody: a border ambush, a nuclear test, constant skirmishes. Yet in its recent dealings with America, China's methods of contact had an entirely different tone: an interview with a famous writer, a photograph from a parade, the release of a dying priest. There was something cultural about many of the Chinese attempts to communicate with America. The next step would be from the world of what the Americans called sports and the Chinese called physical culture. This time the statement was so obvious that every editor at every newspaper in the world, every network television producer, immediately understood its importance. To the Chinese table tennis players idling in Shanxi Province or working in wood-chip factories in Beijing, it was as if a stone had been rolled from their chests.

| **The Seeds of Peace**

In 1971, the World Table Tennis Championships were due to return to Asia, to the Japanese city of Nagoya. Only twenty-five years before, Nagoya had been a central target for US bombing raids, an industrial hub that was home to Japan Aircraft and Mitsubishi Generator. Now an American ally would be hosting Team USA.

Japan's interest in China's attendance at Nagoya could be traced to Ichiro Ogimura. Having read of the Ussuri River clashes in 1969, Ogi had immediately fired off a telegram to Zhou Enlai, recommending that China's 'best opportunity lies in opening the door to the international community through the sport of table tennis.' He had received no answer from the premier.

To his surprise, Ogimura was included in a small cultural exchange programme invited to attend the 1 October parade in Beijing that autumn. For years, relationships between the Japanese and Chinese had involved disparaging each other aloud, disdaining any official ties, but also establishing plenty of low-level trade contacts.

Ogimura, desperate to talk to the premier, was granted little more than a handshake at the event. Deeply disappointed, he started to drink heavily at the banquet that night, until a Chinese official whispered into his ear, 'This liquor has a high alcohol content, Mr Ogimura. If you drink too much of it you'll get drunk, you know.'

At one in the morning he was called to visit Zhou Enlai at his office in the Great Hall of the People, where he pled his case. Zhou was wary. 'Suppose we were to send a team to Nagoya, can you

173

imagine what kinds of trouble might occur? If something were to happen after you have personally involved the premier of a country, how will you take responsibility?'

By the end of the year, Ogi was back in China under the guise of Ogimura Trading, his new company, which exported ashtrays and tablecloths. The former champion was followed everywhere by Toshiaki Furukawa, his employee and table tennis acolyte, a young man so in awe of his mentor that when Ogi once banged his head, he 'immediately banged his head on the same spot so that [he] could feel the same pain.' In November, Ogi asked Furukawa to accompany him on a trade mission to Guangzhou. Checking into the hotel, Furukawa was impressed to see that it had a table tennis table in the lobby.

Two Chinese porters stood on either side 'wearing white dress shirts.' 'You might as well have a knockabout with them,' said Ogi as he checked in. The first porter could barely return a lob. The second started slowly, then raised the pace, until Furukawa, trained by Ogi himself, was being spun around the lobby. The porter put down his paddle, then slowly unbuttoned his shirt. Underneath was the bright red uniform of China's national table tennis team. The player carried with him an invitation for Ogimura Trading to play a friendly game in Beijing.

Furukawa was stunned; fifteen thousand spectators watched Ogimura's next exhibition. The players who emerged from the tunnel under the Workers' Gymnasium had not played on the international stage in years. There was Zhuang Zedong, three-time world champion, a little heavier than before. Beside him was the Handsome Bomber, Li Furong, who had lost all three of those finals. Mao's favourite, Xu Yinsheng, the Ping-Pong polemicist, stood beside them. Ogi couldn't have failed to number his old rival Rong Guotuan and his friend Fu Qifang among the missing. His quiet presumption was that they 'had been sent to their deaths.'

Even with the table tennis team reactivated, Zhou Enlai had other hurdles to jump. The United States would be attending the World Championships. The Americans' political relations with Japan were obviously excellent; it was China that still had no official relationship with either country, something Zhou had to manoeuvre around.

Japanese table tennis was run by sixty-four-year-old Koji Goto, nicknamed Shogun because he resembled one of those proud samurais so frequently disembowelled in Akira Kurosawa's films. Not even a year before, he had been labelled as a 'reactionary' by the Chinese press, having committed the cardinal sin of inviting Taiwan to play in a regional tournament. Table tennis was, as ever, a litmus test for international policies, and Goto had been considered acidic to the cause. Yet suddenly, in January 1971, he was issued an invitation to visit with Zhou Enlai.

It was going to be Goto's second trip to China, but only the first with a visa. In 1937 Goto had arrived in the far north as a noncommissioned squad leader in the despised Japanese army that occupied Manchuria. Guarding communication lines for two years, Goto's work also included training horses and soldiers. He kept his men entertained by teaching them his two personal loves, the martial art kendo and table tennis.

On his way to meet Zhou Enlai, Goto was thinking purely of Sino-Japanese relations. The premier gave no hint of the even greater rapprochement on his mind: the coming together of America and China. The idea would have seemed outlandish to any Japanese, and the implications were frightening. Besides, Goto had no reason to do America any favours. In 1944, American incendiary bombs had set fire to the school his family ran in Nagoya. Worse was to come. Another bomb hit the hospital in which his youngest son was being treated for pneumonia. Though the child survived the attack, he died within the week. Goto had slept alongside the coffin for days before finally giving up the body for cremation.

Goto's decision to visit China wasn't without opposition from Japan's far right. Death threats began arriving by the end of the week. On his flight to Beijing, Goto opted for a disguise. He skittered through the airport terminal wearing a hunting cap, glasses, and a mask, which must have made him only more conspicuous.

In Beijing, the reason for his invitation was made clear. After years of silence, Zhou Enlai was contemplating sending the Chinese team to compete in Nagoya. The price Goto would have to pay for the privilege of hosting their coming-out party was heavy. He would have to step away from his government's policy and abandon support of Taiwan, even within the regional body of the Asian Table Tennis Union. Implicit was Goto's rejection of the Two Chinas solution, which would have allowed both Taiwan and China to be represented. Zhou Enlai was asking a body that was supposed to be nonpolitical to take a highly political stand. It was the essence of propaganda – adapting culture to effect a change in the political world.

On 1 February, Goto finally announced that China would be participating in the World Championships. Chinese and Americans would be in contact. Goto was inundated by calls from TV stations trying to negotiate the rights to air the championships. He was also appointed round-the-clock protection by the government, highly unusual for a Japanese citizen.

Another man was summoned to Beijing that spring. With Montagu finally retired, it was the turn of his former understudy, Roy Evans, a Welshman whose head looked like a ruddy Ping-Pong ball, to helm the ITTF at the Nagoya championships. Before Evans left London, the Chinese chargé d'affaires had passed on a message from Zhou Enlai, asking if he wouldn't mind travelling through Beijing on his way to Japan.

Evans was not like Montagu. Though he had worked under Montagu for many years, Evans was apolitical, albeit a quiet admirer of Montagu's astonishing clout behind the Iron Curtain. He flew to Beijing via Guangdong and was ushered across Tiananmen Square at midnight into the Great Hall of the People. Over green tea, the premier pressed Evans to expel South Vietnam from the World Championships, but Evans held his ground. Zhou Enlai's only satisfaction was that Evans had already rejected Taiwan's latest application to join the ITTF. The ITTF held two Germanys, two Vietnams, and two Koreas, as well as spots for Wales, Scotland, Northern Ireland, and even the tiny island of Jersey, but Taiwan would be excluded again. Evans's explanation in Nagoya would be that Taiwan's 'applications have not been received in the proper form,' followed by a refusal to elaborate. Before leaving, Evans said that the best thing Zhou could do to show that China was now friendly to the rest of the table tennis world would be to invite Western teams back through Beijing after Nagoya.

Finally Zhou had to convince his own table tennis squad to go to Nagoya. For five years they had known they were subject to political headwinds. He called a meeting with the team on 11 March and asked for their opinion as to whether they wished to compete in Japan. A group from the Ministry of Foreign Affairs was there to take their vote.

What were they supposed to say? After handpicking wheat in a field, with callused fingers and sunburned skin, it seemed a ridiculous notion that they would soon be in Japan playing in a televised World Championships. Besides, the Americans were going to compete in Nagoya. What would happen if they were drawn to play them? Though a handful thought they should attend, the majority carried the day and voted to remain in China, indoctrinated for years to believe that there was nothing to learn from foreign countries.

It really didn't matter, explained a player, because the final word came directly from Mao. He agreed with Zhou that the team should leave for Nagoya, wrote them a note conveying his good-luck wishes, and told them 'to prepare for death.' Japan was a rightist country; there was a healthy chance of a bombing or assassination. Mao added to Zhou, 'We should be prepared to lose a few people; of course it will be better if we don't.'

CHAPTER 35 | # Long Hair, Light Heart

The same year that the Chinese world champions had stepped off a plane straight into the Cultural Revolution, Glenn Cowan was still a kid, the oldest son of a middle-class Jewish family from New Rochelle. Just a short ride from Manhattan, in 1966 the New York suburb did a good impersonation of the American heartland. It had a Woolworth's where you could still buy a Coke for a nickel, no stores higher than an elm tree, and a Main Street dominated by red-brick banks. 'We were crew-cut kids,' explained his brother, Keith Cowan, fitting seamlessly into the All-American landscape.

Cowan was one of those boys who seemed to be able to pick up any sport, but he was smitten by table tennis for the simple reason that he'd won the first tournament he'd ever entered within a week of taking up the game. Then he won the next seventeen in a row. His father put a table above the garage, a lopsided affair on an uneven floor. By the age of twelve, Cowan was writing poetry about the game of Ping-Pong:

> This small white ball I hit is quick to lead,
> It travels on the table everywhere,
> Sometimes it happens I'm not always there,
> It surely travels fast with mighty speed.

On the newly built interstate, Cowan's father could commute to his job in public relations at the Manhattan headquarters of

Ivor Montagu's father, the second
Lord Swaythling.

Ivor Montagu's mother, Lady Swaythling.

Ivor Montagu, early childhood.

Ivor Montagu as a teenager.

The Cambridge University team of 1926. Ivor Montagu is in the back row at far right.

A publicity card from Richard Bergmann, world champion, night porter, soldier (1940s).

Ogimura grasps the Cup after his victory in London at the 1954 Championships.

Rong Guotuan, winner of the 1959 men's title, in Dortmund, Germany.

Propaganda photo from Hebei Province showing the supposed benefits of Lysenko's close planting (1958).

Ivor Montagu (right) accepts the Lenin Peace Prize at the Kremlin (1959).

Left to right, Ivor Montagu, Zhou Enlai, and He Long finishing dinner with a cake made up of Ping-Pong paddles (April 1961).

Ivor Montagu in the middle of the rostrum. To his left is Zhou Enlai; to his right, Deng Xiaoping, with He Long in sunglasses farther down the row (April 1961).

Ivor Montagu hands over the Swaythling Cup. Second from bottom is Li Furong, then Zhuang Zedong, and above him, Rong Guotuan (April 1961).

Ivor Montagu smiles as the Chinese team accepts their silverware. Zhuang Zedong is on the highest podium, Li Furong beside him (April 1961).

Red Guards hold aloft copies of Mao's Little Red Book in Beijing (April 21, 1967).

Ivor Montagu holding hands with Zhou Enlai. He Long shares the joke.

Ogimura (left) and Zhuang Zedong—a rare photograph of the two men's champions together (ca. 1962).

The China Watcher, William J. Cunningham (left), shakes the hand of American ambassador to Japan Armin Meyer.

The American team tours the Great Wall. George Brathwaite stands back right. Next to him is Graham Steenhoven. Seated at left is Glenn Cowan. Behind him is John Tannehill; beside Tannehill is Judy Bochenski (April 1971).

Glenn Cowan surrounded by a crowd in Beijing (April 1971).

Kissinger's secret visit to Beijing (July 1971).

The American press awaits the arrival of the Chinese team (April 1972).

Zhuang Zedong grasps Glenn Cowan's hand as he steps off the plane (April 1972).

Zhuang Zedong introduces President Nixon to the team in the Rose Garden (April 1972).

Zhuang Zedong gives a speech
at the UN (April 1972).

The Chinese team visits
Marineland in California
(April 1972).

Richard Nixon
sandwiched by Zhou
Enlai and Jiang Qing
during the president's
1972 visit to China.

Metromedia in twenty minutes on a good day. On the weekends, father would occasionally take son into the city to match up against older players. One of the centres of the New York table tennis scene was a club in the basement of the Riverside Plaza Hotel on West 73rd Street, where a suburban kid could find a glimpse of the city's underbelly. It belonged to Cowan's future mentor and agent, Bob Gusikoff, himself once one of the country's best players. It had a 'smelly, filthy, undersized playing area, poor lighting, and a bathroom that looked like it hadn't been cleaned, ever.' Parents who dropped their children off for the afternoon were horrified to return to find their teenagers 'playing poker with men in their thirties and forties.' The magazine *Table Tennis Topics* explained:

> Most table tennis locations were in skid row type locations. This naturally produces good table tennis. In order for the players to get to their clubs, they inevitably develop great reflexes. They can't help it – avoiding muggers, rioters, falling buildings etc, can't help but improve your footwork, coordination, and general speed of reaction.

At fourteen years old, Cowan was considered a good-enough table tennis player to be asked for an interview by the *Los Angeles Times* during a West Coast tournament. With his big smile and *Leave It to Beaver* crew cut, the teenager explained that table tennis just wasn't that hard for him. 'The most amazing thing,' said the newspaper, 'is that he seldom practices.' The Chinese coaches would have been horrified, but why should Cowan be serious about the sport? His father had been trying to nudge him in the right direction. 'Glenn, if you've got to do swimming or tennis, then do it, because you're never going to get anywhere playing Ping-Pong.' There was no money in the American game. At least the fourteen-year-old seemed to realise this. 'After high school,' the *Los Angeles Times* continued, 'Cowan wants to study law or finance.'

Father and son had enjoyed their trip to Los Angeles so much that they persuaded Glenn's mother and younger brother Keith to move there in 1966. The following year, in 1967, everything changed for the Cowan family. His doting father, his main practice partner and nurturer of his fledgling career, died abruptly of lung cancer.

His mother, determined to keep the family together, started

a small florist business. Without a father figure, Cowan became absorbed by the prevailing trends of everything around him: his hair grew down past his shoulders, and his attitude changed. If anything, his smile seemed to broaden. On top of the suburban New Yorker a new image was grafted: that of the laid-back Californian.

In May 1967, the Beatles admitted they'd dropped acid, Jimi Hendrix's new stage act involved setting his guitar on fire, and Cowan's greatest idol, Mick Jagger, was charged with drug possession in England. It was a time when culture and counterculture overlapped. For Cowan, that meant an odd mixture of hypercompetitiveness and relaxation, namely, table tennis and pot smoking. Unlike his Chinese counterparts, he was content to believe in the myth of natural ability. Ping-Pong was a small-enough sport that Cowan could often just show up at his local spot in Hollywood, hustle a few dollars in winnings, and travel to win a regional tournament on the weekend. By the turn of the decade, his mother estimated that her teenager had won 'over a hundred trophies.'

In early 1971, the best players in the country gathered at the Convention Centre in Atlanta, Georgia, for the US Nationals, which underscored all that was wrong with American table tennis. First came the humiliation of having dozens of competitors show up, only to find that they had been displaced from the main auditorium by El Mongol, a not-so-famous wrestler. Second, the floors were waxed so well that players were sliding into cardboard hoardings. Third, the play was divided between two different floors separated by a maze of passageways. Some players were scratched from the roster for not finding their tables in time. Fourth, attendance was pitiful. Forty-five years before, Montagu had managed to get ten thousand British spectators to pay to watch an unknown sport. Now, about four hundred spectators watched the US Nationals, and most of them were friends or relatives of the players. There wasn't a breath of media coverage. In the hype of American sport, table tennis had been forgotten.

The US team that emerged from Atlanta would bump, trip, and beg its way to Nagoya. The United States Table Tennis Association (USTTA) was still too poor to send a team, and players were paying their own way, just as Ogimura had done before them. Three of the four men's semi-finalists lacked the money.

One player raised her funds at a high school. Judy Bochenski, who at fifteen was the youngest player on the squad, was able to make the trip as a second alternate because her father had taken out a $900 loan from his local bank. Cowan's fare was paid by a semi-retired engineering executive from Detroit. Some team members were solidly middle class – a researcher at Chemical Bank, an IBM computer analyst, another at the United Nations, albeit in the documents section rather than as an ambassador. No one was going to Japan expecting to win a World Championship; it was more of a chance to measure themselves against the world's best to see how far they had to climb, perhaps to learn what the world's finest were capable of and bring back something new to the basements of America.

The USTTA paid for a total of three men to fly. One was Tim Boggan, the USTTA's vice president and an associate professor of English literature at Long Island University. At forty, he wasn't a playing member of the team but was undoubtedly America's ultimate table tennis obsessive, a greybearded Pepys of Ping-Pong who believed that if the unpaid bureaucrats in the American game would just step out of the way, it would shine by itself.

Before leaving for Japan, Boggan had had the effrontery to call the sports editor of the *New York Times*, offering to cover the World Table Tennis Championships on their behalf. There was a pause. 'The US Ping-Pong team!' Boggan recognised the derisive tone. In two weeks' time, the *New York Times* would be begging Boggan to write for them.

Cowan, who would be Boggan's room-mate for part of the trip, was the most colourful but hardly the only character. In fact, Boggan worried that the team wasn't a team at all, just a group of individuals who shared a liking of but no great commitment to the sport. He'd watch in Japan, amazed that women on the team were writing postcards instead of studying the best players in the world.

The generation of Marty Reisman and Dick Miles that had won international tournaments for America was gone. The balding Miles was in Nagoya working for *Sports Illustrated*, the ever grumpy, grumbling reminder of what had been. The squad was now ranked twenty-third in the world. For Japan, according to Boggan, 'there were no expectations.' Some members of the USTTA had

181

even wondered if it was worth sending such a poor team. Boggan violently opposed them. 'How the fuck were we going to get good if we stayed playing in the basement?'

Almost all teams were housed in the Nagoya Miyako Hotel, a bleak box that looked like an inhospitable cheese grater. Glenn Miller's tunes were piped through the hotel corridors. In the lobby a Japanese torch singer warbled American love songs from World War II. Pyjamas and slippers were provided for the players. Buses from the hotel to the Aichi Gymnasium, home of the 31st World Championships, ran every thirty minutes.

On the first night of play, Sunday 28 March, the fifty-eight teams paraded through the arena for the opening ceremony. The Chinese entered in much the same manner as their army stomped through Tiananmen Square every October to celebrate the foundation of the PRC, arms swinging vigorously back and forth, perfectly synchronised in their red tracksuits. Every country had outfitted their players in uniforms for the event except for the beleaguered American team, which made its lap of honour in an assortment of colours and styles.

The matches proceeded just as the Americans feared, starting with the sad sight of the empty-handed team captain, Jack Howard, stepping forward to greet his counterpart although the USTTA hadn't provided him with a pennant to swap. They lost five–one to Hong Kong and five–zero to South Korea. Cowan was swinging away, losing again to a better player. He desperately beseeched Howard for advice. 'You got to tell me what to do out there. You got to tell me what to do!' But Howard was a captain, not a coach, and had no cure for the desperate state of American table tennis.

Thanks to Ivor Montagu, Ping-Pong was now a game in which state-sponsored professionals dominated amateurs. There were really only a handful of countries that competed at the top. All the other fifty-three competing nations lagged far behind. The American team dropped into the third tier with nothing to play for.

The team went sightseeing, but Boggan barely moved from the Aichi arena. He walked past Japanese students curled up in sleeping bags, reading copies of Ogimura's books while waiting for tickets to the championships. Boggan himself was scheduled to play at Nagoya in the Jubilee Cup, a sop to the over-forties. Just before the tournament began, he had been practising in the auditorium with a team-mate. As he bent over to pick up a ball, Boggan noticed the entire Chinese team filing into the stands one by one. The team was 'thirty or forty strong'; they descended 'like they were out of a spaceship' and walked straight past him to sit en masse behind a skinny Swedish teenager, Stellan Bengttson, the fifteenth seed. At nineteen, Bengttson looked more likely to win the role of Peter Pan than a World Championship. The Chinese squad sat transfixed behind him.

What Boggan didn't know was that Bengttson was enough of an athlete and Ping-Pong addict to have travelled to Japan, slept on Ogimura's floor, and withstood Ogi's merciless training regimen. Within ten days, Bengttson would seize Zhuang Zedong's former crown as the men's singles champion. But Bengttson's achievement would be eclipsed by the Chinese in other ways. While he was playing table tennis, the Chinese were there to play a different game.

| Could the Great Wall Crumble?

The Chinese team had arrived in Nagoya on not one but two planes for maximum safety. Zhou Enlai had chosen a decorated air force veteran to organise the flight details, telling him 'to treat the journey as a special campaign.' He'd gathered the team one last time. 'Go,' he'd told his ambassadors, 'and rejoin the international family.'

The team had spent much of their last five years in either Beijing or the farms of Shanxi. When the first plane landed, security was tight. Among the advance party was one of the men's team coaches, Liang Youneng. To his relief, he saw among a large crowd on the tarmac a handful of people holding aloft the *Little Red Book*. 'Long Live Mao!' they shouted. Across the runway, he saw a larger group swarming toward them, furiously bellowing 'Down with Mao!' The police tried to hurry the Ping-Pong players toward safety. 'I couldn't even feel my feet on the ground,' remembered the Chinese coach. 'I was pushed by the crowd to the car.' Perhaps Mao's warning wasn't an exaggeration. Ping-Pong players might really be killed on the streets of Nagoya.

Everywhere the Chinese went, they were accompanied by a convoy of police officers on motorbikes. While most of the teams would be sharing a hotel and transport, the Chinese had their own buses and had made their own hotel arrangements. The assigned Japanese security wore tiny pins so that the Chinese players could identify them in an emergency. At night, as the team tried to sleep, they could hear the chants of Japanese demonstrators drift up to their windows. 'Drive! Drive! Drive! Drive away the Chinese!' The team watched the Chinese national flag burning on the street beneath their hotel. They watched portraits of Chairman Mao spark, light, and burst into flames. To ensure their safety, a handful of Japanese Communists would sleep in the corridor outside their rooms 'with only some newspapers underneath and overcoats for covering.'

Though most of the foreign press believed that Nagoya was the first international tournament for the Chinese team, they had actually played their first comeback match almost eight months earlier. Straight from cutting wheat stalks in Shanxi Province, the Chinese players were suddenly sent to play at the king of Nepal's sixtieth birthday party in Beijing before Zhou Enlai. It was the exhibition match against Ogimura and their oldest rivals, the Japanese national team.

Before the match, on an airless July night, Coach Xu Yinsheng, Mao's favourite speechmaker, gathered the squad to watch two patriotic films about atrocities that China suffered during the war against Japanese Aggression in the 1930s, which had cost the lives of 20 million civilians. All the tenets of the Cultural Revolution – to care only about the domestic and ignore the foreign, to serve the people and disregard competition – were immediately forgotten.

'The aim was to emphasise the hatred toward Japanese militarism,' explained Xi Enting, who was present that night. By the end of the movie, the team was thoroughly worked up. The domestic oppression that had plagued the squad over the last few years was cast aside. 'We all stood and started swearing, our hair was standing straight up, we were sweating away and chanting "Down with the revival of the Japanese army!"' Had Montagu been there, he would have been thrilled by the moment – his three great loves, table tennis, film, and politics, rolled up into powerful propaganda.

After the final reel ended, the team 'marched to the arena like an army entering into battle.' It was the first time the Japanese players had seen their great rivals in five years. Zhuang Zedong remained an idol to them and was surrounded by Japanese admirers. He refused their autograph requests and looked 'so angry that his face was pale. He jumped up onto the table and shouted loudly. It scared the Japanese. He was like a madman.' The Chinese won the match with ease, 'terrifying the Japanese into submission.' What the king of Nepal made of his celebrations wasn't noted. Ogimura seemed bemused.

The game was covered by Peking Radio. Though the Chinese could not have been hungrier for victory, the new rules accepted by Zhou Enlai to allow the reintroduction of sport insisted upon 'Friendship First and Competition Second.' The radio commentator wasn't even allowed to announce the score. All you could hear was the ping, pang of the ball going back and forth and polite, entirely political commentary. Even the manufacturing of the balls had become political. In factories, only balls that rolled out of the machine straight were chosen. Those that rolled left or right were labelled deviationist and destroyed.

China's only preparatory tournament in late 1970 had been deeply depressing. Humiliated three–one by the Hungarians at the Scandinavian Open, the team had slunk back to the Chinese embassy, where 'some started to cry.' The cook sent up bowls of hot noodles, but they couldn't eat or sleep. The following morning, the squad opened a Swedish newspaper and understood nothing except for a cartoon that showed a picture of the Great Wall of China crumbling.

When they were coaxed by Zhou Enlai into travelling to Nagoya, it had been understood that they weren't necessarily there to win the tournament. There had never been a more political trip. They were supposed to report to Beijing three times a day. Still, as ever, the officials were in the know, and the table tennis players were the pawns to be moved where they were needed.

In Nagoya the Chinese were doing better than they had hoped – slowly pushing aside their Swaythling Cup competitors and heading toward the inevitable clash with Japan. Their faltering visit to Sweden seemed a long time ago. They practised feverishly on the days when they didn't have matches and occasionally mixed with the North Koreans and players from other friendly countries.

In Nagoya, the Chinese could spot an American at a distance; they were like small clouds of radioactivity that were best avoided. As the players had already learned, the Cultural Revolution moved in uneven rhythms. Both players and officials knew that direct contact with Americans could still be interpreted as counter-revolutionary behaviour.

Liang Geliang, Zhuang Zedong's young acolyte, was about to step away from a table when an odd apparition appeared before him. Glenn Cowan was gesturing to Liang to practise with him. Liang was horrified. Not only was the long-haired, head-banded teenager an American, 'he was a really bad player . . . third ranked.' Liang thought of his invitation as 'almost an insult,' an American attempt to hoodwink him because he was so young. Liang retreated to ask an official what he should do. What if Cowan had been told to approach the Chinese by an American official? Go back, was the advice from the Chinese delegation, play for a short time, and then excuse yourself.

The Swaythling Cup came down to the usual ending. The Chinese men scraped off the rust and edged the Japanese. And in the singles? Could Zhuang Zedong recapture his crown after six years? Instead of a highly anticipated matchup against a fancied East European, Zhuang held a press conference and suddenly withdrew from the tournament. Before he could meet such a high-ranking player, he would have to defeat a young Cambodian. Zhuang sat in front of dozens of microphones and patiently explained that he refused to compete against 'players who represent governments [that are] enemies of the Cambodian and the Vietnamese people.' The squads representing these countries in Nagoya, Zhuang insisted, were simply 'puppets of US imperialism.' It was pure strategy, devised a month before by Zhou Enlai.

The Chinese team had now made two statements. First, in the all-important team competition, the Swaythling Cup, they remained the best. Second, in the men's singles, withdrawing their three-time world champion signalled that the Chinese did not value personal glory. Zhou had walked sport across a political tightrope to satisfy both sides of the Chinese political spectrum. The hard-liners of the Cultural Revolution could claim the victory for the masses. But Zhou and his pragmatists had not only re-entered international competition; they were practising international diplomacy.

CHAPTER 37 | **A Measured Coincidence**

On Monday 5 April, Glenn Cowan walked out of the practice hall after a game with a young Englishman. There was a bus waiting outside; Cowan presumed it was one of the shuttle buses running between the practice hall and the stadium, but it seemed to be full. According to the Chinese, Cowan stumbled up the steps, the bus doors shut, and the driver drove off. Only then did Cowan realise that he was the lone American on a bus full of Communist Chinese.

Cowan's version was significantly different. 'I was invited actually to board the Chinese bus with the team, which shocked me of course.' All agree that there followed minutes of silence, other than the mechanical roar of a large bus changing gears. Cowan was in a country where he couldn't even read a street sign with players representing a supposedly hostile nation. These were the dreaded Red Chinese.

Ever since he'd approached Liang Geliang for a knockabout, he'd been convinced that the Chinese were watching him. He looked up at one point and spotted Zhuang Zedong staring at him from the crowd. 'It was really weird,' he told Tim Boggan later. To Cowan, he felt he was getting the Bengttson treatment: the Chinese were learning from him. They weren't. They were studying him.

If this was diplomacy, then who would be the diplomat? Cowan decided to defuse the awkwardness and started talking to the entire bus through the English-speaking interpreter. 'I know all this,' he began, 'my hat, my hair, my clothes look funny to you. But there

Central Library
Newport City Council

Issue Summary

Patron: Fowler, Stuart Reginald
         James
Id: G001***
Date: 10/1/2019 2:23 PM

Loaned today

Item: Y015061
Title: The first wave : the D-day warriors
       who led the way to victory in the
       Second World War
Due back: 22/10/2019,23:59

Item: Z973956
Title: One minute to ten
Due back: 22/10/2019,23:59

Item: Z935331
Title: Ping pong diplomacy
Due back: 22/10/2019,23:59

Remember that your library
membership
also gives you access to free
eBooks,
eMagazines and eAudiobooks,
available
to download online any time of day or
night!

*Visit LION to renew, request
and search for books online
https://opac.newport.gov.uk*

Thank you

are many, many people who look like me and who think like me. We, too, have known oppression in our country and we are fighting against it. But just wait. Soon we will be in control because the people on top are getting more and more out of touch.'

The translator translated. Was Cowan actually talking about Mao's continuous revolution coming to America? Who was Cowan speaking on behalf of? Cowan told his room-mate later that he was trying 'to think like a revolutionary.' The Chinese players exchanged sideways glances as Cowan's words were translated. Who would speak to an American? The orders had been strict back in Beijing: Americans could be greeted politely, but they were the only country at the World Championships with whom the Chinese players shouldn't shake hands. What to do now? Which of them had waved him onto the bus? Why had they done it if they didn't even want to talk to him?

From the back of the bus, Zhuang Zedong, China's greatest player, stood up and walked forward. His team-mates tugged at his sleeves. One whispered, 'What are you going to do?' Another said quietly, 'Don't even talk to him.' Zhuang walked all the way to the front, where Cowan was sitting. In Zhuang's right hand, he carried a gift. Not just a Mao pin, a badge with the Chairman's profile, but a silk-screen portrait of the Huangshan mountains. He offered Cowan his hand to shake and handed him the gift. Cowan beamed in surprise. 'Even now,' said Zhuang thirty-five years later, 'I can't forget the naïve smile on his face.'

'Do you know who's giving you this gift?' asked the interpreter.

'Sure,' said Cowan. 'It's Zhuang Zedong.' He looked at the champion and smiled again. 'I hope you do well this week.'

There are only two ways to interpret Zhuang's behaviour. The first is to take every interview he's ever given at face value. All his actions that day, he claims, were influenced by Confucianism – a general belief in openness and reconciliation. Add to that a touch of topicality. He remembered that Chairman Mao had had several talks with the American Edgar Snow just months before. By Zhuang's account, he was willing to go against everything that had been drilled into the team over the last five years, including the knowledge that 'during the Cultural Revolution a lot of people got arrested from contacting foreigners and everyone was afraid.'

Or were Zhuang's actions premeditated? This was the man who had seen three of his oldest colleagues and mentors driven to death as counter-revolutionaries because of their ties to foreigners. He'd stood onstage and been interrogated in front of tens of thousands; he'd been beaten and tortured and had his head shaved. Under extraordinary pressure, he'd signed a big character poster denouncing He Long and team officials. The accusations against them were weak; none of those deemed guilty had ever instigated contact with a citizen of a hostile nation.

Zhuang had already shown that he was in Nagoya to act as an individual representing the wishes of the Chinese Communist Party. He had withdrawn from the men's singles on direct instructions from Beijing. As the most senior player, he was, in his own words, the first to be asked to 'represent our team.' Even if the actual moment was spontaneous, the context was premeditated in the extreme. Cowan was more like a mark in a con game than an accidental diplomat.

Cowan had most likely been selected because he'd already tried to reach out to the Chinese in the practice hall, making them almost certain that he'd behave in a friendly way. The bus had waited for him even though the Chinese had their own bus, hotel, and training facility. The fact that it picked up Cowan and then departed without waiting for other players suggests it was Cowan they were waiting for. Would Zhuang, a player who knew the high price of political crimes, do something so obviously political without permission from above?

Besides, how could Zhuang explain the fact that he was carrying such a gift when even the most senior players were allowed to carry only tiny souvenirs, like Mao pins, to exchange? Despite always maintaining that the moment was spontaneous, he once admitted, 'Before I left China, I went to a warehouse to get a large silk screen portrait, for an American. I thought it had to be a large one.' The Chinese Foreign Ministry 'kept a warehouse, very carefully graded,' filled with gifts for foreign dignitaries. It was always decided in advance exactly what level of gift a diplomat would receive.

When, minutes later, the two men stepped down from the bus at the Aichi stadium there was a group of photographers waiting. Photographs of the two grinning players were printed on the front pages of every Japanese newspaper the following morning and immediately picked up by the Associated Press. They were also included in one of the world's most important newspapers with a tiny circulation, specially edited for the leaders of the Chinese Communist Party. When he reached page seventy-eight, Chairman Mao peered closely at the photograph of the two beaming athletes. The Californian and the former world champion had the Chairman's full attention. 'Zhuang Zedong,' mused the Chairman. 'He's not just a good table tennis player. He's a good diplomat as well.' Mao immediately gave instructions that phone calls between the Ping-Pong team and Beijing increase from three to five times a day.

Now that the players had reached out to each other, the officials might be able to do the same. But instead, there was silence. The Chinese were convinced that the US team was being run by Washington. There had even been a rumour that the CIA had stocked its Langley headquarters with Ping-Pong equipment in anticipation of the Chinese team's trip to Nagoya. They feared that an American intelligence agent was going to be trained to infiltrate the tournament. The Chinese believed that the idea had been discarded by the CIA only when table tennis proved harder to master than the Americans had thought.

Cowan, son of a PR man, knew an opportunity when he saw it. From underneath the shaggy hair came an accent that swayed back and forth between New York and California. He didn't have any more games to play, having crashed out of the first rounds of both the singles and the consolation tournaments. Instead, he went shopping for a return present.

Cowan ended up buying two T-shirts, one for him and one for Zhuang. They were white and long-sleeved, with a peace symbol in the corner of a painted American flag. Underneath in large letters sat the Beatles' epigram, 'Let It Be,' that Paul McCartney had written two years earlier at the height of his acrimony with John Lennon. All Cowan had to do was confirm from the schedule that the Chinese were due to play the following morning at 8:30 and go along to wait for Zhuang. The second photo op within twenty-four hours would be even better attended than the first.

When Zhuang arrived, Cowan was waiting for him. Cowan had already been walking around the practice hall, showing off the silk

191

screen; now he stepped forward in front of the photographers he'd gathered. 'He gave me a big hug,' remembered Zhuang, and the cameras blazed.

The press would turn the moment into a spontaneous gesture of two innocents thirsting after world peace. For Zhou Enlai, it was the seamless projection of state policy; for Richard Nixon and Henry Kissinger, it would be perfectly acceptable since it furthered their own designs. Kissinger would later suspect the friendship might have been manufactured in Beijing. In 1979, he wrote that 'one of the most remarkable gifts of the Chinese is to make the meticulously planned appear spontaneous.'

The incident seemed to contain all of what the world thirsted for. The truth was subtler. It was the justification of Ivor Montagu's belief in Ping-Pong as a form of diplomacy. The correct deployment of propaganda in sport provides the illusion of a space that *seems* neutral. The instigator can then step forward to gain the ground. You get the advantage of being seen as openhanded at a moment of thorough calculation. Ping-Pong diplomacy was a tribute to Zhou Enlai's exact preparation. Table tennis had been political in China since its official adoption in 1953 and had remained malleable enough to be the correct tool at the correct time – but only if the last step was pulled off correctly. And the very last step would have to be made by officials.

CHAPTER 38	**An Invitation Home**

The point man for Zhou Enlai in the Nagoya delegation was Song Zhong, the general secretary of the National Sports Commission. Song had previously worked for the People's Liberation Army analysing military intelligence. He was charged with conducting sporting diplomacy of the most delicate level. Chairman Mao's initial reaction to Zhuang Zedong's overtures had been positive, so Song now had to orchestrate the dance with the American officials. He had to prepare for the possibility of inviting the US team to Beijing but also to engineer matters to appear that the Americans had requested the invitation.

By the end of the first day of the tournament, a rumour had spread that the English team had been invited to Beijing to play an exhibition. Word soon followed that the Chinese had also invited Colombia, Canada, and Nigeria. That was particularly frustrating to Rufford Harrison, the US delegate to the ITTF Congress, who had accompanied the team to Nagoya. He was English by birth and had jokingly asked his English counterpart if he could finagle an invitation to China for the US team.

Back in 1959, when Ivor Montagu had proposed giving the 1961 World Championships to Beijing, Harrison had been the lone US representative in the room. Harrison, who regarded Montagu as a genial 'iron hand in a velvet glove,' had always believed that the Englishman was behind China's bid. By the time Harrison voted, he had already tallied up the numbers and knew that the proposal had been accepted, so he gave his vote to the Chinese in the hope that it might count for something down the road.

The ITTF meetings usually coincided with the start of the World Championships. Harrison expected nothing from the Chinese, still believing that 'they were the pinko-commie bastards and we were the lickspittles of capitalism.' Beside him sat Graham Steenhoven, president of the USTTA. Like the rest of the American team, the president had a day job. Steenhoven was an English immigrant who had spent his entire life working for Chrysler in Detroit. He wasn't, as many thought, an executive, just an employment supervisor at a stamping plant, anxious to toe the line. Genial and doughy, he was benign to his perceived betters but a stern parent to those placed in his charge, no matter their ages.

During the meeting the South Vietnamese made a motion for the inclusion of Taiwan in the championships, a proposal that was answered with a vicious harangue against American plotters from the Chinese delegation. Harrison and Steenhoven, long inured to the Chinese dragging politics into the ITTF, sat stoically. Between sessions, the two Americans bumped into Song Zhong in a narrow corridor. Harrison wryly complimented the Chinese on the skills of their interpreters. He'd noted that the quality of interpreting had risen considerably and had quietly wondered why.

Steenhoven had brought handfuls of Kennedy half dollars with him and had been giving them out to maids in the Nagoya hotel as inexpensive mementos of the States. Now he smiled widely and handed one to Song. 'I heard you Chinese people are gentle,' he joked. 'Why were you so aggressive just now?' Song laughed loudly, pocketed the half dollar, and immediately went to file a report with Beijing.

Without realising it, Steenhoven and Harrison had made a key contribution to one of the first reports that whistled back to Zhou Enlai: the Americans were deemed friendly. There's no word on how closely the half dollar was examined. On one side of the coin, the American eagle holds an olive branch in one claw and thirteen arrows in the other claw, symbolising both the original colonies and the United States' willingness to go to war if need be. It was entirely accidental and entirely appropriate. Was it an aggressive overture or a peaceful outreach?

Qian Jiang, the Beijing-based author of a book on Ping-Pong diplomacy, explained that 'Song Zhong was really like a spy,' though in truth, he was more like a thermometer, gauging American temperatures five times a day. Did the Americans know, for instance, that one of their female players had already been seen buying a pin with a picture of Zhou Enlai on it?

Perhaps because he already knew what Zhou wished to happen, Song was reporting steady progress, painting the Americans as eager for an invitation. Years later, he told Qian Jiang that in retrospect, he'd been a little naïve. When Steenhoven and Harrison had been merely polite, he called Beijing to elaborate on their choice of words. 'Glad to meet you' had been interpreted as something other than a banal welcome.

A series of high-level meetings leading to the final decision to invite the Americans to Beijing involved the Foreign Ministry, Zhou Enlai, and Mao himself. Zhou tried to promote contact and refute it at the same time. He talked about inviting the American team only if it was 'progressive' and then railed against US actions in Vietnam, walking the line between his own desires and the radicals' fervent isolationism. As his friend Edgar Snow recalled, he was a man who 'never gambles – without four aces.' The report summarising China's options in Nagoya sat on Mao's desk for several days. The opportunity to reach out to the Americans through table tennis was slipping by. Like Zhou, Mao followed the games on the radio. He was well aware of Ping-Pong's foreign-policy credentials over the previous fifteen years. But was table tennis really the best way to deal with Americans?

Mao waited until the tournament was almost over to decide. The Americans were supposed to be heading out to Mie Prefecture for three days to play exhibitions against teams from a Japanese ball bearing factory. It didn't matter what Zhou thought; for all his power to execute ideas perfectly, this decision was so large that it could only be made by Chairman Mao himself.

Now seventy-four and recently diagnosed with amyotrophic lateral sclerosis (ALS), Mao's restful nights depended on his nurse supplying a steady dose of sleeping pills. Having personally authorised the Chinese table tennis's team trip in the first place, he was still wavering over whether an invitation should be extended to the US team.

That morning, he had 'endorsed a Foreign Ministry recommendation to turn down the request.' Now, having taken the pills, Mao still couldn't sleep. According to the Chairman's explicit rules, decisions he expressed after swallowing the drugs were to be ignored. 'Invite the American team to China,' he said, as he began to doze. His nurse leaned in closely, 'dumbstruck.' 'It was just the opposite of what he had authorised during the day!' His nurse decided to play it safe and pretended she hadn't heard the Chairman. 'Little Wu,' he said. 'Why don't you go and do what I asked you to do?'

She then spoke loudly so there could be no misunderstandings, 'Please say it again.'

Once more the Chairman repeated his words. 'Invite the American team to China.'

'You've taken your sleeping pills. Do your words count?'

'Yes they do!' said Mao. 'Do it quickly. Otherwise there won't be time.'

The emergency message arrived in Nagoya early on 7 April, just as the Chinese team was sitting down to a farewell meal. Had it really been a last-minute decision, or had Mao deliberately waited until the last moment so that the Gang of Four would have no time to oppose such a drastic move toward America? The message was couched in language familiar to anyone who had ever read an imperial edict about 'solicitous barbarians' seeking an audience with the emperor:

Considering the fact that the American team has requested several times to visit China, and that they have expressed warm and friendly feelings, the decision has been made that we will invite them, including the team leaders, to visit our country. Entry visas can be obtained in Hong Kong. If the travel funds are insufficient, we can subsidise them.

Zhuang Zedong insists the message was followed up by a personal call to him directly from Chairman Mao.

At 10.45am Rufford Harrison was standing just outside the Miyako Hotel, 'trying to hail a cab and none would stop.' Frustrated, Harrison stood waving his arm until 'Finally one stopped and two Chinese got out.' It was the head of the Chinese delegation,

196

former military analyst Song Zhong, along with his interpreter. Harrison presumed they were on the way to see the English delegation to organise their trip to Beijing. Instead, Song walked right up to him and asked, 'How would you respond to an invitation to visit China?'

Harrison stood there on the street, trying to keep his mouth closed. 'I was thinking, how can I avoid showing too much outward signs of joy? How can I keep a straight face?' Trying to think of something to say, he mentioned that it might be hard for the younger members of the team to afford the fees to reschedule their airline tickets. 'Don't worry,' said Song. 'It can be arranged.' The wealthiest nation in the world was about to accept a handout from a country still in the process of industrialisation. 'It was,' remembered Harrison, 'the sort of offer you couldn't refuse, in *Godfather* terms.'

Song's wording was precise, brilliant, that of a professional dealing with an amateur. From the beginning, it was important for the Chinese to adhere to their marshaled version of the truth. America was going to play the role of supplicant. China was the Middle Kingdom. America was arriving empty-handed; China was the generous host, without a care in the world other than the health and comfort of her guests.

Harrison hurried back in the hotel to talk to Steenhoven. He was nowhere to be found. Harrison asked team captain Jack Howard to call all the players to a meeting at 3.30pm and then decided to ring the American Embassy in Tokyo. He quickly explained the situation. Was there any problem with the American team entering China? 'Just go,' came the immediate answer. The answer was delivered, Harrison remembered, in an '"everybody-goes-to-China" sort of tone.' Harrison was confused. It seemed a preposterously curt response to what he was beginning to understand was a momentous question.

Still puzzled, Harrison made his way over to the stadium, where the American team was gathering. As the meeting got under way, Steenhoven finally walked in. He had been out shopping with his wife, or, as Steenhoven would later put it, tied up with administrative matters. The biggest moment of Ping-Pong history had almost passed by without him. For a moment 'he was livid,' feeling thoroughly slighted that the Chinese hadn't approached him directly –

he was the head of the delegation. He even contemplated declining the invitation.

Once Steenhoven had settled down, the conversation continued. Should they go? 'We knew there were some rather horrible people in the Middle Kingdom,' said Harrison. They had no idea if they would be safe, be kidnapped, be humiliated by Red Guards, be used as propaganda puppets. The USTTA was an organisation without any knowledge of China whatsoever.

How long should they go for? They settled on one week. There were those who believed they'd be fired from their jobs if they stayed away any longer, those who missed wives or boyfriends too much, those scared to stay longer. Ultimately, only two felt they couldn't go at all, including America's number one, DJ Lee, who had been born near Seoul and 'regarded Beijing as being responsible for the Korean War' and his family's suffering.

By now the press had become aware of the invitation. This strangely representative group of Americans was suddenly in the vanguard of international politics. As the meeting drew to a close, the first thing Steenhoven had to make sure of was that it wouldn't be against State Department policy for them to enter China. What if they were portrayed as pariahs on their return? What if they never returned? Besides, how could Harrison feel so sure about the legality of their entry? Did he even know whom he'd talked to in the embassy in Tokyo? What on earth was going on here?

| Surprise

Two hundred miles to the east of Nagoya, in the Japanese capital of Tokyo, the China specialist in the US Embassy Political Section, Bill Cunningham, received a phone call. It was the press attaché from the United States Information Service (USIS), explaining that the Italian Press Agency was leading with a story that an American table tennis team had just been invited to China. What was their official line? If it was true, continued the press attaché, it was going to 'be the story of the year.' For Cunningham, it was the diplomatic equivalent of being handed a live grenade. Should he distance the United States government, persuade the team not to go, or embrace the moment and encourage contact, albeit through table tennis? Cunningham, like the press attaché on the other end of the line, sensed at once the potential commotion about to come his way. They would have to come up with an appropriate answer immediately. Anything less would not only embarrass the State Department but also make the Japanese nervous. Silence on so obvious an issue as China policy was not an option.

Cunningham's usual day involved gleaning information on China and transmitting it back to Washington. By 1971, Cunningham felt that the United States 'had developed a fairly good picture of what was going on' inside China. Back in Washington, dozens of translators read the output of the New China news agency. At the American consulate in Hong Kong, the *People's Daily* was examined in mimeographed form. Anyone leaving China and heading through Hong Kong was intensively interviewed.

For all of the State Department's efforts to keep an eye on the Communist Chinese, its knowledge was scant compared to an earlier generation of China watchers. Back in 1944, the United States had been open-minded enough to set up an observation base just outside the Communist enclave of Yan'an. The Dixie Mission, as it came to be known, had been one of the many unlikely unions of World War II.

Twelve Americans spent over a year living next to Mao and Zhou Enlai, aiding the fight against Japan, reporting on weather conditions for B-29 bombers passing over northern China, and, with the help of the Communists, establishing escape routes for downed pilots. They would go hunting with the Communists or head out together on reconnaissance behind Japanese lines. Sometimes they'd hold volleyball matches. Sometimes they'd play Ping-Pong together.

The Americans had the only generator in the whole of Yan'an. The men who would come to rule China could often be found over at the American caves when the Americans were screening films; the Chinese favoured anything starring Ivor Montagu's old friend Charlie Chaplin. Montagu had sent Chaplin a copy of *The Jews Are Watching You*, the German book that lay behind Chaplin's decision to make *The Great Dictator*, the perfect film for Chinese Communists and American officials to watch together during their fight against Fascism.

American opinion of Communist intelligence in those key years had been high enough for one officer to recommend that the Dixie Mission be made permanent. On the other hand, opinion of Chiang Kai-shek was devastating. General David Barr, Chiang's own chief military adviser, attributed the collapse of the Nationalist armies fighting against Mao's force to 'the world's worst leadership . . . widespread corruption and dishonesty throughout the Armed Forces.' Or, in the words of General 'Vinegar Joe' Stilwell, 'We are allied to an ignorant, illiterate, peasant son of a bitch called Chiang Kai-shek.'

The beginning of the end of any lasting relationship between the Communist Chinese and America had come with the arrival of Ambassador Patrick Hurley, a man who believed he could negotiate with the Chinese because 'they're just like Mexicans and I can handle Mexicans.' He had called Mao Zedong 'Moose Dung.' The

Communists thought little of him. The Office of Strategic Services (OSS), precursor to the CIA, apparently didn't think much of him either; his code name was ALBATROSS.

Still, back in Washington, Hurley's reports carried weight, as he stormed around making excuses for Chiang Kai-shek's squandering of US aid. In November 1945 he wrote that 'the weakness of the American foreign policy together with the Communist conspiracy within the Department are reasons for the evils that are abroad in the world today.' He reserved much of his hatred for the very best China watcher out in Yan'an, John Stewart Service. Service, fluent in Mandarin, not only had the ear of Mao and Zhou Enlai, but had been a school friend of Chen Yi's in Sichuan. He was guilty of accurately reporting the current situation: the cohesion of the Communists and the utter incompetence of their Nationalist rivals.

In the anti-Communist hysteria that would soon grip America, Hurley's evidence was wielded against Service and his colleagues by Senator Joe McCarthy, who was conducting a witch hunt against Communists he claimed were infiltrating US institutions. They were kept as far away from China as possible, 'blown like dead leaves all over the earth' to posts as incongruous as Dusseldorf, Liverpool, and Bern, or, like Service, they were fired. Once they were gone, what was left was a 'wasteland' that came to be known as 'the China generation gap.' The mistreated were the Foreign Service officers who had presciently compiled a report on Vietnam in the mid-1940s declaring that the French, or anyone else who got themselves involved, would find that 'guerilla warfare may continue indefinitely.'

Twenty years later, capable men like Bill Cunningham in the embassy in Tokyo were in charge of watching China; a country they had never been able to visit. It was, as one China scholar declared, closer to astrophysics than diplomacy.

Cunningham was attentive 'any time the PRC gained a step forward in any organisation.' This was the 'termites in the basement' theory; without a close watch, an institution could be slowly rendered ineffective by Communist infiltration. By the end of 1970, the likelihood of the US mustering enough support to keep Taiwan in the UN and China out was waning. American diplomats not privy to Kissinger and Nixon's intentions with China were closely monitoring the situation and working on damage control for what was beginning to seem an inevitability. A table tennis tournament, on the other hand, had been so obscure an entry point for a termite that it had passed under Cunningham's radar.

The question of an American team entering China reminded Cunningham of a document he'd kept in the bottom of his desk. It was an annual report on foreign relations from the president to Congress – one of Kissinger's innovations on Nixon's behalf. A sentence had caught his eye that January, a single line buried in the four volumes. It stated that 'the United States is open to educational, cultural and athletic exchanges with People's Republic of China.' Cunningham's career would rest on that one sentence. Despite the fact that the public face of Washington was still set against Communist China, Cunningham based his decision on these sixteen words. Cunningham, along with the rest of the State Department, had no idea about Kissinger's and Nixon's attempts to reach out to Mao and Zhou Enlai.

The USIS attaché who called with news of the US team's invitation to China pressed Cunningham about what their response to the media should be. Both men knew instinctively that a deluge of calls would follow. 'Tell them we know about it,' said Cunningham, 'and that if they decide to go it will not be against United States policy.' Minutes later, the embassy's public affairs officer, Alan Carter, called Cunningham. 'Don't you think you've gone awfully far?' he asked. Cunningham paused. 'You better go see the ambassador' advised Carter.

What had Cunningham just done? Was a team representing the United States necessarily political? A Chinese team would certainly consider itself political. Cunningham read the sentence again and again and went to get a grudging approval from the ambassador.

His next call was from the deputy director of China Affairs at Japan's Foreign Ministry. What was the United States government doing? Was it behind this development? Cunningham assured the official that the table tennis team in Nagoya was a private group. 'Who's the leader?' pressed the official.

'I haven't the slightest idea,' replied Cunningham.

| **Decisions to Be Made**

At 6:30 that evening, as he was clearing off his desk, Cunningham received a piece of paper with Steenhoven's name and phone number. When Cunningham dialed Nagoya, the first words out of Steenhoven's mouth were 'Thank God you've called.' He was due to meet with the Chinese in under an hour and explained that he was 'barricaded in his hotel room' in order to make a final decision while, in their eagerness, the team outside 'was pounding down his door' in their desire to go. Was that really okay with the United States government?

Cunningham calmly read him the vital sentence from the annual report on foreign relations. 'You're saying that we should go,' said Steenhoven.

'No, I am not saying that you should go,' explained Cunningham carefully. 'The US government is not going to tell you what to do about this. What I am saying is that the US government has said that we are open to athletic exchanges with the People's Republic of China.'

Steenhoven paused for a moment and then rebuilt his question. 'Okay. It won't be against US policy if we go?'

'No,' said Cunningham, 'it will not.'

For all of Zhou Enlai's wrangling to reach this moment, had Cunningham been less adept or more cautious, the opportunity would have passed.

In Nagoya, the final meeting to hammer out the details took

place in a windowless room beneath the stadium as the finals were played above them. Song Zhong awaited them. What would they like to see in China? What would they prefer to eat? While the Chinese had such a good grasp on negotiation, with a marshalled bureaucratic hierarchy of ten thousand heads, they were unaware that Steenhoven had no right to control the movement of his own group. At that stage, Steenhoven knew that the only thing he had control of was the team's passports.

There was no time to prepare; very little time even to panic. The Chinese invitation meant that the Americans were due to fly in thirty-six hours. Some players began to write their wills. Tim Boggan admitted, 'We were all nincompoops; none of us knew what we were doing. None of us was a China watcher. Nobody knew from shit what we were doing.' USTTA president Steenhoven later summed up his own knowledge about China before the trip as pigtails, satin pyjamas, and pirate junks. Most of the team still clung to the belief that the Ping-Pong invitation was about Ping-Pong. Why not? They were Ping-Pong players invited to play against the world's best players in the world's biggest Ping-Pong stadium. Would Little Leaguers refuse a chance to play against Joe DiMaggio in Yankee Stadium? Few were thinking of the media; as Ping-Pong players, they were used to the absence of media coverage.

For international travel, the Chinese team had always been run by the Protocol Office of China's Foreign Ministry. The American team was barely run at all, something Steenhoven was very much aware of. They were typical in the very best ways of 1971 America. They were racially and sexually diverse; they were students and chemical engineers, professors and file clerks. What could possibly go wrong?

By the end of his call with Steenhoven, Cunningham had decided to invite the American table tennis officials to Tokyo so they could meet face-to-face. The pretext was that the US Embassy would need to validate the team's passports, even though that would normally be done at the consulate.

The following day, 9 April, Harrison and Steenhoven shot from Nagoya to Tokyo by fast train, taking a quick breakfast of beer and seaweed on board. They wandered into the US Embassy, and the team's passports were sent down the hill to the consulate. Steenhoven entered Cunningham's office in a blue suit with an American flag on his lapel, eager to please. 'He looked like everyone's grandpa,' noted Cunningham, 'perfect for the American public.' He'd have been a lot more alarmed, thought Harrison, had he seen Glenn Cowan.

Back in Washington, Kissinger's staff was trying to figure out who on earth was about to enter China. Herbert Levin, a friend of Cunningham's from the Tokyo Embassy now working under Kissinger, remembered that they 'had to find out who were these fellows? I mean, were there warrants for their arrest outstanding, some child molesters . . . who were these guys?'

Cunningham gave Steenhoven and Harrison some advice. The Cultural Revolution was ongoing. They were about to enter a puritanical society, so they needed to act accordingly. 'Never call a Chinese a Chinaman,' remembered Harrison from the pep talk. 'The second was, never touch a woman. He gave an example of a Russian diplomat who had groped a Chinese elevator operator and was arrested.' That gave Harrison pause for thought. On a previous trip with Cowan, he'd watched amazed as the young Californian had sat down next to a foreign airport official and draped 'his arm around her shoulder, and his hand was on one breast.'

Steenhoven's first worry was that the team 'would be attacked by the Chinese,' a fear that Cunningham believed totally unfounded. Steenhoven also worried about gifts. They knew the Chinese would present them with mementos in Beijing and Shanghai, but they didn't want to give the Chinese Japanese gifts in return. The present had to be made in America. Cunningham believed there were three acceptable gifts in Beijing in 1971, wristwatches, transistor radios, and ballpoint pens that 'could fit nicely into the outside pocket of a Mao suit.' He immediately sent a Japanese colleague out to all the army post exchanges within reasonable distance to purchase American-made goods.

The team's passports were returned. To all three men's surprise, there was no official stamp on any of them. Down in the consulate, someone had simply drawn a black marker over the line that said 'not valid for travel into or through mainland China.' There was no official etiquette for what was happening.

As they left Cunningham's office, Steenhoven and Harrison had a good sense of the sort of quasi-diplomatic mission they were undertaking. It was like being in a Western where they'd just been deputised by the sheriff, only to be refused the tin star and pistol. In the corridor outside Cunningham's office Harrison and Steenhoven bumped into John Rich, perhaps the most experienced of all Asia-based journalists. Cunningham didn't even know how Rich had made it inside the embassy, but forty years later, still remembered his doorway smile, polished for Steenhoven and Harrison. The US team wouldn't be escaping from the press for weeks.

By the time Harrison and Steenhoven made it to a lunch near the international airport, boxes filled with hundreds of American-made ballpoints were being driven out to meet them. Cunningham had considered seeing the team off but decided it was best no representative of the government be seen anywhere near this group. American table tennis wasn't political, was it?

| # The Worries

The madness began as the American team reached Hong Kong. It became increasingly obvious that this might be the biggest story of the year. There was no avoiding the media. 'You go to eat, and they're there at the same table as you. You go to take a leak, and they go and take a leak with you,' remembered Harrison. The story had so many perfect ingredients: the importance of Sino-American relations combined with the faintly ridiculous scent of Ping-Pong. Throw in the unexpectedly diverse group of Americans heading into unknown Beijing, and something would simply *have* to happen, and when it did, every single TV network and newspaper wanted the news at once.

Because it seemed at first that no Western journalists would be allowed into China, it looked as though the players themselves would be the only witnesses to history. They were asked by media outlets to act as reporters. Boggan alone was tracked down by *Time, Life, Newsweek*, CBS, an Australian newspaper, and the *New York Times*, until recently uninterested in Ping-Pong but now anxious for his services. The younger girls would be approached by *Seventeen* magazine. George Brathwaite, a Guyanese immigrant who worked at the UN, would hear from *Ebony* magazine. He carried four cameras from different newspapers around his neck. Sitting in their hotel rooms in Hong Kong, the Ping-Pong players were provided with equipment and given crash courses in how to use the cameras. They were told what to ask, what to look for, and how to write.

Before he'd even left Nagoya, Steenhoven had called Cunningham to inquire about returning China's invitation. A visit from the Chinese team to the United States would generate much-needed domestic publicity for the sport. But it wasn't as simple as it sounded. Steenhoven would need clearance from a different government department to have Communists admitted to the States. The McCarran Act of 1950 restricted visas for citizens of Communist countries. In the normal order of things, applicants for visas were supposed to be interviewed in a US consulate, and of course there wasn't one in all of China. There was also the question of funding a Chinese tour, an impossibility for the impoverished USTTA. As Steenhoven put it, he'd be relieved if 'a fairy godmother could be found.'

To Steenhoven's relief, a cable awaited him at the Golden Gate Hotel in Kowloon, announcing that the National Committee on United States–China Relations had agreed to fund-raise for the trip. The committee began six years earlier as a forum for Americans to promote a public discussion that might delve beyond knee-jerk negativity against Red China. Steenhoven kept the good news to himself. He didn't trust anyone else on the trip with the information, worrying that something might happen and that he was the one who was 'going to look like an asshole.'

Cowan, the maverick, was thinking ahead. He placed a call to his old mentor Bob Gusikoff, back in Los Angeles, and decided that Gusikoff would act as his agent on his return. Cowan planned to hit the ground running, starting with a press conference the moment they landed back in the United States. Gusikoff returned his call within hours to tell him that he'd already negotiated the front cover of *Life* magazine. He felt Ping-Pong had a good chance to become as big as golf on the team's return and advised Cowan to concentrate on getting rights to Chinese table tennis equipment.

To anyone who'd listen, Cowan shared his optimism for the future, 'Don't worry, baby, we're gonna play 50,000 tournaments when we get back.' For the moment, Cowan was completely relaxed. He'd promised Jack Howard, the team captain, that he'd flushed the last of his stash down his hotel toilet in Tokyo.

Steenhoven's other worry, asides from Cowan, was eighteen-year-old John Tannehill. He had had a shoulder-length hairstyle similar to Cowan's but had mowed it down to stubble before heading to Japan. His only long hair now grew from the point of his chin in a wispy, youthful beard. A psychology student from the University of Cincinnati, Tannehill was a loner by nature who carried with him a novel by Norman Mailer, a book on Che Guevara, and a copy of the *Teachings of the Buddha*. One of his team-mates considered him so smart that 'he could play chess against eight people at the same time without looking at the board.'

On the eve of their departure, Tannehill disappeared from the Hong Kong hotel for a mere twenty minutes and returned, claiming to Boggan that he'd just visited a hooker. 'I won't do that again,' he said. Boggan doubted that he'd had time to do it at all.

His rival from hundreds of youth tournaments, Glenn Cowan, one-upped him and went missing before midnight. Cowan's roommate, team captain Jack Howard, was seen scouting the hotel lobby at 2:30 in the morning. 'Has anyone seen Glenn?' Cowan had remained so relaxed the night before their entry into China that he'd headed to a bar in Lang Kwai Fong, where he picked up a local prostitute for $12, smoked some dope, and ended up at her apartment, relying on her to wake him up for his trip into China. The alarm went off at 5.00am, and Cowan's day began with his new friend 'giving him a blow job.' By 5:30am he was back in the Golden Gate Hotel being dressed down by his captain, who had begun the night with Cowan searching for hookers before getting cold feet.

If Cunningham had been comforted by Steenhoven's blue suit and American flag pin, Cowan's bag of dirty clothes, condoms, and marijuana would have horrified him. Tannehill's Che Guevara tome would have raised a little red flag in the State Department, too. Ambassadors were nominated by presidents and approved by the Senate; Ping-Pong players weren't vetted quite so closely.

More worrying still was Cowan's mental state. Boggan paused by his open hotel door the next morning as Cowan was preparing for an interview with a TV reporter. He obsessively brushed his hair before suddenly leaping on his bed, rolling in circles clutching his pillow. He hoped the girls in China liked him, he said. The Japanese girls had been keen on him, so why not the Chinese? 'Christ,' thought Boggan, 'I reckon this guy's still on something.'

CHAPTER 42 | **Crossing the Borders**

Glenn Cowan wore his white 'Let It Be' shirt, a yellow floppy hat, and purple tie-dye pants. It seemed to have been his outfit of choice, no matter where he went or whose hand he was told to shake. Cowan sensed that he could become a one-man brand – his own spokesman, model, and salesman. It was already obvious to all that Cowan craved the spotlight. On the railroad bridge between the freedom of the New Territories in Hong Kong and the stricture of Communist China he was 'given explicit directions . . . to lag behind the others' and then turn to give 'a smile and a great big wave.'

As the team-mates stepped across the border, 'there was music playing from the sky.' Chinese loudspeakers accompanied their arrival, giving many members of the team the sensation that they 'were in a movie.' Even as he traipsed across the red-and-white bridge, Cowan was cognisant of his unique position – a hippie in China to play Ping-Pong with real live Communists. Another American paused on the bridge and silently wondered, 'Am I going to come out again?' In the watching crowd of newspapermen lurked an official from the US Consulate, an unnamed exception to the firm orders for all American diplomats to avoid the team. A report shot to Washington. The team 'crossed the border at 10.18 local time . . . we welcome this development.'

The photograph of Cowan waving goodbye to the Western world hit the front page of the *New York Times* and the front pages of newspapers across the world. Zhou Enlai couldn't have designed a more favourable layout. Mao's invitation to the table tennis team shared the front page with news of the ongoing Paris Peace Talks, Kissinger's and Nixon's incessant push and pull to extract America from the Vietnam War with a vestige of honour. The coincidence would not be lost on Washington this time. For a reminder of why Nixon needed Mao's influence with the North Vietnamese, just below was an anguished article about a rise in American casualty rates. And should Zhou have wished one more nudge to remind Kissinger and Nixon that China was going to re-establish contacts with or without their help, in the bottom corner of the front page was an article on China's quiet surge into Africa.

As they boarded the train from the border to Guangzhou, Cowan was in his own world. He stared out the window at the workers labouring in the paddy fields that lined the tracks. 'I really believe life is simple. It's all the other people that make it complicated,' he said to nobody in particular. Earlier, he'd approached Tim Boggan with a strange request: 'You gotta watch me, please watch me.' He would raise more eyebrows at their first lunch in Guangzhou when he suddenly stood up and left the room in the middle of a speech by their host.

If Cowan was playing the role of Californian counter-culturalist, then on that train to Guangzhou, Tannehill was undergoing a quieter, more earnest conversion. He was dressed in his Farmer Brown bib overalls, more suitable to a Nebraskan homestead than a train to a Communist hub, sitting alone eating a box of cereal and almonds, playing chess against himself. At the Customs House at the border, he'd picked up a copy of Mao's *On the Correct Handling of Contradictions among the People*. On the train he declared it 'one of the best books I've ever read.'

After flying from Guangzhou to Beijing, they were put up at the Xing Qiao Hotel, just as the last generation of Ping-Pong playing Westerners had been a decade before. Everything that happened to this US team was seen as new, yet everything that they were going through was entirely familiar to their Chinese hosts. Ping-Pong was ambassadorial politics, and the US team was one of the few that had never received this treatment. During the next week, the world's press ignored table tennis history. The 1961 Beijing Championships, and the fact that dozens of foreign Ping-Pong players had already been sent on exactly the same kind of tour that the Americans were about to undergo were brushed over to emphasise the strangeness of the situation.

The team's biggest immediate danger wasn't Steenhoven's fear that they would be torn apart by Red Guards but gluttony. Every way they turned at all times of day, they were met with banquets with double-digit courses. Even after their first banquet in Beijing, a tableful of food awaited them on their return to the hotel. Opinions on the dishes varied from the diplomatic ('I haven't acquired a taste for it yet') to the repelled ('a vat of vomit').

On the first morning in Beijing, as the others discussed their breakfast, eaten in the hotel restaurant under a banner of 'US aggressors and all their running dogs,' Cowan and Tannehill ran breathless back into the hotel. They had been up before 4.00am and managed to slip out alone onto the gray streets. They had walked around followed by children, then more children, until Cowan was convinced that they had a crowd of thousands in tow. Cowan and Tannehill had decided that if this was a truly communistic society, then everything must be shared. As they tried to get on bikes propped against a wall, they realised that the kids 'glared at us. It wasn't such a socialist country after all.'

To Tannehill, it seemed like the crowd was closing in on them. 'The only way we could stop them from getting on top of us was that we had a camera and we took pictures of them as we were going away and I don't think they'd seen a camera or a white person before and they were kind of startled.'

A newsman went to check on Cowan's crowd, which Cowan numbered at five or ten thousand. Cowan was losing his credibility among the reporters. 'In fact, there was only the usual collection of onlookers, about fifty of them, mostly children, who always collect outside the hotel to wait for foreign guests staying there.'

Cowan's enthusiasm was unabated. He walked around 'whistling at the girls, following them down the street,' remembered Tannehill. He got Jack Howard to play a game of imaginary Ping-Pong with him in a street, which did attract a huge crowd, stopping traffic all around them until 'the meanest-looking guy in China came along.' Intimidated, Howard stopped their game and dragged Cowan back toward the hotel through the crowd.

'This is getting a little dangerous,' said Howard.

Cowan disagreed. 'Don't be silly,' he said.

Then a rock came flying out of the crowd and landed between them. Howard was suddenly worried that he, the captain of the American Ping-Pong team, would end up 'stoned to death on the streets of Peking.' Cowan just casually shook his finger at the crowd and kept walking.

During the preparations for the visit to China, the table tennis team hadn't even made the sports pages of an American newspaper. Now, after less than twenty-four hours in China, they dominated the broadsheets; five articles inspired by their trip appeared in the *New York Times* alone. On their second day in China, there were eight articles in the *Times*. All were in the international news section, placing Ping-Pong in columns usually reserved for foreign policy. The Chinese press coverage was quite different. The other teams, from England, Nigeria, Colombia, and Canada, were given equal ink. The stories were short, bland, and placed on the back pages.

At first, the Chinese players had no idea of the impact the US team's arrival was having. 'It was,' after all, 'a crime to listen to the Voice of America.' Xu Shaofa, one of the country's top players, crept into officials' offices once a week to steal the newspapers, including those published specially for the Communist Party hierarchy. It was from him that the team learned of the influence Ping-Pong diplomacy was having on relations with their 'American enemy.'

Zhou Enlai had played another subtle card, suddenly granting visas to three veteran American newsmen and one Englishman who had covered Asia for decades. Why, at the last minute, would the Chinese do such a thing? It was a considerable rise in the stakes. These weren't the British sportswriters of 1961 nor members of the thin line of sympathisers, such as Edgar Snow, who had dripped into China over the years. John Rich, Jack Reynolds, John Saar, and John Roderick, representing NBC, the Associated Press (AP), and *Life*, were considered some of the shrewdest Asia reporters on the continent. Roderick was among those who had made it to Yan'an to visit the Dixie Mission back in the 1940s.

Norman Webster, the correspondent for Toronto's *Globe and Mail* who was accompanying the Canadian tour, believed that the Chinese were shocked to find the American press, denied access for their experienced reporters, had recruited athletes who knew nothing about China. Early on, he heard one player turn to another and ask, 'What's this Cultural Revolution they keep talking about?' Perhaps, he thought, the Chinese had decided that the risk of poor coverage would lessen if veteran reporters were allowed in – the compromise was that they would be tied to covering the Ping-Pong team's progress. It was a savvy move; the reports of AP man John Roderick were front-page news across the world.

Though some of the would-be reporters on the squad felt aggrieved by the presence of professional journalists, Cowan was thrilled. 'He thought they were going to do all the work and he was going to get all the . . . glory.' They gave Cowan $50 as spending money and told him, 'From now on, we'll tell you when we need you.' But Cowan wasn't so easy to dismiss. By the end of the week, Cowan explained to the reporter and photographer from *Life*, 'I thought instead of doing "Inside China" you could have done a piece on "Americans in China" with a big picture of me on the cover.'

The rest of the team could be timid around the experienced pressmen, but not Cowan. He muscled aside Roderick, interrupting the interview of a professor at Tsinghua University. 'These are really strange questions, man.' 'You think you can ask better questions?' snapped Roderick. Cowan nodded and took over the interview. At the same university, a spontaneous game of basketball erupted in front of hundreds of students. It was another event in which Cowan could shine. 'They liked me as much as the Harlem Globetrotters,' he beamed afterward.

The team had the wonders of the Cultural Revolution explained to them. Steenhoven played the parental role, making small speeches of thanks that were painfully in line with the Chinese, urging his squad to applaud 'the peasants, the workers, the students who are in the room.' The older players knew when to keep their mouths shut, but John Tannehill and Glenn Cowan were still teenagers. They were in college at a political time, found themselves in a political place, and, unsurprisingly, were thinking about politics. Everywhere they went, the newsmen followed, and passing conversations were slapped down on paper.

On the bus ride to the Great Wall, weaving 'through a stream of

oncoming Mongolian ponies, trucks and bicycles,' the two turned
to the question of how America might be transformed by resistance
to the Vietnam War. Cowan thought that the country was on the
cusp of an intellectual revolution, though he worried it was coming
across more like 'a lot of hippies doing their own thing – and protesting the government.'

'How are you an intellectual?' interrupted Tannehill.

'I don't know,' said Cowan. 'How are you an intellectual?'

'I don't know,' said Tannehill. 'I read.'

'Oh,' Cowan said slowly, 'is that how you're an intellectual?'

'It helps,' said Tannehill.

'I think,' said Cowan. 'That's how I'm an intellectual.'

Tannehill had an awakening on the Great Wall that would horrify
the American heartland. First, he riffed on Steenhoven's constant
harping on the word 'responsibility': 'I've decided to be political
and suffer the consequences. Not being political, it's like not having
any mind. China knows it can beat us at table tennis. They brought
us over here for the political consequences.' Instead of listening to
Graham Steenhoven, the Chrysler company man, president of the
USTTA, and holder of American passports, Tannehill decided that
the truth lay with Mao, 'the greatest moral and intellectual leader
in the world today. He reaches the most people and influences the
most people. His philosophy is beautiful.'

It was said in earshot of Webster and made the front page of
the next day's Toronto *Globe and Mail*. It wasn't what Steenhoven
wanted to hear, it wasn't what Nixon wanted to hear, and most of
all, it wasn't what Chairman Mao or Zhou Enlai wanted to hear.
They were looking for bridge-builders, not converts who might
inspire opposition to China back in America. 'The Chinese,' said
Tannehill, on a roll, 'had this Great Wall to keep out the Mongols.
The US has its paranoia in its ghetto suburbs, its missile defence
systems.' Back in his hotel room that night, Tannehill taped a silk-
screen portrait of Mao above his bed. And then, to his surprise, he
felt very, very sick.

At four in the morning, an unconscious Tannehill was found by
his room-mate, George Brathwaite, wedged behind the toilet bowl,
slumped in his own shit. It's tempting to presume the Chinese had
targeted him with a well-placed dumpling, but many on the team

suffered during their trip. Team captain Howard was missing from the team's *Time* cover photo on the Great Wall because he was bent double over a hole in the ground at the foot of the steps. Another player, Errol Resek, had to stop a bus ride and leap into the neighbouring field.

Tannehill was rushed to the hospital by Howard. As the team captain headed back to the hotel, he heard Tannehill screaming 'Jesus, don't leave me here! Don't leave me here!' Tannehill watched as a man was rolled past him in a wheelchair, holding up Mao's *Little Red Book*. It was helping his recovery, explained the translator. By the time Tannehill made it back to the hotel, John Roderick, the AP man, was there to capture his first doubts. His initial enthusiasm had been tempered by a day of Chinese health care: 'From his sick bed, Mr Tannehill said, "I wouldn't want to spend the rest of my life here, but I'd like to see more of it."'

Steenhoven was by now seething with anger at the *Globe and Mail*'s reporter. It was the worst possible scenario, a stain on the tour fully documented by a veteran reporter. Was Tannehill a Maoist among them? Or simply a young man strung along by an old hand? Steenhoven called Webster to his room, accused him of yellow journalism, and told him he might be ruining a young man's entire career. He threatened to get back at Webster. He wasn't sure how, but Steenhoven planned to make the effort. Webster shrugged it off. He was a reporter and he was reporting. What else was he supposed to do?

| # All Eyes on America

A stadium devoted to Ping-Pong, 'grander than Madison Square Garden,' was now packed with eighteen thousand fans. It was an intoxicating moment for the Americans. If the crowds of five thousand in Nagoya had surprised them, what to make of this? The Chinese played it safe; the reporters noted that almost the entire stadium was made up of conscripts from the PLA. The only person missing was the ailing Tannehill.

Cunningham had been right about Steenhoven. His geniality and refusal to take offence made him a perfect ambassador. At that first match, he noticed that behind a huge banner saying 'Welcome American team' was another message painted in large red letters, four feet high: 'Down with the Yankee Oppressors and Their Running Dogs.' He asked the interpreter why they hadn't taken it down. It was said in a joking manner. The interpreter just smiled and didn't say anything.

The team had been introduced to the crowd by the song 'As a helmsman is necessary to navigate in high seas, so the thought of Mao Zedong is necessary to make a revolution.' 'Probably carried away by the music,' Cowan had started to perform 'a twist-like shuffle.' Then he pulled out his red headband and strutted out to the table for his match. The crowd applauded. No member of the American team knew that Zhou Enlai had personally overseen the schedule and dictated how the event would be covered by television cameras. He had personally drafted the text for the announcer.

Even the timing of the applause Cowan heard as he stepped forward had been ordered by the premier.

For all of Cowan's posturing, he was one of the few natural entertainers on the team. The crowd, regimented and breathless, began to react to him. Here was a man doing exactly what he wanted – clenching his fist to celebrate a point rather than dedicating it to Mao; putting his foot up on the table to tie a shoelace instead of discreetly bowing to the floor; jumping over barriers to get a ball back instead of stepping around them. Even Steenhoven appreciated Cowan's antics. Though Cowan was playing well, after he lost a point he walked back to the table and picked it up, shifted it an inch, and put it back down, implying that his last shot would have been a winner if the table had been in the right place. Steenhoven listened as laughter rolled around the stadium.

The Chinese were masters of the fixed match; a thousand games of friendship had preceded this one. Cowan won his first game twenty-eight–twenty-six. He thought it was a legitimate match up to the point when he was leading sixteen–twelve in the second game, when his opponent let Cowan win the remaining points. 'Fuck you,' said Cowan as they finished up. 'I'd have won anyway.' The words weren't translated. By the time he took his seat, he had comforted himself. 'Eight hundred million people are watching us!' he told Boggan.

What was left unsaid was that to the Chinese crowd, hosting and throwing a match wasn't just a sign of friendship but a symbol of superiority. 'A team of their most powerful players could have humiliated their American guests,' noted the AP's John Roderick, but the Chinese men won by only five–three and the women by five–four. Roderick roamed the arena trying to balance the table tennis with a touch of politics. He kept pestering his interpreter to ask questions about Liu Shaoqi, Mao's old number two, once chairman of the People's Republic. Roderick was assured that Liu was 'alive and probably being re-educated,' which, Roderick noted, 'is a Chinese Communist way of saying he was being punished and brainwashed.'

Roderick wasn't even close. It had been two years since the Red Guards had found his body. Excommunicated from the Communist Party, constantly persecuted, he had been cremated under an alias. The pathetic state of his corpse had been hidden from his family.

A year after the Americans left Beijing, Liu's family would finally learn of his death. The man who had helped to draw up China's constitution could not be protected from Mao.

If Ping-Pong was the friendly face of China, it was also tied to the ugly fate of so many who had founded the country. Peng Dehuai, who had asked a journalist for a shipment of Ping-Pong balls four decades before, had challenged Mao on the success of the Great Leap Forward and had died in jail. He Long was another casualty of Mao's cruelty, and Chen Yi was still marginalised.

After Cowan's performance, the rest of the team was beginning to lose any good feelings they had for him. The more he began to shine as a celebrity, the less his team-mates liked him. They didn't even know what to call him as the newspapers began to claim him as representing the youth of America. He couldn't really be a hippie, because 'Hippies aren't rude.' Another agreed. 'He doesn't represent anybody. Just himself.'

The Americans toured the Summer Palace, just as the teams had done at the 1961 World Championships. Dick Miles had been allowed to accompany the US squad from Nagoya because of his history as a table tennis player, not because of his current status as *Sports Illustrated* reporter. Out by the lake, he asked an official what he thought of Americans. The official tried to brush the question off but Dick persisted. 'I mean, in what ways do you find them peculiar? Have you ever seen an American before?'

The Chinese looked Miles right in the eye. 'On the battlefield,' he said, 'in the Korean War.'

History and politics were never far away. Brathwaite, the Guyanese immigrant who worked at the United Nations, was approached by a delegate who wanted to know whether Brathwaite thought China belonged in the United Nations. Brathwaite held his ground and tried to explain he had no official capacity and simply worked in the documents section. The delegate pushed him, just as Miles had pushed in conversation with the Chinese official. 'I would vote for all the countries of the world to be admitted,' said Brathwaite, Ping-Pong player and diplomat.

The news filtered through that morning that let the last doubters see that this really was about politics and not Ping-Pong: they were to be granted a meeting with Zhou Enlai that afternoon. There were politicians who had been in Beijing for years without gaining such an audience.

They walked up the stairs of the Great Hall of the People and were ushered past huge portraits commemorating Communist victories. Howard casually asked the interpreter if Mao was dead or alive; the interpreter 'turned white.' They were led to sit alongside the other Ping-Pong delegations in a room like so many others they'd waited in on the tour – big bulky chairs and davenports, all with crocheted dollies on their backs, and small tea tables with all the makings for a pot of tea, an open pack of cigarettes, an ashtray, and a writing desk with envelopes and an ink bottle.

Zhou Enlai arrived promptly. Jack Howard clocked the time Zhou spent with the Nigerians, Colombians, Canadians, and Americans at ten to twelve minutes each; then he moved on. This wasn't how it seemed to the other delegations. A chagrined Canadian player claimed the United States received most of the publicity and hogged almost all of the premier's time. 'It was quite the tea party,' carped a Canadian news channel.

Zhou asked if any of the American team had been to China before. Steenhoven burnished his diplomatic credentials and answered for the team. 'Well, no, none of us are familiar with China, but we have become familiar with Chinese hospitality.'

'What joy it is to bring friends from afar,' said Zhou, quoting an old Chinese proverb.

'Good friends can be found anywhere,' said Steenhoven and then, because he couldn't resist pushing the thought of a Chinese team pouring Ping-Pong fever across America, 'and we would welcome the Chinese in the United States.'

The premier talked of his own fondness for the sport and how he still played despite his age. Then came the line that would be carried on the front pages in America. Zhou congratulated the table tennis team for having 'opened a new page in the relations of the Chinese and American people. I am confident that this beginning again of our friendship will certainly meet with the approval and support of the great majority of our two peoples.'

Just as it seemed that there would be no more questions for the premier, Cowan waved a hand. He was, thought Boggan, 'the only one undaunted' before the meeting and 'probably the first person in purple, bell-bottom trousers received by Mr Zhou,' the *New York Times* observed. What did the premier think of the hippie movement in the United States? It 'seemed to catch not only Mr Zhou off guard but also the rest of the Americans.' Zhou said that he didn't know too much about it, but 'youth wants to seek the truth and out of this search, various forms of change are bound to come forth . . . when we were young,' he continued, 'it was the same, too.'

The premier of China had spent more time with Cowan than anyone else in the room. The world's press loved the comparison of the two men talking together. Cowan went from hippie to 'our hippie' overnight. The team was won over by Zhou Enlai, especially Graham Steenhoven, who now believed the premier could have been a top executive at Chrysler.

CHAPTER 44 | **Tension**

The next morning, as the team gathered in the hotel lobby ready-ing themselves for the short flight to Shanghai, a pair of Chinese bellboys galloped down the stairs. They were holding Cowan's and Tannehill's dirty underwear. The Americans boys, having received an abundance of gifts from the Chinese at every stop, had had to make some strategic packing choices. But they were not allowed to leave a thing behind. They stuffed their underwear into their pock-ets and trudged out to the bus. Later, another player was chased down by a man waving his forgotten toothbrush. To Americans they seemed like acts of honesty, but the Chinese were only trying to sidestep political trouble. Who, for instance, would want to be caught wearing a pair of imperialist underpants?

On the plane to Shanghai, Tannehill and Cowan went at it again. Tannehill thought hippies were fine but useless, like parsley on America's steak dinner. Their true weakness, thought Tannehill, was their fondness for drugs.

'Drugs help me think,' said Cowan. 'Every time John gets stuck, he attacks me for drugs. You have a million crutches, John. Every-body has crutches.'

'Glenn needs dreams,' said Tannehill. 'Because he's a product of a society where the dreams are taken away.'

'I do escape in drugs,' said Cowan. 'I choose to because they give me a world that fits my needs.'

Tannehill's disdain was mounting. Later, he'd say that 'Glenn

222

was going to lay his long-haired hippie thing on the Chinese, was going to bring hippiedom to China – like he was a missionary, like he was Jesus Christ himself come back.'

In Shanghai, Cowan roamed the streets with the *Life* writer and photographer. He wasn't the Pied Piper, because the Pied Piper was independent. He was more like a pot of honey, made by others, attractive to many. The Chinese gathered around, the photographers took pictures. To Cowan's delight, the crowd slowly broke into applause as they realised he was an American Ping-Pong player. This was Shanghai, rumoured to be the birthplace of Ping-Pong in China. They had walked past toddlers using table tennis racquets as teething tools.

For Boggan, who strolled beside Cowan that morning, it was the turning point, when Cowan began to suspect how 'innocent and vulnerable' he was before the media – perhaps he was the one being controlled. As Cowan disappeared after breakfast, the *Life* reporter leaned toward Boggan and asked, 'Who's the real Glenn Cowan?' Boggan didn't answer. 'As if I knew,' he wrote in his notes.

In Shanghai the team played another exhibition game in front of a large, enthusiastic crowd, including every foreign diplomat in the city. The only one who boycotted the evening was the head of the North Vietnam Mission, who remained 'extremely upset' at the American presence. China watchers in Hong Kong picked up what they considered an 'intriguing statement' made over the public address system: 'The great leader Chairman Mao teaches us that it is necessary to distinguish between the American people and their government and between the policy makers in the US government and the ordinary work personnel at lower level,' as it was reported by telegram. Did that mean the Chinese were thinking that the American Ping-Pong team was in some way official, albeit at a low level? Did the Chinese presume that Ping-Pong was political in America as well?

All players would play this time, including Tannehill, now recovered. What he remembered afterward was not so much the constant applause but how that applause would increase for certain players. Brathwaite, Tannehill believed, received 'very special treatment' because the Chinese were trying to demonstrate that they knew 'blacks were oppressed more.' 'They especially liked Cowan, he flopped around with his long hair,' recalled Tannehill. 'He lost his match, but the Red Guards loved him.' There was something to be understood, but for the moment, Tannehill couldn't put his finger on it. Cowan 'was the exact antithesis of what the Chinese should stand for and for some unknown reason, they loved it.'

Feeling better again, Tannehill hadn't totally dismissed the idea of remaining in Beijing or Shanghai. 'I could very easily have switched over to China without a problem. Get some yellow paint and I'd be done.' To the young Tannehill, what he was seeing looked like 'a perfect society. There was nothing out of order.' The people 'behaved very properly, like seventeenth century puritans . . . Plymouth Rock people.'

Even the *Sports Illustrated* reporter, Dick Miles, was asked to play – a rematch against a man he'd beaten on his way to the semi-finals in Dortmund twelve years before. To the stubborn Miles, throwing a game meant you were the better player. But what to do when both players were trying to lose? The game, which had started off as a fast-paced match bringing huge cheers from the crowd, turned into a farce near the end. Both were shanking shots out or into the net. Miles said to the interpreter, 'Look, this is silly. Let's call it a draw.' The man's face collapsed. Even the combative Miles finally got the message and accepted his hollow victory with a bow.

The next day, as they toured Shanghai, Miles made a play for freedom. He had to get back to the States to do his voice-over for ABC's *Wide World of Sports*. All he needed was his passport from Steenhoven.

'Do you think I'm a fucking idiot?' said Steenhoven, seething. 'You're going to go back and tell the story before all the rest of them do.'

'Then I'm going to have you arrested,' said Miles.

Steenhoven finally silenced him by threatening to have his Chinese friends keep Miles behind a day or two extra.

At their last stop, a commune outside Shanghai, Boggan's worries for Cowan increased. According to Cowan, he'd drunk one too many cups of ginseng tea. Boggan presumed that he'd lied and was now traipsing through the Chinese commune high on pot. He was being guided around in the arms of the Chinese, who also seemed to have noticed his strange behaviour.

'I was getting into the chickens,' said Cowan as they walked through the commune. 'They were yellow and really fascinating. You don't see them at zoos. And they were right up close to me.' Boggan started to laugh at him, but Cowan was 'quite serious.' He finally confessed to Tannehill that he'd smuggled drugs into the People's Republic of China. Right now he wanted to talk about the chickens. They weren't in cages. They just walked around. How many eggs were there?

Cowan next began to explain how Californian hippie communes were different from their Chinese counterparts, that theirs was an American revolutionary culture. That was too much for Errol Resek, the Dominican immigrant. 'Why the hell do you keep talking to them about revolution?' Resek interrupted. 'What do you know about revolution? I come from the Dominican Republic. I know about revolution. You don't.' Cowan stared at him nonplussed. Where did the aggression come from?

Dick Miles interviewed Tannehill before they left Shanghai. Did he really want to stay in China? No, said Tannehill, he wanted to go back to Cincinnati and keep on 'developing myself and helping others. Like living for the revolution.'

'Nonviolent,' asked Miles, 'or violent?'

'Nonviolent for now. Till we get enough people behind us.'

On the steps to the plane back to Guangzhou, Tannehill squeezed the last round of applause from Shanghai by waving his silk-screen portrait of Chairman Mao at the small crowd who had gathered to see the team off.

Their last evening in China was spent with Jiang Qing, Chairman Mao's wife, who treated the team to a performance of her revolutionary ballet, *The Red Detachment of Women*. It was a stultifying political polemic crafted by Jiang herself to explain the central tenets of the Cultural Revolution, yet some of the team managed to find things to admire in the grace of the flying bodies that crossed the stage. They were at least more polite than Kissinger would be. Months from now, when he was subjected to his first piece of revolutionary opera, he'd call it 'an art form of stupefying boredom [in which] as far as I could make out, a girl fell in love with a tractor.'

The next morning, they boarded the train to the border. As they walked back across the bridge into Hong Kong's New Territories, they could see the dense pack of press waiting for them. Boggan estimated that six hundred newsmen were now covering their story. Cowan looked up at the mass of men draped in cameras and recording equipment and said, 'There are the vultures.'

As the Chinese waved goodbye, the calculations were already being computed in Beijing. The 'Chinese had carefully analysed each member of the US team on their arrival and had found an array of attitudes towards China.' And now? 'On departure, however, Chinese found all team members unanimous in expressing satisfaction over warmth of reception, treatment received, and progress of China.' By Chinese standards, the visit had already been judged a success.

The press rode beside the Americans on the second train from the bridge into Hong Kong. Judy Bochenski, the youngest of the group, remembered the trip as mayhem, with 'cameras and elbows in our faces.' An AP reporter bought the film right out of her camera for $200 without any idea of what it might contain. The Ping-Pong players hadn't seen how the world had covered their trip. Now the reporters slapped copies of various front pages into their laps. 'Look,' said a man pushing a newspaper at the teenage Bochenski, 'there you are with Zhou Enlai!'

For the first few minutes, Steenhoven presumed to speak for everyone, muttering one or two of his paternal aphorisms. The newsmen swept over the party. The group was bound to splinter. Individuals were surrounded and dragged away into private conversation. But something strange happened that the players didn't notice.

The usual routine for any American coming out of China was for the US Consulate in Hong Kong to interview them extensively and send the information directly to Washington. Kissinger had decided against this and ordered the consulate 'to stay away from these people coming and going,' saying that they should stick to the channel already open – Bill Cunningham waiting in Tokyo, where they would board their flights home. The telegram from Washington was very specific. 'No *repeat* no contacts should be initiated without prior direct approval.'

Once in Tokyo, Steenhoven and Harrison checked into a hotel. Steenhoven changed into a rumpled blue suit, walked out the door without telling Harrison, and waited on a street corner a few blocks away. A taxi pulled up with the passenger window wound down. 'Steenhoven?' Graham Steenhoven nodded and got in. Cunningham looked at Steenhoven, noted his exhausted appearance, and gave the driver the address of his house about three miles from the centre of Tokyo.

While the US team had been touring eastern China, Cunningham had been manning the phones, inundated by calls and accusations. The Japanese Foreign Ministry and most embassies had hounded him with the same questions: 'Was the United States government behind this? Was Steenhoven working for the CIA?'

When Steenhoven walked into Cunningham's house, he was immediately greeted as Fred by Mrs Cunningham. Steenhoven corrected her. 'Graham,' he said. Mrs Cunningham replied, 'Our kids will just be delighted to tell everybody that Fred Graham had breakfast with us this morning.' Finally, it clicked – the house was most likely bugged. The truth was less dramatic. Cunningham didn't want his five young children blurting Steenhoven's name in a local playground and having locals tying the trip to the Tokyo Embassy.

To Steenhoven's credit, he immediately brought up his concerns about Tannehill, calling him an 'unsophisticated youth in unusual circumstances.' What Cunningham really wanted to know was whether there were any specific messages from the Chinese. Yes, said Steenhoven, he was carrying a message that the Chinese wanted conveyed directly to President Nixon. 'Zhou Enlai told me that they want to send a team to the United States.'

Back in Beijing, Zhou Enlai was magnificently coy. 'Sometimes, one single event can bring about strategic changes,' he noted. 'The inevitability of things usually appears in the contingency of things. Similarly strategic changes often express themselves in trivial details.' A State Department spokesman tried to downplay the moment, calling it a 'conscious if limited diplomatic initiative by Peking.' But a Gallup poll quickly conducted in the United States revealed something else entirely. For the first time ever the number of Americans in favour of China's inclusion in the United Nations had vaulted to a positive majority.

| **Nixon's Game**

That summer, in the dusty hills of Pakistan, Henry Kissinger's car wound up the sweeping roads to the Pakistani presidential retreat near Murree. The national security adviser had announced his plan to spend the next two days recovering from a serious bout of stomach flu. It was far from the truth. The suited man resting in the backseat of the government car wasn't even Henry Kissinger but a double.

The elaborate deception had begun at a state dinner the night before, with the full cooperation of Pakistani president Yahya Khan. Kissinger rose at 3.30am and drove to Chaklala Airport in a red Volkswagen Beetle. He boarded a Boeing 707, where seven Chinese awaited him, including Mao's own interpreter, the Brooklyn-born Nancy Tang, herself so high-ranking 'that she did not hesitate to argue with Zhou En-lai' in the presence of visiting diplomats. Three months earlier, she had sat next to Glenn Cowan at the revolutionary ballet in Shanghai and explained 'how every move, every gesture, every line had a symbolic meaning.' In Chinese culture, Cowan had learned, everything meant something.

Kissinger was accompanied by six Americans, including his special assistant, Winston Lord. Lord waited until they were at 30,000 feet and nearing the Himalayas before entering the cockpit to sit with the pilots. As the plane whipped over the border toward Beijing, Lord secured his position as the first American diplomat in China in two decades. Only when they were in Chinese airspace did

Kissinger realise he had failed to pack a clean shirt. He would be meeting Zhou Enlai in a borrowed white shirt three sizes too big. It still carried the Made in Taiwan label inside the collar.

The US table tennis team had been invited to China just three months previously, on 8 April. In the Oval Office that morning, toward the end of a ranging conversation, Kissinger mentioned to President Nixon, 'I don't know whether you've noticed, incidentally, but the Chinese have invited the American Ping-Pong team.'

'No,' said Nixon.

'To visit China,' continued Kissinger. 'Maybe it doesn't mean a damn thing. On the other hand—'

'A lot,' said Nixon, interrupting.

'Exactly,' said Kissinger.

There followed a pause in which, it's tempting to imagine, the minds of both men rushed through the momentous possibilities that might unfold. What were the Chinese up to? Nixon and Kissinger had fired off their last message to Zhou Enlai over three months before. The main worry was that the entire initiative had died. Ping-Pong was obviously a signal, but what kind? Was it official? Should the White House count it as such? If so, was it their turn to respond?

After the American table tennis team had landed in Beijing and the reports started to flood back, both Nixon and Kissinger were fascinated at the speed with which the fairy dust of table tennis was changing the way Americans thought about Red China. Nixon wrote, 'I had never expected that the China initiative would come to fruition in the form of a Ping-Pong team.' Kissinger had other worries. What if the table tennis team 'screwed up all these back channel plans that we had very carefully been trying to put in place?'

In the days to come, Nixon's favourite line with visitors to the Oval Office was, 'Have you learned to play Ping-Pong yet?' The last time the game had been so keenly noted in Washington was during its first crazed boom and bust in 1902, when 'justices of the Supreme Court, members of the cabinet . . . play and talk about Ping-Pong as though it were one of the most important affairs in life.' Now, apparently, it actually was.

On 13 April, the day before Glenn Cowan 'laid his rap' on Zhou Enlai, President Nixon was on the phone with his assistant for international economic affairs. If the Ping-Pong team's presence truly heralded a détente, then Nixon knew that history was up for grabs. The memorandum they were preparing was fine, announced Nixon, 'except that rather than thirteen months ago, it was twenty months ago that we started this initiative with regard to the Chinese.' Nixon deserved much credit for the initiative, but success without recognition was worthless, especially nearing an election year.

> Be sure we get the tone, The Chinese thing is going just the way we want it. . . . I don't want us to appear to be exploiting it. . . . Say that the President took the initiative and it was my decision . . . you can honestly say that there was some opposition in the Foreign Service, some of the Kremlinologists, because they were concerned about . . . our Soviet relations. That Ping-Pong team is worrying them right up the wall.

Russian anxiety was obvious from the reports of American ambassadors stationed around the world. In Australia, the Soviet ambassador 'warned that US did not understand what kind of people it was dealing with in China.' The Soviet ambassador to Uganda, Kurdyukov, advised that the Americans 'must be very, very careful with PRC.' The Chinese, he assured the State Department, 'are racists' and 'very, very tricky.' In Laos, the Soviet ambassador 'made big show of demonstrating annoyance at recent developments in US-PRC situation' and suggested that the US ambassador 'learn Ping-Pong quickly.' He facetiously told his American counterpart that if there were any questions about Southeast Asia, 'Nixon could ask Mao when he visited Peking' or when the Chinese came to New York for a UN session. These would turn out to be extraordinarily prescient words.

On 16 April, after 11.00pm, Kissinger and Nixon were discussing China again. Nixon was seeking reassurance that he hadn't gone too far in talking to the press that morning, when he'd expressed his hopes that maybe his children, or even the president himself, might one day visit China. No, said Kissinger, 'it was a human touch. Very moving.'

'If we make the breakthrough in China, this is the biggest thing that's ever happened in twenty years, Henry.'

Kissinger agreed. 'It's a historic turning point.'

There was a small pause. Then the president said, 'No dove could have done this.'

Winston Lord, Kissinger's special assistant, remained sceptical. He knew that there still might be an edge to China's positive gesture. Zhou Enlai's table tennis overtures contained a 'subtle warning.' The North Vietnamese had already proved that they could undercut American leverage by 'dealing publicly with the Jane Fondas of the world' while remaining tough in the actual negotiations. What if the Chinese started to play with the goodwill engendered through table tennis? One worrying report was filed from the American Embassy in Rome, where an 'unknown Chinese' was overheard explaining that 'The recent visit of American Ping-Pong players meant strengthening of friendship with American people and, therefore weakening of imperialist camp.' The report went on to insinuate that the recent antiwar protests in Washington were the fruit of Chinese policy. Was this really a breakthrough, as Kissinger and Nixon were now presuming, or could it be a setup?

Lord kept his worries to himself. Vice President Spiro Agnew did not. He ruffled Nixon's feathers by calling in nine reporters for a three-hour off-the-record chat that went straight into the next day's papers. Agnew called the Ping-Pong visit 'a propaganda beating' for the United States.

If Agnew's comment upset Nixon, what really rankled was Beijing's official silence. The US decision whether or not to respond to the table tennis tour would have to be taken in a vacuum. Nixon and Kissinger decided to hold back to avoid seeming over-eager. To do otherwise, despite the ocean of newsprint inspired by the table tennis players, would be to suggest that Ping-Pong was directed by the Chinese Ministry of Foreign Affairs. On 23 April, the White House suffered a reminder of how the Vietnam War could grab the headlines again. More than a thousand veterans marched on Washington, 'approached the wire fence around the Capitol and pitched the medals . . . over the fence.'

Four days later, on 27 April, contact with the Chinese was finally re-established through the Pakistani channel, ending an American anxiety that had dated back to the unanswered communication in January. Zhou Enlai made no reference to table tennis. 'The Chinese

Govt,' he wrote, 'reaffirms its willingness to receive publically in Peking a special envoy of the President of the US (for instance, Mr Kissinger) or the US Secy of State or even the President of the US himself for a direct meeting and discussions.' Since the secretary of state had been kept out of the loop, Nixon chose Kissinger, quelling his own worry that despite being the instigator of China policy, he was about to let his national security adviser become 'the mystery man of the age.'

Kissinger first proposed that he meet Zhou Enlai 'preferably at some location within convenient flying distance from Pakistan to be suggested by the People's Republic of China.' Kissinger would be 2,800 miles from Islamabad, 7,000 miles from Washington, DC. Zhou would be a short walk from his own bed. Not only was Zhou the more experienced statesman by some twenty-three years, but he was the premier of a country deigning to meet with a mere national security adviser. Just as he had soothed the table tennis players into the role of grateful guests, in Beijing Zhou could now play the role of a welcoming dean to Kissinger's bemused freshman.

Nixon and Kissinger deserved much credit. They had been like a pair of fishermen skimming international waters with a dozen hooks trailing their boat. But Zhou made sure that when he bit, their boat was in Chinese waters. The speed, the method of delivery, and the chosen moment were all controlled by the Chinese. Considering the difference in the strength of the two nations, it was a diplomatic feat by Mao and Zhou when compared to the utter chaos of Mao's domestic policies. With Soviets on their borders, a nation traumatised and isolated by the Cultural Revolution, and a still largely agricultural economy, they had played their hand well against industrialised, powerful America. Table tennis had been the catalyst but, vitally, one that the Americans had not seen coming.

Kissinger's mission in Beijing was to establish contact with Zhou and lay the groundwork for a possible meeting between Mao and Nixon. To the rest of the world, that idea still seemed preposterous. But for the four men at the centre of this vortex, Kissinger and Nixon, Zhou and Mao, it remained highly desirable.

As Kissinger's plane descended, he had much to be preoccupied by. Play his cards well, and he could hasten the end of the Vietnam

War, bring the Soviets to heel, and draw 800 million Chinese out of self-imposed isolation.

Zhou led off the discussion:

The first question is that of equality . . . all things must be done in a reciprocal manner. . . . Recently we invited the US table tennis delegation to China – perhaps you met some of them – and they can bear witness that the Chinese people welcomed this visit of the American people. We have also received many repeated invitations from the US Table Tennis Association to send a delegation to the US. We feel this shows that the US people want to welcome the Chinese people.

'We have talked to Mr Steenhoven,' said Kissinger.

Zhou nodded. 'He recently sent us a cable.'

The conversation wandered far and wide. Kissinger reasserted Nixon's wish to keep their meeting secret, 'so we can meet unencumbered by bureaucracy, free of the past, and with the greatest possible latitude.'

'You don't like bureaucracy either,' said Zhou.

'Yes,' said Kissinger, 'and it's mutual; the bureaucracy doesn't like me.'

Both men showed off a deep and supple knowledge of the world's balance of power over hundreds of years and, above all, a mutual suspicion of Russia. The Soviet Union, said Zhou, 'will also be defeated as it stretches out its hand so far.' Kissinger sympathised, 'Even today their constant probing makes it very hard to have a real settlement with them.' Zhou allowed himself something close to self-congratulation, 'You saw just throwing a Ping-Pong ball has thrown the Soviet Union into such consternation.'

| CHAPTER 46 | Political Ping-Pong |

If Zhou Enlai believed he held any leverage, it was partly thanks to the publication on the front page of the *New York Times* of information about the Pentagon Papers just weeks before, revealing the desperate state of America's involvement in Southeast Asia and how the prime objective of policy for years had been to avoid a humiliating defeat.

Zhou was also aware that Nixon had an election to win. When Glenn Cowan was talking to Zhou, the president and Kissinger had been almost giddy at the relief the Ping-Pong story was providing them. Nixon asked how the coverage of the table tennis tour had been that day. 'It was tremendous,' Kissinger answered. 'The lead item on television.' 'Rather than Vietnam for a change,' exhaled the president. And the newspaper editors Kissinger had just met with, asked Nixon. What did they think? 'Intrigued by China,' said Kissinger.

To remove Vietnam from the front pages, Kissinger was willing to put almost anything on the table with Zhou Enlai, especially the issue of Taiwan – the sine qua non for China's Communists. As Nixon would soon write, '1. Taiwan – most <u>crucial</u>. 2. V. Nam – most <u>urgent</u>.' By the end of the two days, both men were talking as if Taiwan returning to China was an inevitability, despite the fact that America and Taiwan shared a mutual defence treaty. As an added bonus, Kissinger made it clear that Chiang Kai-shek's seat in the United Nations was within reach, something Zhou probably thought probable with or without Kissinger's help. 'You would get the Taiwan seat now,' Kissinger told Zhou, suggesting that the United Nations and the United States were suddenly on track to follow Montagu's move to bring China into his federation by nudging Taiwan into limbo.

If Ping-Pong remained a metaphor for communication, attack, and defence, then Kissinger's talks with Zhou were the real thing. Kissinger wrote to President Nixon as he flew back from Beijing; at first his tone was almost breathless: 'It is extremely difficult to capture in a memorandum the essence of this experience,' since it was 'an event so shaped by the atmosphere and the ebb and flow of our encounter, or to the Chinese behaviour, so dependent on nuances and style.'

Kissinger was hardly naïve, though it seemed he was occasionally in danger of being overwhelmed by his sense of his own place in the American narrative. 'We have laid the groundwork for you and Mao to turn a page in history,' he wrote to Nixon. 'But we should have no illusions about the future. Profound differences and years of isolation yawn between us and the Chinese.'

Back in Beijing, Marshal Chen Yi felt deep relief. His advice had been followed. He might have been acting unofficially, but his recommendation to stride toward America and distance China from the Kremlin had been followed by Mao. 'With this move by the Chairman,' said Chen, 'the whole game is enlivened.'

In the middle of July 1971, the president appeared on television with an urgent message for the nation. Nixon explained to America that Kissinger had been in Beijing and that he himself would fly to China to meet with Mao Zedong the following February.

In his mother's house in California, William Cunningham was stunned. He wasn't alone. The moment actually introduced the word *shokku* (shock) into the Japanese language. The US ambassador to Japan had already noted that the table tennis invitation had caused 'exquisite nerve twitching' in April. But now, in July, he was halfway through a haircut when he heard the news; he was so upset that he threw the barber out of his office. The State Department's top Asia hand, Ambassador Marshall Green, had also been kept out of Kissinger and Nixon's tiny loop. Thanks to his exclusion, he was considered by his colleagues to have been a broken man at the time.

In February 1972 Nixon rolled into China in the wake of the

largest advance team in presidential history. Air force planes touched down carrying 'tons of equipment,' including everything from cameras, microphones, and Xerox machines to whiskey and American toilet paper. When the president himself finally arrived, his wife was by his side in a startling red coat. It was her own fashion gesture to the Beijingers who greeted her, the colour of celebration favoured for the New Year. Once again the Chinese were the hosts, and Americans watched their every word. Not once in the State Department's official record of the trip, 'including the speeches, toasts and press conferences,' was the word 'Communist' used.

The banquet Zhou Enlai hosted for Nixon garnered the second-largest television audience in American history, after the first lunar landing. The images were as incongruous as the previous year's Ping-Pong visit, but this time they were live. They showed 'the Chinese army playing American songs in the Great Hall of the People, and Nixon and Zhou Enlai clinking glasses at a banquet.' This was the same Beijing administration that had compared Nixon's first foreign visit to Europe as a presidential nominee to 'a rat running across the street.'

Zhou himself chose the song 'America the Beautiful.' It rang out across the world and caused either amazement or conniptions, depending on your politics. Enver Hoxha, Albania's dictator and old friend to China, emptied his bile into his diary. 'The orchestra at the banquet played "America the Beautiful"! . . . America, the centre of fascism and barbarous imperialism!'

With such startling images being broadcast simultaneously on every US television network, it was easy to forget the sequence of events that had led to the president's visit. Before his banquet had come the American table tennis banquet. A decade before that was the banquet for the teams from thirty-two Ping-Pong-playing nations, held in the midst of the famine. And another decade before that, when an American secretary of state refused even to shake the hand of Zhou Enlai, there was a handshake and a banquet for Ivor Montagu.

For the audience watching back in America, those most amazed were the missing generation of China watchers – not because a breakthrough had been made, but because it was clear their absence had left a wasteland. Watching Nixon and Kissinger 'as they hobnobbed with their hosts in Peking and Shanghai, they kept explaining to each other, "My God, they don't know who's sitting next to them!"'

Mao had not attended the Nixon banquet. Increasingly frail, he had signalled his approval of the president's visit by inviting Nixon to meet with him within two hours of the president's arrival. To enter Mao's room, the visitors had to walk past the table tennis table. Kissinger, Nixon, and Lord shook hands with the Chairman. They talked of everything from Mao's recent betrayal by Lin Biao, his number two, who had objected to the détente with the Americans and then died in a suspicious plane crash, to Mao's opinion that Nixon had been correct in wanting to meet rather than let the most contentious issue of Taiwan separate them forever. 'I saw you were right,' said Mao to Nixon, 'and we played Ping-Pong.'

Ping-Pong remained the metaphor through which to study the Chinese. On Nixon's second night in Beijing, when the city's populace was ordered to clear a sudden snowfall from the streets, the president was treated to a performance by Chinese athletes and table tennis players. There was Zhuang Zedong, dashing around in front of the first lady and her husband. Nixon called their performance 'superb.' Later that night he confided to his diary:

> Not only we but all the people of the world will have to make our best effort if we are going to match the enormous ability, drive and discipline of the Chinese people. Otherwise we will one day be confronted with the most formidable enemy that has ever existed in the history of the world.

If Nixon always regarded the détente with China as the pinnacle of his presidency, then Ping-Pong had provided not only the catalyst but also a sobering coda. Table tennis, Kissinger admitted, 'had played a huge role' in April 1971. As propaganda it had opened a new door and opened it wide. Since Zhou Enlai stressed how important reciprocation was, the onus was on America to host a return visit. A Chinese Communist Party delegation would be heading to the United States for the first time. These were not political innocents, like the US team; they were the Ping-Pong-playing extension of the Chinese government, or, as one player put it, not just an 'important adjunct in the communist struggle' but 'an instrument of subversion.'

PART FOUR | **Aftermath**

| # Return Game

In the spring of 1972, the National Committee on United States–China Relations was putting the last touches on the upcoming visit of the Chinese table tennis team. Since the USTTA had trouble raising enough money to attend a World Championship, let alone funding an eight-city whistle-stop tour, the National Committee was in charge of organising the two-week event and had turned to more than 125 sponsors. If the China tour the previous year had smelled strongly of politics, this was a more American recipe of individuals, businesses, cities, and states.

China's input in the tour would come from its new UN mission, itself a direct result of the warmth engendered by Ping-Pong diplomacy. To help coordinate the trip, the National Committee's president, Carl Stover, had set up a tiny temporary office in New York's old Delmonico Hotel on Park Avenue, where he worked with his young consultant for press affairs, Marcia Burick. As the two returned from lunch one day, Burick unlocked the door to the hotel room. It swung open. The room had been ransacked.

Burick had been shopping at Saks that morning; for an instant, she worried about her purchases. Oddly, they were still there. In fact, as she and Stover rummaged through the mess, it seemed as if 'the only thing missing was the tour schedule for the team with the plane flights, hotels, everything.' Stover reached into his back pocket, 'pulled out a piece of paper,' and sat down to use the phone. The call went directly to the White House.

The response was simple. The State Department would have to assign agents to cover the visit. There were three main threats. First, the American antiwar movement might bubble back to boiling point at any US surge in Vietnam. Second, the Chinese Nationalists, Chiang Kai-shek's vocal supporters, still regarded him as the rightful ruler not just of Taiwan but of all China. They had been horrified at the prospect of a 'Bandit Table Tennis' team touring the United States and thought of the visit as an opportunity to plead their case in front of the American people, hopefully steadying what they now knew was the declining power of the Taiwan lobby in Washington.

The third threat was the strange figure of Carl McIntire, a firebrand minister from the Bible Presbyterian Church in New Jersey who had a taste for publicity that far outshone Glenn Cowan's. Among his other attention-seeking projects was the rebuilding of the Temple of Jerusalem in Florida, as well as a plan to assemble a replica of Noah's ark off the Jersey shore. A rabid anti-Communist, he planned to hound the Chinese players from coast to coast.

The Chinese team's point of entry on 12 April 1972, was Graham Steenhoven's hometown of Detroit. The first to step onto American soil at Willow Run Airport in Ypsilanti, Michigan, outside Detroit, were members of the Chinese press contingent, taking a hundred pictures of the American crowd gathered to welcome them.

Next out of the plane was Steenhoven, who had flown to Ottawa as the Chinese passed through Canada so he could escort the team south. Only months before, rumours had Steenhoven considering a run for Congress. He had, after all, had a private audience with Nixon. Nixon had been given a list of talking points but was unable to cope with a conversation about table tennis. 'Let's talk about anything,' said Nixon. 'Like what?' asked Steenhoven. Nixon looked stumped. 'What's the price of a Ping-Pong ball?' he ventured. The important thing for Nixon had been the photograph with Steenhoven in the American press, sure to be picked up by the Chinese as another positive signal.

Zhuang Zedong emerged from the plane twenty pounds heavier than the year before. As a reward for his performance in Nagoya, he had been promoted to vice president of the Table Tennis Association, and more surprisingly was a newly established deputy from Beijing to the National People's Congress. Instead of being an embodiment of politics within Ping-Pong, he was something new in China – the Ping-Pong within politics.

Zhou Enlai had announced some of his picks for the travelling squad at the Great Hall of the People. 'It's not the turn for the officials' to head to America, he explained. The players came first. Those selected were a mixture of young and old, but mostly they were chosen because they were considered politically reliable enough to travel to the heartland of imperialism.

The American team awaiting them on the tarmac was positively shiny in their new uniforms, the men in white pants, blue turtlenecks, and bright blue blazers, the women in orange turtlenecks and white pants. They looked like the crew of a cruise ship. As Zhuang moved away from the airplane, he spotted Cowan, hard to miss with his mop of hair. Zhuang stepped toward the Californian, and they raised their hands into the air together. It was a generous move. The music behind the two table tennis players suddenly changed to a brassy version of 'She'll Be Coming 'Round the Mountain When She Comes.'

Even before the team had landed, a professor from Columbia had briefed all who would come into contact with the Chinese. 'Those of you who expect country bumpkins, be disabused,' he'd declared. 'They are, most of them, well-travelled. They consider themselves political personages.' They weren't in the United States for the shopping. Last of all, be careful with food choices. 'Do not serve them lamb – they find its odour offensive.' A *New York Times* reporter heard one of the American table tennis officials grumble, 'Nobody told *them* we don't like sea cucumber.'

Though the tour was supposedly apolitical, Nixon had handpicked an informational aide to welcome the team. The aide's speech was built around Zhou Enlai's vague promise to send the team 'when flowers bloom.' The language was friendly, but in the Sheraton hotel that awaited the delegation, security agents were using a dog to check for explosive devices.

The team was shown to their rooms, then quickly came down for lunch, where a moment of awkwardness awaited them. Each member of the Chinese delegation had a map, a copy of *Audubon's Birds of North America*, and a Polaroid camera sitting in front of their plates as welcoming gifts. One of the translators, Perry Link, noted that it was painful to watch that 'kind of awkward, naked commercial pitch' as a Polaroid representative explained how the cameras worked.

Another American translator, Vee-ling Edwards, who had been born in Fukien in 1918, found the tension hard to bear. 'The air was like a solid piece of ice,' she noted. 'People didn't even dare to talk.' In the hotel, the Chinese were apprehensive. The members of the Xinhua News Agency accompanying the tour included a smattering of undercover Chinese security officers. One of the translators remembered a Xinhua man briefly taking off his coat to reveal not one but two revolvers – adequate protection, thought a player, in a country where he'd 'heard that everyone carried a gun.'

The players had been raised knowing that America was really the land where a handful of rich ruled the desperately poor. It was quickly apparent to them that this wasn't the full truth. They passed scenes of unthinkable abundance – malls surrounded by hundreds and hundreds of parked cars, enormous supermarkets bursting with colour, hardware stores with stacks of building materials on the sidewalk. The *Los Angeles Times* lamented that 'the Chinese got a glimpse of the American consumer society at its zenith, from billboards proclaiming cars and whiskey to hotels that offer colour TV in every room.' To the Chinese, it was enlightening. Perhaps, thought one player, America had become such a strong country because of its 'combination of different people.'

A banquet was hosted for the Chinese delegation on the first night by the mayor of Detroit. The Chinese 'were extraordinarily quick to feel condescension.' In China, the dignitary would have greeted a visiting delegation on the street and walked them inside. Here, the mayor awaited them on the first floor, which they saw as an act of 'coldness.'

The Chinese weren't the only ones feeling ill at ease that evening. Cowan attended, but seemed to be hiding behind his friend and agent, Bob Gusikoff. Where was the confidence, the easygoing chit-chat? The man who had offered to negotiate between Zhou Enlai and Nixon seemed to struggle negotiating the buffet table. Before the dinner was even over, Gusikoff escorted Cowan from the room and whisked him back to his mother's house in California. Was he high on pot again, or using stronger drugs, or was he actually mentally disturbed? Soon Cowan would enter a frightening downward spiral. On that night in Detroit, it left Cowan's counterpart, Zhuang Zedong, drifting between dignitaries, carried by his wide smile.

Stanley Karnow, an old China watcher from the *Washington Post*, was finally given time with the Chinese officials during supper. Perhaps fearful that he wouldn't be given a second chance, he immediately asked the question that haunted the whole tour: 'Don't you find it ironic that you are visiting the United States while our Government is bombing North Vietnam, who are your country's allies?' The question was sidestepped like a well-marked land mine.

Despite the stuttering start, eleven thousand people showed up at Detroit's Cobo Hall for the first exhibition match. Was Steenhoven right? Was Cowan right after all? Was there a future for table tennis in America? Best of all, the game was covered by ABC's hugely popular TV programme *Wide World of Sports*. 'It's a very spectacular kind of sport to watch,' enthused host Jim McKay. 'I think you're going to be quite surprised by it, if you haven't seen it at this level before.'

Once again, the Chinese were in full control of the outcome of the matches. But this was America, and the one thing they couldn't predict was the crowd. A banner unfurled above the seated teams: 'Send us our POWs not Ping-Pong players.' Next, hundreds of anti-Communist leaflets spiralled from the upper levels of Cobo Hall. Finally, dead rats came floating down in miniature parachutes. One 'had a red coat on it and the name Kissinger.'

The two teams marched out amicably, except for Tannehill, who stood in line with a clenched fist raised high. Was that for Black Power? Solidarity? Solidarity with whom? The protesters, the Chinese, his fellow students? Perhaps he already knew that Steenhoven had decided not to let him play. 'Steenhoven didn't want to take a chance on me,' he'd say, before calling the Chrysler man 'a motherfucking racist bastard' for picking local CPA Dell Sweeris over George Brathwaite for the televised match. Steenhoven sent him home. So now the two youngest men, Cowan and Tannehill, the most controversial players on the China visit, were gone.

In Cobo Hall, the Chinese were showing their preparation. They had figured out where each of the American players were from and let the hometown players shine in front of their own fans. Dell Sweeris, one of America's best, was from Grand Rapids, Michigan, northwest of Detroit. Playing against Liang Geliang, he seemed to get better and better as the game continued. The American crowd took the game as they saw it, celebrating a hard-earned win in front of the cameras that were providing the coverage table tennis so badly needed.

During the commercial break on television, Haggar, a men's clothing company, premiered a commercial for its new red Dacron polyester pants. A Communist Party official in China smiled into the camera. He was very, very happy with his red slacks. They were only $17. 'We make *everybody* look good,' came the voice-over.

The next day was spent in Ann Arbor at the University of Michigan, where the Chinese got a taste of campus life in the 1970s. There were friendly faces, pamphlets, and protesters. 'We recognise the lies of the Nixon administration for what they are,' one leaflet began. There were long beards and short skirts, effusive welcomes, earnest handshakes, and only a few backs turned. There was also Carl McIntire, the minister of the Bible Presbyterian Church, shadowing the team with his faithful demonstrators, waving a 'Mao Killed More Christians than Hitler Killed Jews' placard. The Chinese documentary team following the players added a simple voice-over to the footage: 'The young Americans express their friendly feelings for New China.'

Despite Carl McIntire, the opportunity to meet regular students was sweet relief from the initial stiffness of the tour. 'How do you like American food?' one student asked as he approached the Chinese. 'We're getting used to it,' said their interpreter. 'So are we,' replied the student.

CHAPTER 48 | Capital Performance

A day later, the Chinese delegation touched down near Colonial Williamsburg, the heart of Virginia. The Chinese remembered this as their favourite place on their tour. It was well chosen, a sly nod to the revolutionary past of the United States. The Chinese walked past the apothecary, past the tavern, past the Authentic Barber and Peruke Maker, past windmills and bowling greens. Dinner was served by candlelight. 'I thought it was beautiful,' said woman's champion Zheng Huaiying, 'to see all the old customs were still kept.'

As the Chinese politely listened to a potted history of America, the US Air Force was launching a heavy air assault on the Vietnamese port of Haiphong, six thousand miles away.

The first to feel the painful awkwardness of their position were the interpreters. 'It was like putting a dagger in their back, and you then shake their hands,' thought Vee-ling Edwards. Bob Woodward of the *Washington Post* called to interview her and asked why the Chinese didn't refuse to continue the tour. 'They could never do that,' she explained. 'They were guests.' Though the conflict in Vietnam magnified the opposing interests of the United States and China, the Chinese team never mentioned it. Obviously, though, the bombing of Haiphong did not go unnoticed. Every morning, when Edwards went to greet the team, she'd find the officials going over the *New York Times*, the *Washington Post*, and the local papers, scissors in hand, creating a scrapbook of their journey.

Before leaving the revolutionary past of Williamsburg, Zhuang Zedong stood up in a Virginia restaurant after finishing his apple pie and led the team in singing 'Home on the Range.' Some songs were more controversial, such as 'Row, Row, Row Your Boat'; Vee-ling Edwards was interrupted by Chinese objections when she reached the line 'life is but a dream.' It was politically incompatible with the teachings of Mao.

One of the translators solved the problem, and the Chinese resumed singing: 'Merrily, merrily, merrily, life is full of steam.' After they finished their songs, the bus chugged north toward Washington, where the team was due to meet with the man who had ordered the bombing of their North Vietnamese allies, Richard Nixon.

In the Cole Field House, on the University of Maryland campus in College Park, just ten miles south of the White House, thousands came to greet the Chinese. Tim Boggan stood up in the stands and looked around him at the sea of Americans gathered for a game of table tennis. 'Would you believe it! Would you believe what's happening! After all those fucking years in dirty subterraneous basements!'

Seated neatly together in reserved seats were the US secretary of state Bill Rogers, Graham Steenhoven, and Zhuang Zedong, next to President Nixon's daughter Tricia. Nixon had been encouraging Tricia to take her honeymoon in China, but the Vietnam War still loomed over the president and his family. A big banner was unfurled saying, 'Tricia Nixon Watches Ping-Pong While Her Father Bombs Haiphong.'

The Chinese team entered, and a huge roar went up. It wasn't welcoming. 'Kill Mao!' screamed the Nationalists who'd bought a block of seats near the floor. A boisterous Taiwanese woman heckled the team with obscenities. Neither Zhuang nor any of his players ever turned in her direction. Sometimes, part of Ping-Pong politics was to maintain that the politics did not exist. This wasn't only a Chinese trick. Toward the evening's end, Tricia Nixon and Secretary Rogers walked down from their seats to shake the players' hands. 'The [American] students changed their chant without let-up to "Rogers is a murderer." And it was the Secretary's turn be inscrutable and imperturbable.'

The demonstrations and counter-demonstrations in Maryland were so large that after the match, the local section of US Route 1 was shut down for two days. The governor of Maryland called out the National Guard, giving the Chinese ample proof of what domestic troubles Nixon and Kissinger were facing and how important a solution to Vietnam would be to them.

The situation in Washington, DC, was worse. The Haiphong bombing had stirred up furious antiwar protests yet again. At campuses around the country sporadic violence broke out, 'as rock-throwing student groups tried to seize buildings while police used clubs and tear gas.' For the first time in six months, hundreds had been arrested on Pennsylvania Avenue, and the White House was surrounded by a defensive ring of buses as the Chinese neared.

The day was bright. The Rose Garden was in bloom. On arrival at the White House, the two teams were separated. The Chinese, 'the first group from the People's Republic of China ever to visit the nation's capital,' stood in the middle of the Rose Garden, while the Americans were herded behind a slim rope with the press and public. The president emerged to say a few words. 'In the course of your contest,' he intoned, 'there will be winners and losers. But there is one big winner and that's more important than who wins a match. The big winner is Friendship – between the people of the US and the People's Republic of China.' It was the echo of Zhou Enlai's words a year before: Nixon's pong to Zhou's ping.

The American team had never looked smarter. They were almost fluorescent in their blue-jacketed brightness. But no one in the White House had thought about introducing them to Nixon. Those who had gone to China, who had somehow not contaminated twenty months of strategic planning, would not be given so much as a handshake. The slight was all the more cutting because it was obvious that such a step had not even been considered.

The Americans watched Zhuang Zedong shake hands with Nixon and lead him down the line of the Chinese delegation. The president had a word and a handshake for every single one, despite the shrill cries of 'Come enter the free world!' wailing from the protesters on Pennsylvania Avenue. By that point, explained a Chinese player, they'd come to realise that this was 'the American way of doing things.'

The president was guided back toward the White House. Just before he disappeared, a voice piped up in indignation: 'Don't you want to meet the team that went to China?' 'Oh, yes,' said Nixon, turning around. 'I didn't know you were here.' Finally Nixon stepped toward them. 'I noticed as I came out that some of you were in uniform,' he added, 'and I wondered who you were.' He shared a few gracious words and then moved on again. Consultant for Press Affairs Marcia Burick cringed at the memory of neglect. 'It was awful.'

There was another conflicted team in Washington that day: the American interpreters. Should they boycott the White House event as a political statement over Haiphong in support of their guests, or toe the line so that they could be there to assist the Chinese? One of the interpreters, Perry Link, considered 'the bombing of Haiphong too contradictory' for him to participate in the Rose Garden ceremony. Another three interpreters agreed, including Vee-ling Edwards. Their decision was met with fury by both the White House and by Graham Steenhoven, who recommended that all the offenders be fired at once. Their only comfort was from a Chinese official who had noticed their absence. 'One day,' he said to Vee-ling Edwards, 'we'd like you to come visit the Ping-Pong team in China.' It was the subtlest way the delegation could find to let Edwards know that their stand had not gone unnoticed.

| **United Nations**

As their motorcade, accompanied by circling helicopters, reached New York for their visit to the United Nations, the US table tennis players seemed to have dropped into the role of extras. The press was always there in great numbers, often more than two hundred. They had their own 747 that followed the Chinese plane and their own bus that followed the Chinese bus, but they weren't interested in covering the American players. If some of the American team had chafed at Glenn Cowan's hogging of the limelight the previous year, it turned out that without him, there was no limelight at all.

What the US players had failed to recognise was that they had already done their jobs. Thanks to them, politicians had more room to manoeuvre without being restricted by a surprised or angry public. A few more games in front of thousands, and then Ping-Pong would return to the basement. You could almost smell the neglect reclaiming American table tennis.

The visit to the United Nations brought out the contradictions, joys, and disappointments experienced by the attendees. In the wake of America's warm receipt of the Chinese table tennis overture in 1971, countries had rushed to re-establish diplomatic relations with the People's Republic. America's UN ambassador and future president George HW Bush fought hard for Taiwan, but the mood had turned thanks to Ping-Pong diplomacy. Bush's efforts were undercut by his own president.

The man the Chinese chose to be their first ever ambassador to the United Nations was none other than Huang Hua. Thirty-four years earlier, he had been the translator who guided Edgar Snow into the mountains to find Mao and Zhou Enlai, and he slept along-side Snow on top of a Ping-Pong table after surveying the Red Army.

The Chinese documentary voice-over was at its most breathless inside the United Nations. 'This is the Security Council chamber, the seat of the permanent representative of the People's Republic of China.' The fact that for twenty-two years that seat had belonged to Taiwan was left unsaid. Ping-Pong diplomacy was changing the shape of the world. The camera cut to Zhuang Zedong sitting in Huang Hua's chair. Zhuang leaned back, smiled broadly, and pat-ted the armrests, the perfect hybrid of player and politician. Why not smile? His actions the previous April had helped cause more countries to re-establish relations with China since the year Mao had come to power.

The American Ping-Pong players' experiences were very differ-ent. At the drinks that followed a brief exhibition game, Steenhoven looked around him at his players and their spouses. Steenhoven hadn't invited any spouses. The players had smuggled them in for the tour of the building. Minutes into the drinks, Steenhoven ordered all his players to leave. He accompanied them back to the hotel where a spontaneous meeting took place.

The players voiced complaints. Being ignored, not playing, not being paid, husband not allowed into hotel room, no invitation to a drink or to a dinner. It was a bizarre inversion of the criticism meet-ings that the Chinese squad had endured in previous years. So many American players believed this was their one dance in the spotlight, and the spotlight was gliding past them.

Most criticised of all was Steenhoven, but his closing remarks had a quieting effect. 'I've fought for table tennis every step of the way,' said Steenhoven to the group. 'And they don't know me. They don't know Steenhoven. Zhuang Zedong takes my hand when I'm introduced. He introduces me.' The neglect ran from top to bottom.

The next stop was Memphis, Tennessee. It contained exactly three registered table tennis players but was the world headquar-ters of Holiday Inn, which was keen to make an impression on the Chinese. The chairman of Holiday Inn welcomed them with a few well-chosen words. 'We're going to have a Holiday Inn in every city of the world,' he said, 'and I hope we can soon have one in your great country.' A mortified Vee-ling Edwards chose to translate such an aggressive pitch as politely as possible. 'We hope we can include you in this grand design.'

That evening the team was invited onto a riverboat called *The Memphis Queen,* filled with buxom 'Southern Belles . . . in their antebellum costumes.' It steamed down the river followed by a helicopter that swept 'the banks of the Mississippi with powerful searchlights . . . as if to flush out the snipers.' The *New York Times* reporter called it 'an unfortunate reminder of the Vietnam war.'

As they headed west to Los Angeles, the American team riding in the aircraft provided for the Chinese, Boggan watched Zhuang Zedong entertain the teams with card tricks and sleights of hand, amazed by the man's ability to charm. Zhuang hadn't just sat next to the US secretary of state nor simply taken President Nixon by the arm and introduced him to all thirty-four members of the Chinese delegation, he'd also bowled on a lawn in Williamsburg, tossed a frisbee with college students, hit a single at a high school baseball practice, signed an orange, and would soon play Ping-Pong with a dolphin named Peppy at Marineland. He was, as Chairman Mao had said, a very versatile diplomat.

In California, the mood was more relaxed. On a visit to Disneyland, 'they were greeted by Mickey Mouse, Donald Duck, Pluto and a six piece band' and got dizzy riding in swirling giant teacups. At Universal Studios, players shook hands with Frankenstein, saw a dog show, and survived a flash flood. They took the train past the man-made lake, where a submarine periscope appeared and a torpedo hurtled through the water toward them to soak the team with water. A year before, real Russian warheads had been aimed at Beijing. How quickly life could change.

The first to jump off the bus at Universal that morning was Doug Spelman, designated as the main interpreter for the day. He landed at the feet 'of this large, fat man standing right there.' Spelman looked at the familiar face. 'Hello,' said the man, 'I'm Alfred Hitchcock.' The director was spotted later in the Universal cafeteria. 'Jeez,' said one player, 'I might be in the middle of a mystery and not even know it.' The team finished their meals and walked down a corridor past the poster of one of Alfred Hitchcock's earliest films, *Sabotage*. If the team had paused to squint at the credits, they would have seen that the name of the producer was the same as the original architect of all Ping-Pong diplomacy, Ivor Montagu.

For the press officers, players, and interpreters it had been a long two weeks. Even though few friendships had managed to jump the language barrier, there were plenty of odd and touching scenes. At a last, unscheduled stop in Napa, California, the Chinese players were left alone with their State Department security agents. One of the players came up with a bottle of the scorching alcohol mao-tai. One of the State Department bodyguards borrowed a set of golf clubs. The Chinese and Americans, not a golfer among them, started trying to drive balls down the valley.

As they hit, the Chinese noticed people below tending to the vines. Throughout the trip, they'd been asking their hosts when they would meet peasants. 'We don't have peasants in this country!' Rufford Harrison kept explaining. 'We have farmers . . . but no peasants.' Here at last were peasants. After the golf concluded, the Chinese strolled toward the vines to shake hands with migrant workers to express their solidarity. Zhuang Zedong helped plant a vine, but little communication was possible because the Chinese interpreter spoke no Spanish.

Plenty of problems on the tour were caused by the Chinese carrying the rigidity of the Cultural Revolution on their backs. In Detroit, they'd refused to enter a local church. In Washington, they'd walked out on a high school choir that 'began the programme with a sacred song.' They balked at entering the Kennedy Centre of the Performing Arts after spotting a Taiwanese flag outside. At the National Gallery of Art they cancelled their tour after finding a Taiwanese reporter in the media entourage. They'd refused a tour of the *New York Times* after taking issue with an article in that morning's paper. The same evening, at an Alvin Ailey performance of modern dance, they'd risen as one when told it was an interpretation of Jesus's life, until Vee-ling Edwards chided them, 'Don't you walk out on Christ: he was a friend of the poor.' They took their seats again.

Yet by Chinese standards, nothing big had happened. The bombing of Haiphong, demonstrations, Carl McIntire, dead rats, the National Guard, and Frankenstein had all been greeted with equanimity. The cumulative effect of the tour only strengthened the goodwill between the two countries. Anyone who doubted it hadn't seen the footage from the tarmac as the Chinese players departed. Genuine tears flowed on both sides. Vee-ling Edwards, at the age of fifty-four, realised that it was only the third time she had ever cried. They weren't the tears of indelible friendships but the recognition that something remarkable had happened. In twelve short months, the majority of Americans no longer 'considered citizens of the People's Republic of China their enemies,' and the proof remained in the Ping-Pong players.

Not all the Chinese left at once. Consultant for Press Affairs Marcia Burick chaperoned a handful of Xinhua journalists who lingered on to file reports. She escorted them to a Cincinnati Reds baseball game, where they were disappointed to find out that Cincinnati wasn't the birthplace of American Communism. She did her best to explain baseball terminology. 'Do you know what a "sacrifice" is?' 'Yes,' said one newsman, 'when you throw yourself under a tank.' Burick leaned in to explain, 'This is a little less dramatic.'

CHAPTER 50 | **The Hippie Opportunist**

The year before, as the team was about to touch down in Los Angeles, Cowan casually broke the news to Steenhoven that he planned to be first off the plane to meet his mother, hoping to get a jump on the group and reach the press ahead of the team. Steenhoven explained he could arrange for Cowan to be the last off the plane. If he wanted to meet his mother, Steenhoven would arrange a small room where he could do so quietly.

Steenhoven had guessed correctly that Cowan had tried to arrange his own press conference. It made sense: Los Angeles boy, Los Angeles press. Minutes later, Steenhoven was unable to prevent Cowan from dominating the USTTA press conference, but at least Cowan was still representing the team. Who else would have dipped his yellow hat and said, 'I think I could mediate between Zhou En-lai and Nixon quite easily.'

At the airport, Cowan had shaken the hand of an undersecretary of state sent out west by Kissinger because the White House didn't want Beijing to think that the US team was 'being cold-shouldered by their own Government.' In China the Chinese players knew that they represented the state, but what was the role of an American player once they had returned? Now that the game had achieved its goal and American politicians were stepping in to take over, what was going to happen to a frontline diplomat like Glenn Cowan?

The young Californian emerged from the terminal into the sort of whirlwind of media attention reserved for the celluloid denizens of his hometown of Hollywood. Cowan was whisked into and out of talk shows, radio interviews, even a guest spot with Johnny Carson. His agent, Bob Gusikoff, fielded a stream of calls from businesses. Maybe, said Cowan, 'with this China thing' table tennis 'will even turn into a money-maker.'

Cowan finally held his own press conference two days later, announcing his plans for 'appearances on the lecture circuit, and the opening in several cities of Glenn Cowan Table Tennis Centres, which he hopes will become hangouts for the young.' Two publishers were offering advances for one or more books. Best of all, he'd been asked to shoot a pilot for a syndicated talk show called *Reach Out*.

Perhaps companies were hoping that the kid who had said he was willing to negotiate between governments would be able to reconcile generations. Maybe Glenn Cowan could bridge the fearful chasm between campuses teeming with antiwar protesters and the aging establishment. He seemed a perfect fit. He was confident, handsome, youthful, 'a hippie opportunist.' Within weeks, he was standing under the lights being introduced by Dinah Shore on her popular NBC daytime TV show. Cowan's bashful smile comes across as half 'Aw shucks' and half 'I could get used to this.'

Dinah Shore's questions were earnest but still couldn't step away from how Americans thought of Cowan's game. Did eighteen thousand Chinese really come to watch a Ping-Pong match? Did they have to use binoculars to see the ball?

Cowan dealt with the questioning well. He showed Dinah Shore his exercise routine, standing back to back with her, linking their arms, and lifting her off the floor. 'Boy,' said Cowan, laughing. 'You really are heavy.' 'You didn't have to tell them,' she said glancing at the studio audience. 'How'd you become a diplomat with a line like that?' She looked Cowan up and down, stared at his long hair and relaxed demeanour, and said, 'We're so proud of you. You kept your own identity.' She couldn't help sounding like a concerned aunt wanting to drag Cowan to a barbershop.

As the show ended, Cowan held up his now famous 'Let It Be' T-shirt to the audience. The applause was warm. The last shot was of Shore; she called Cowan's efforts in Ping-Pong diplomacy 'remarkable' and 'beautiful,' then opened her mouth and concluded,

'The whole world . . .' and the microphone went dead as the commercials took over. The whole world what? Should thank Glenn Cowan? The whole world had been saved by Glenn Cowan?

It was the pinnacle of his fame. The ride down would be rapid. In early May, *Business Week* remained positive, noting that 'US history is full of individuals who got rich quick by being in the right place at the right time. The latest could be Glenn Cowan, the luxuriantly maned nineteen year old in the flamboyant threads who rode a Ping-Pong ball to Peking.'

The other players were enjoying the moment. They went on *To Tell the Truth* and *The Phil Donahue Show*, and a handful were flown to Paris to be on French television, including Tim Boggan, who was followed by a reporter who believed he might fly on to Hanoi for peace talks. The youngest player, Judy Bochenski, travelled to New York to be interviewed by Barbara Walters on *The Today Show*. Back in Oregon, she was the grand marshal of the 1971 Portland Rose Festival Parade. Resek and Brathwaite made a record called *Ni Hao (Hello)* featuring the two repeating the phrase again and again. Neither quit their day jobs.

Not everyone's experiences were positive. Tannehill received 'all kinds of hate mail' for his brief embrace of Chairman Mao. His fellow students at the University of Cincinnati took a knife to his bed and carved a big X. He'd be invited onto talk shows, only to be told to go ahead and move to China.

Cowan wrote his book, a lazy work full of photographs of Glenn Cowan, which sold poorly. The next disappointment was the TV show *Reach Out*. No network picked it up. He held on to his fame longer than the other players, but it kept slipping through his fingers as easily as a buttered ball. In July, the best that Gusikoff could drum up for Cowan was a side table at the Orange County Teen-Age Fair at Anaheim Stadium, where they played table tennis between the sets of fifty local bands. By September, Cowan was judging a fashion show of models on bicycles held in a parking lot on Wilshire Boulevard.

The rest of the team either were so young, like Bochenski, that they had the stable surroundings of high school to protect them, or else they returned to their old jobs at the United Nations or IBM. But Cowan was untethered to begin with. He thought what had happened in China was a firm foundation for a new life, one in which he had a starring role in front of thousands.

What came first: the disappointments or the loosening grip on reality? After the TV deal fell through, it became obvious that the market for table tennis equipment wasn't strong enough for Cowan to earn any kind of salary as a spokesman. Nor would there be any Glenn Cowan Table Tennis Centres. His mother described his behaviour as 'a little erratic' during 1971, when he was caught on film swearing at a news commentator and throwing papers at the TV camera. By the end of the year, he had been 'diagnosed, variously, as being bipolar and schizophrenic.' 'When he was in one of his crazy states,' said his brother, 'there were a lot of paranoid delusions that had to do with Russian spies planting stuff in his head.'

Ironically, the Chinese *had* most likely been spying on him in Nagoya, probably intensely, albeit for less than a week. His mother didn't notice his paranoia until his return, but Cowan had told Boggan back in Nagoya that he had seen the Chinese watching him while he practised. 'He went into the hospital,' explained his mother, 'and they gave him medication to keep him on an even keel.' The problem for Cowan was obeying the doctor's orders. 'Pot was his thing,' said his mother. 'He took the drugs and didn't take his medication.'

The real reason he abandoned the tour in 1972 was that 'he had freaked out.' There was little doubt that what was happening to Cowan was tied to the China trip. His grip on reality began to slip. He could do a very good impression of normal and attended therapy paid for by his mother, but every spring the same thing would happen: Cowan would stop taking his medication and end up in a psychiatric institution in the San Fernando Valley or Pasadena. 'It was a very tough time,' explained his brother Keith. It took Cowan a long time to graduate, and because his mental health collapsed with the anniversary of the China trip every April, it was almost impossible for him to hold down a job. He lost his apartment and declared bankruptcy.

In the mid-1970s, Cowan made a new friend, Sandy Lechtick. They shared a passion for playing paddle tennis on Venice Beach, and Lechtick was impressed by Cowan's level of concentration. He called him 'the toughest guy I ever saw on court.' Lechtick ran a headhunting personnel agency and took a gamble on hiring Cowan. 'He had the gift of the gab,' said Lechtick, and 'with his powder blue eyes' and 'total confidence,' he did well for a while.

But April always came, and Cowan would appear with 'ketchup stains on his tie and mustard stains on his shirt,' and then wouldn't appear at all. Lechtick knew that he'd stopped taking his medication once again.

Cowan was unable to keep a job. Eventually he lost his rented apartment and began living out of his car, driving up to Venice Beach to hustle on paddle tennis. He had borrowed money from friends and his mother, but no one could support Cowan year by year. 'It was exhausting for the family,' explained his mother, 'and there was nothing in the world you could do about it.' 'Eventually,' agreed his brother, 'you've got to give up because it just wears you down.'

Cowan became a substitute teacher. On occasion, he sold shoes at a discount store in Venice Beach. His one true attempt at a comeback in table tennis in his midthirties ended when his entry cheque for a local tournament bounced. That April, he wrote to a Beijing author, asking about an ivory carving of himself playing table tennis that he'd heard was for sale in Beijing's markets.

Finally, Cowan's car stopped working and he began to sleep on the streets. Every now and then, Lechtick would get a call. 'I miss the fine dining,' Cowan would say. 'Why don't you come over to Venice Beach and bring me a pack of cigarettes?' They'd partner up on the doubles courts and win a few dollars. It wasn't enough. Soon, Cowan didn't even own a pair of sneakers. All he had left was a small backpack. Inside it was his last copy of his book on table tennis.

'People sanitise what happened to Glenn,' says Lechtick. 'It was tragic.' One day he watched his friend sitting by the side of the court, picking crabs from his crotch; he asked Lechtick if he had any extra underwear he could borrow. His motto had become 'MGM,' which stood for Mao, Glenn, and Mick. He convinced himself that he had written some of the Rolling Stones' biggest hits and would soon be playing guitar for them onstage. It hadn't been that long ago, back in 1972, when he'd tossed that famous yellow hat of his up at Elton John onstage at Carnegie Hall. John had finished his set with the hat on his head, but backstage, Cowan had had to explain who he was. 'I'm the guy who went to China. Here, I'll autograph it for you.' Maybe even then his fame had been stretched too far. Boggan remembered that *Rolling Stone* magazine had mocked Cowan as its groupie of the year.

Lechtick suspected the end was near when a friend called him to say that he'd found Cowan's battered book by the side of the paddle courts one afternoon. It was almost inevitable that he would die in April. His heart stopped on 6 April 2004, on the eve of the thirty-third anniversary of the invitation to China. There were no obituaries in the *Los Angeles Times* or the *New York Times*. For his old rival Tannehill, it was obvious what had happened to Cowan. 'After China, everything seemed to be useless.'

Cowan had stood before Zhou Enlai. He had played a vital role as liaison between two worlds that hadn't yet been bridged. Lauded by Johnny Carson and Dinah Shore, he had appeared on the front cover of every newspaper in America. The *Los Angeles Times* wrote that Cowan and his team-mates had done 'what the Paris peace talks, striped pants and Homburg hats, and the State Department couldn't do in decades – unthaw one-quarter of the world.' Or as John Tannehill explained, 'How can you do better than world peace?'

When Zhuang Zedong, his mirror image on the Chinese team, heard about Cowan's death, he found it impossible to believe that the nation had paid no attention to him. 'When I die,' said Zhuang, 'everyone in China will know.'

Cowan's trajectory had been very American. He had been shot into the stratosphere, tested against the market without a safety net, and then cracked in two by a hard fall.

| **The Heights**

Zhuang Zedong's path was more incremental and yet in many ways much more terrifying than Glenn Cowan's. In October 1976, Zhuang was incarcerated for the second time in his life. He was driven from his home in Beijing to 'an anonymous building in rural China' and found himself behind bars with every reason to fear for his life. For a three-time world champion, the apparent instigator of Ping-Pong diplomacy, the head of the first Chinese Communist delegation ever to visit America, it was a stunning fall.

Two years after singing 'Home on the Range' at a restaurant in Virginia, he was raised to the post of minister of sport and physical culture, a member of the Central Committee of the Communist Party. An American journalist had watched him on tour in 1972, 'murmuring niceties at teacup and cream-puff receptions and sight-seeing,' and quickly concluded that Zhuang had chosen the right side in the Cultural Revolution.

In 1974, Zhuang Zedong was guest of honour at a dinner given by George HW Bush, Gerald Ford's China envoy at the US Liaison Office in Beijing. Zhuang treated Bush to a long harangue over dinner on how sports existed in China to give strength to 'the million troops on the Northern border,' interrupted only when Zhuang paused to stub out one cigarette and light another. But Zhuang soon relaxed, and the future president and the Ping-Pong politician had a long discussion on international relations. 'I like the man,' confessed Bush to his diary, and a few weeks later accompanied

Zhuang to a Sino-American athletic meet, where 'red flags fluttered from the top of the stadium and nationalistic slogans were discreetly covered with red swaths of cloth.' Zhuang was still pushing the Cultural Revolution slogan 'Friendship First and Competition Second,' but the American college students flown over for the friendly meet had no such qualms. They took sixteen of the seventeen medals on offer. An American athlete saw a Chinese 10,000-metre runner 'meditating by the side of the track. "You are thinking of your lap times?" asked the American. "No. I am thinking of friendship."'

Back in 1971, when the Ping-Pong team returned from the Nagoya World Championships, Zhuang and three other champions were summoned to the Great Hall of the People to greet touring players from Canada and Australia. After his ceremonial duties were over, Premier Zhou Enlai approached the small group of Chinese players. 'Come on,' he said. 'Let's go and play some Ping-Pong.' The game stretched into the afternoon, despite the fact that it was 1 May, International Workers' Day. All four knew the premier would soon have to join Chairman Mao at the Gate of Heavenly Peace in Tiananmen Square to watch the workers of China parade before them. To their surprise, the Ping-Pong players were also called up into the reviewing stand along with Zhou Enlai. It was the place for generals, or the country's greatest heroes. As Zhuang headed up the stairs in front of women's champion Zheng Minzhi, she wondered why they'd been invited. Did their achievements in Nagoya really rank that highly?

Chairman Mao approached the Ping-Pong players. His outings were less and less frequent, and still, years after the first gatherings of Red Guards, his presence caused ripples of hysteria to shimmer across Tiananmen Square. Zheng Minzhi found herself applauding as he approached. Zhou Enlai leaned in toward the Chairman, and Zheng listened as the premier introduced her. Mao reached forward, smiled, and shook her hand, leaving her in shock. Zhuang Zedong stepped forward to greet the Chairman, no stranger to the leaders. As Zhuang talked to Mao, Zhou Enlai's wife, Deng Yingchao, came up to Zheng and whispered, 'You've contributed so much to Chinese Ping-Pong. The Ping-Pong ball is very important, you know. It can shake up the whole earth.'

It was less than two weeks after the American team had left Beijing, and the Chinese players didn't fully understand the effect of their outreach. After all, the Chinese newspapers had played down the event, even as coverage around the rest of the world intensified. Not until later in the year, after China was welcomed into the United Nations and Nixon's visit to Beijing was confirmed, would Zheng finally understand what Deng Yingchao had meant.

The Nagoya triumph had sent a firm signal to China's National Sports Commission that slowly echoed out through the root system of provincial teams: sports could be practised again. The achievement was attributed to the strength of the Cultural Revolution rather than recognised for what it was – a deliberate rebuttal of all the limits on thought and action the Cultural Revolution had imposed on the Chinese people.

Yet there was something in the air in 1971 that had not been there in the early 1960s: distrust. Looking along the line of China's greatest athletes, one young sportsman saw in their faces 'omnipresent shadows. No one laughed cheerfully and openly. It was as if they were constantly watching out for something, something so vicious and fearful that it could devour them any time it wanted.' It was the experience of fear. The older athletes knew their lives were lived on a public tightrope. One misdeed, and an athlete could be dismissed to his or her hometown with no position and no career training to fall back on.

| # The Costs

In the wake of the thaw with America, the Chinese players couldn't afford to relax. Rumours kept sliding back to Beijing. The table tennis team heard that one of the highest-ranked officials in the National Sports Commission was still in Shanxi, beginning each morning waist-deep in pig shit, filling and dragging carts of manure to the fields. If he could fall, then anyone could. Every sport had not only a political director but an army representative, and it took little to receive a dressing down. One athlete peeled the skin off his potatoes in the vast dining hall and was humiliated by the political director, who lectured him in front of hundreds for such 'decadent bourgeois habits.'

It was a given in Chinese politics that no one was independent; everyone was attached to a faction. If you were not recruited by one side, it was presumed you were working for the other. In Zhuang Zedong's case, one of his biggest fans was Mao's wife, Jiang Qing. She had nurtured a coterie of young, handsome men, and some insinuated that all were ordered directly into her bed. By then Jiang was receiving blood transfusions from healthy young PLA soldiers because she'd heard it was a way to live longer. Zhuang fit her concept of vigour and success.

The further Zhuang was pushed up the political ladder, the more precarious his position. At the top, overseeing all sports from January 1974, was Deng Xiaoping, considered by Jiang as a main rival in the race to succeed Mao. Once again the National Sports Commission became one of the battlegrounds for the future of power within China.

Zhuang Zedong believed there was only one centre of power, Jiang Qing's Gang of Four. Given personal instructions by Jiang on whom to attack, he began to chisel away at Deng Xiaoping's position. When Jiang called, Zhuang responded. Jiang ordered him to the Summer Palace, where he was filmed playing table tennis. During a period when the number of films deemed fit for public consumption numbered less than ten, Zhuang Zedong's image was committed to celluloid. He had become Jiang's 'cat's paw,' to help her knock Deng from his position of power in 1975.

With Deng Xiaoping gone, Zhuang Zedong was tempted to believe that the future was secure. But he was cautious, as he explained to the *Times*:

> It was a huge honour to be a member of the Central Committee. But it carried huge risks. It was like being taken to the top of a mountain only to find a steep precipice at your feet. If one was going to survive, one had to form an alliance that would please the Chairman and offer oneself protection.

From his perch under Jiang, Zhuang continued to swipe at the old guard. Once Deng fell, the next target was revealed; none other than Zhou Enlai himself. If the Gang of Four could pry the premier away from Mao, their succession would be all but guaranteed.

Zhuang Zedong claimed that Zhou Enlai and Deng Xiaoping 'worshipped foreign things and toadied to foreign powers.' Denunciation meetings were held on Zhuang's orders, where men and women had their scalps shaved and were 'beaten around the head.' Once again, the Cultural Revolution targeted the premier, but this time he was a decade older and suffering from cancer. His old comrade Mao Zedong kept the news of his cancer from him, deciding it was better to extract more work from the premier than to send him to the hospital for lengthy treatment.

Under Zhuang, criticism of anything foreign in the National Sports Commission was ferocious. Referees were markers of 'capitalist privilege.' When the head of FIFA came to visit Zhuang, he had to suffer through a meeting so absurdly political that the FIFA president 'didn't know whether to laugh or cry.'

In 1976, the Tangshan earthquake killed a quarter of a million Chinese in a morning. The same year also brought the deaths of China's first Communist sportsman, Zhu De, then Zhou Enlai, and finally Mao himself. Mao's death may have been greeted with shock, but it was Zhou's death that had the greater emotional impact. As all of China braced for the coming struggle for succession, Zhou Enlai's funeral was shown live on television. One young athlete watched in horror, realising that the premier's tortured grimace indicated a slow, painful death. 'He was the second most powerful person in China,' mused the athlete, 'but he was also the most miserable victim.'

What kind of society had this become? What must men like Zhuang Zedong have done to secure their own positions? And the real fear was that Jiang Qing could make things worse. The country could remain in the grip of the Cultural Revolution forever. Back in England, the aging Ivor Montagu enthused about its continuation. 'You keep on having to wake people up' with revolutions if you wanted to keep the populace involved in politics, he told an interviewer.

After Mao's death, however, the Gang of Four was seized in a sudden move orchestrated by members of the old guard. Jiang Qing went from talking openly of her affinity with past empresses to defending herself against criminal allegations. 'I was Chairman Mao's dog,' she said when she was finally brought to trial. 'When he said "Bite," I bit.' Impromptu banquets in Beijing factories celebrated her downfall. Workers 'paraded on the streets setting off firecrackers until the shells were a crackling red carpet underneath.' Jiang Qing would spend fifteen years in solitary confinement. She was released after being diagnosed with throat cancer in 1991 and hanged herself in her hospital bathroom.

Zhuang Zedong was caught up in the first round of arrests; he was far too close to the Gang of Four to avoid repercussions. After his arrest, he 'was forced to appear before a meeting of 10,000 athletes and sports officials in a Peking gymnasium in November and read aloud a long article that attacked the conduct of the "Gang of Four."' Zhuang was called the 'black hand' of the Gang of Four, used to 'topple numerous officials,' and was accused of turning the

National Sports Commission into a fascist dictatorship. Questions were screamed at him. Why had he sent Jiang 'a pair of embroidered shoes as a present'? Was it true that he was 'afraid of Jiang Qing's calls'? How did he 'usurp the supreme power in the Sports Commission'? He was prohibited from answering at the struggle sessions, and he realised that in this game of thrones, he had chosen the loser.

Eight years after his death, He Long was officially rehabilitated by the party. The marshal who had overseen Zhuang Zedong's rise, who had selected him over Li Furong to take the gold medal at the World Championships three times in a row, returned to haunt Zhuang. Zhuang's earlier criticism of He Long had been recorded and was now turned against the Ping-Pong player. It was Chinese politics as usual. Ghosts rose to walk again, and the living were condemned to live as the dead.

It was hard to reconcile the two images of Zhuang Zedong. Was he the man whose arrest brought a round of cheering from those who worked under him or the warmhearted sportsman who had toured America? In New York in the spring of 1972, after the crowds at an exhibition match at Nassau Coliseum had dispersed, Consultant for Press Affairs Marcia Burick remembered him quietly passing a paddle to her small son and spending five peaceful minutes hitting back and forth with him. It was an unnecessary kindness, not a public performance.

For four years, Zhuang Zedong suffered in solitary confinement at a garrison outside Beijing, 'in a cramped room containing a small bed and a reading lamp.' For two of those years, he had no contact at all with his wife or two children, who believed he had been executed. One hour of exercise a day was all he was permitted. 'I was not allowed to play table tennis,' he said. 'I was shut away and I was always reading, reading and learning by myself in those years. I armed myself through learning.' He was allowed a copy of *The Count of Monte Cristo*, and he read the novel of incarceration and escape again and again. 'The book taught me to hope when I was at my mental limits.'

He was exiled to Shanxi on 6 October 1980, where he had sent so many from the National Sports Commission. One of China's most famous men was allowed out of captivity to start his new life as a sweeper of streets.

Many of his old team-mates had suffered under his rule: Li Furong, who had patiently accepted a lifetime in second place and whom Zhuang had struggled against; Xu Yinsheng, his old doubles partner, whom he had publicly humiliated and exiled from Beijing; Xu Shaofa, whose party membership he had turned down. Zhuang Zedong had written letters to Jiang Qing against all three, but he didn't talk of these things. He diluted the truth to a less incriminating level: 'What I did never caused anybody to die.'

And what would have happened had he done as the protesters on the American tour screamed at him to do: defected? In 1961, when Zhuang won gold at the Beijing World Championships to lift the country during the famine, the Hungarian pre-tournament favourite wasn't beaten by Zhuang himself but by an obscure team-mate, Tan Cho Lin, ranked thirteenth in China. In practice sessions, Tan was Zhuang's preferred sparring partner. But by the start of the Cultural Revolution, Tan knew there was little left for him in China. As the madness of Mao's politics destroyed any chance of a future, Tan, along with tens of thousands of others, dreamed of escaping to either Hong Kong or Macau.

Some tied themselves to a plank of wood or a tire and tried to float their way to freedom across Deep Bay or the Pearl River estuary. Most ended up as bloated carcasses on rocky shores, additions to the statistics used by the American State Department to measure the turmoil inside China. But Tan Cho Lin had trained for years with the table tennis team. His body, hardened by the state and for the state, pulled against the tides, and after three straight hours of swimming, Tan found himself in Macau. Most arrivals would be carried to Casa Ricci, a residence run by a Catholic priest who roared around the tiny island on 'an ancient scooter.' They were allotted two weeks' rest and then encouraged to leave. Tan passed through Hong Kong, stayed long enough to play for the national team, and was banned under Chinese influence from taking part in the 1971 Nagoya Championships.

By the time Zhuang Zedong landed with his squad in Detroit in 1972, Tan had moved to Austin, Texas. Soon Tan was once again a concern for the Chinese government, which was anxious that he not be included in any friendly matches during the Chinese team's US tour. Instead, he fished for his dinner in Texan rivers or roamed graveyards looking for 'coffin crickets' to keep him company. Occasionally, he played in regional table tennis tournaments. Boggan had heard he was unemployed.

Was this the choice? Stay in Beijing, compromise ideals under party pressure, and rise as high as Zhuang Zedong, now minister of sports, or escape to America? For what – a fishing rod, an expensive smoking habit, unemployment, and the pittance of regional table tennis prizes? But also for the deep peace of knowing that you would not have to gird yourself against another political campaign for the rest of your life.

Many of Zhuang Zedong's old team-mates still find it hard to speak his name. 'Let's talk about something else,' one told me, as I interviewed him at a Beijing hotel under a vast glass atrium that stretched upward for six floors. 'If we're going to talk of him we need to find a bigger room,' he said. 'I could blow the roof off this place,' he continued, shaking his head as he considered his past with Zhuang. 'I could bust it wide open.'

Finally, in 1984, Zhuang Zedong was allowed back to Beijing to teach in a local sports school. His protégé, Liang Geliang, who won six gold medals in World Championships, stayed true to him. 'He'd been in a difficult position,' Liang said, 'and made mistakes.' Now Liang went to treat his old friend to dinner, the old friend who had once taken Liang around Beijing by bicycle to find medicine for Liang's mother's cancer. As they walked, Liang noticed they were being followed by two security officers, who stood outside the restaurant throughout the meal. The midnight shadows of Communist China escorted the two champions all the way back to Zhuang Zedong's modest apartment.

During Zhuang Zedong's absence from Beijing, the vast city had begun its transformation, and new buildings were starting to rise above the old quarters. It was hard now to see the wrongs of the past. The government preferred that they were acknowledged quietly, if at all. With a crime like the Cultural Revolution, both victims and criminals could be counted in the millions. Zhuang Zedong was the personification of everything Montagu had once hoped for, the political within Ping-Pong, a racquet-wielding diplomat who held power. And yet he had returned to nothing.

In 2005, when Zhuang Zedong wanted to set up a table tennis

club, he had to make a series of phone calls to the men who had once played beside him, those he had once punished. Slowly, they came around. They even showed up on the opening day. A photo from that day shows Zhuang Zedong and Li Furong holding either end of a banner, looking but not smiling at the camera. 'The old players get together often,' explained former coach Liang Youneng. 'But not with Zhuang Zedong.'

Zhuang Zedong would still be dragged out for the Americans every time China hosted a memorial event for the 1971 American team. In 2006, on the thirty-fifth anniversary reunion in Beijing, Boggan noticed that when they sat for dinner, Zhuang was exiled to a distant table, while all the other world champions were at the centre tables. 'The officials sitting there,' he'd write, 'seemed cool to him.'

Zhuang Zedong was the sole Chinese volunteer to travel in the American bus during the reunion, a strange inversion of Cowan's famous ride back in Nagoya. He acted as the veterans' guide as they travelled out to the Great Wall. During their 1971 trip, the Americans had had the Great Wall to themselves, but now the crowds clogged the crenellations as far as Boggan's eyes could see. There were camels to ride and T-shirts to buy if you were willing to haggle. Heading back into Beijing, they passed McDonald's, KFC, and a Mr Donut. The next day, when Zhuang Zedong showed them around the Forbidden City, Boggan paused in front of a kiosk that had certainly not been there in 1971. It was a Starbucks, a splotch of American green among the red roofs of the emperor's palace.

Zhuang Zedong persuaded the National Sports Commission to let the Americans play at his own table tennis club. In the audience, he confided to Boggan, there were relatives of Mao. Was it true? Or was Zhuang trying to impress the visitors to compensate for his loss of status in his hometown? Zhuang led a karaoke session after the final banquet of the week-long trip. He chose the song based on the shirt he still kept, 'Let It Be.' Glenn Cowan was dead, but his ninety-year-old mother had travelled in his place. The Americans rose to join in, and Cowan's mother wept.

After the Americans left, Zhuang Zedong was not alone. With special dispensation from Deng Xiaoping, the man he had once helped exile from Beijing, he was permitted to marry his second wife, a Japanese citizen. In 2007, he was diagnosed with colorectal cancer and given a year to live. He decided in his remaining time to travel with his wife to Jinggangshan, the birthplace of the People's Liberation Army back in 1928. It's a sparse mountainous region with little to recommend it: no flashing lights, no theme rides, no camels, nor guides to lead a tourist up the side of a mountain. 'Can you imagine,' he said, 'in a place as desolate as that, our predecessors dared to dream of founding a brand-new China and actually made it. I was there to see, think and learn.'

Jinggangshan was where Mao retreated with only a thousand men, where Zhu De and Zhou Enlai and Chen Yi congregated just as Montagu was paying a visit to Leon Trotsky. The Communists were still twenty years away from victory over Chiang Kai-shek, and Edgar Snow had not yet appeared over the hill to sleep on a Ping-Pong table.

Like Zhou Enlai before him, Zhuang Zedong lived with his cancer, travelling when necessary in a wheelchair. The state treated him inconsistently. Premier Wen Jiabao was rumoured to be funding his ongoing treatments. Players of Zhuang Zedong's calibre are supposed to have their treatments paid for by the National Sports Commission, yet it often ignored Zhuang. More revealing still was the list of Zhuang's hospital visitors, including Mao Zedong's daughter Li Min and Zhou Enlai's nieces and his old secretary. The ties really were still there. He had not forgotten his past and the past had not forgotten him.

His death in 2013 provoked dozens of obituaries around the world. Most concentrated on his sporting past, a few on his political rise. All commented on his meeting with Glenn Cowan. However, by characterising that meeting as spontaneous, none gave Zhuang Zedong the credit he deserved for executing a very deliberate strategy. He made up for that himself. 'The Cold War,' he once told a reporter, 'ended with me.'

What lies between Zhuang Zedong's disastrous career as a politician and his glory days as a Ping-Pong player is an understanding of what it meant to be part of a new country. In 1961, when Montagu was a retired spy and president of the ITTF, Zhuang was just a sportsman, but even then he knew the weight of his burden. As Mao's famine hushed the nation, people looked to Zhuang and his team for good news. 'If I won, the whole country won,' he explained. 'If I lost, China lost.'

Epilogue

When I began this book in 2008, my research in China soon led me back to the city of my birth, London. Months later, about a mile from where I was born, I stood in front of 28 Kensington Court, the house where Ivor Montagu had been raised. It turned out that this man I first heard mentioned by a Chinese Ping-Pong player was the uncle of my father's closest friend. My father had spent a few days at Kensington Court in the 1940s, the guest of Montagu's nephew. Montagu, I found out, was never allowed to meet his nephew. Much of this book was driven by another early question I asked myself: What exactly does an uncle have to do to be kept away from his own family?

Montagu's relatives may never have known the extent of his betrayal, but his espionage didn't have the same long-term effects as his role in bringing China into the International Table Tennis Federation. As Russia's man, if Montagu had lived another five years, he would have seen the fall of the Berlin Wall as a searing loss. Would he have acknowledged the Sino-American détente as one of the reasons for the fall? Did Ping-Pong diplomacy help push the Soviet Union into strategic errors that brought an end to a seventy-year-old experiment? Did his chosen game help bring about the demise of the only country he was ever faithful to?

Ninety years ago, Montagu revived a sport that really did fit the best and worst of Communism. It was suited for airless, cramped factories, it was humanistic and competitive, it kept the brain engaged and exercised as much as the body. Table tennis became, as Montagu wrote, 'a weapon for peace.'

273

But as a retired president of the ITTF, Montagu had to witness 1971's Ping-Pong diplomacy from the sidelines. He had placed the game in Chinese hands when China had been in Russian hands. Now the band in the Great Hall of the People was playing 'America the Beautiful.'

Just months before American Ping-Pong players touched down in Beijing, Montagu released his autobiography. *The Youngest Son* was evasive and covered only the first twenty-three years of his life. The reviews were mixed. 'Few men have achieved anything by the age of twenty-three to justify putting their life story on paper,' huffed the *Times Literary Supplement*, 'and Mr Ivor Montagu is no exception.' Even the most perceptive review, by former Communist Philip Toynbee, dismissed Montagu as 'deeply naïve' in writing that he'd been incapable of 'convincingly maintaining deceit.' Toynbee remembered that in his own time as a Communist he had 'told more lies, and with more relish, in three years than I have told, or relished for the rest of my life.'

Montagu's book sold well enough for his publisher to ask him to produce a second volume. It was rejected for the simple reason that Montagu didn't write a new book; he rewrote the old one. Who would write about the same twenty-three years twice? Only a man who was still trying to sort out his own story. He omitted World War II, the rise of the Cold War, his trips to China, and many of his Moscow visits. Yet in that rejected handwritten memoir, he included the revelation that he had been ordered back to Moscow by the Comintern. Was Montagu, now entering his seventies, edging toward the full truth or merely confessing to the life of a propagandist to blur his role as a spy?

In his final years, he would step forward every now and then to speak about Russia or China, giving rapturous summations of Mao's legacy in the wake of the Chairman's death. When the Chinese table tennis team toured England in January 1972, Montagu awaited them as they took tea at 10 Downing Street with the prime minister. He took the squad to London Zoo to introduce them to Chi Chi the panda. Mostly though, he was true to his *Who's Who* entry, where he claimed his hobbies were 'washing up, pottering about, sleeping through television.'

To his great-niece, Nicole Montagu, perhaps the only one of his relatives to track him down after the family split, he was a warm, kind character, always dressed in 'a green cardigan with slightly tufty hair.' He'd lead her to his study, where they'd sit for hours over mugs of tea. She may have reminded Montagu of his younger self as she 'tried to understand why there were so many injustices in the world.' She remembered him as patient and gentle even when she started to make choices that contradicted his own views. In 1984, while she was working in drug rehabilitation in the slums of Hong Kong, Ivor's wife, Hell, died. Ivor followed her two weeks later, passing away on 5 November, Guy Fawkes Day.

There was a handful of obituaries. Like the best of spies, Montagu had receded quietly into the shadows. Only five thousand miles away was his value recognised. 'The Chinese people will never forget Ivor Montagu,' said an official in Beijing.

Glenn Cowan and Zhuang Zedong were the casualties of his ideas. Montagu built Ping-Pong for the state, not the individual. The Chinese grasped that and were willing for their athletes to pay the price. Cowan unwittingly bet on table tennis and failed.

And what of Montagu's greatest gift to China, the game itself? If you're young and Chinese, you're wearing a Houston Rockets shirt and bouncing a basketball on Beijing asphalt or you're in a Manchester United kit, sprinting after a dusty ball and dreaming of a green field. Your dad plays table tennis. The numbers still amaze – 300 million play the game – but the shine is off.

For a sport to be effective, even politically, it needs at least the perception of drama. The Chinese tried everything to make the international competition in table tennis more equitable. They benched their A team and still dominated tournaments. They sent coaches abroad to try to raise the level of play. Yet they still win.

Once upon a time, table tennis was the only option, the very first foothold on China's journey to international respect. Nowadays it's a living fossil like the horseshoe crab; both were formed in volatile eras. Other sports have evolved in China over the decades. A richer country has a boundless horizon to explore, but table tennis remains the nation's one perfect specimen.

Acknowledgements

First and foremost, thanks to those who granted me interviews. The book relies heavily on the memories of the men and women who travelled to Beijing in 1961 and 1971.

I am even more indebted to the Chinese players, coaches, and officials who lived through the extremes of that decade and chose to talk with me. In Beijing and Shanghai, thanks to Qiu Zhonghui, Xi Enting, Liang Geliang, Han Zhicheng, Liang Youneng, Li Furong, Shen Ji Chang, and Wang Ding Hua. Thanks to Xu Shaofa, Xu Yinsheng, Yao Zhenxu, Zeng Chuan Qiang, Zhang Xielin, Zheng Huaiying, Zeng Minzhi, Zhuang Jiafu, and Qi Da Zheng.

In England, so many thanks to Jennifer Montagu, Jeremy Montagu, and Nicole Montagu for sharing their memories. Thanks to Diane Rowe. Thanks to Robert Sinclair and Diane Webb and all those at the English Table Tennis Association in Hastings for access to the archives. Thank you to Ben Macintyre, Nigel West, and Boris Volodarsky.

Thank you to Chuck Hoey of the International Table Tennis Federation Museum for his guidance.

Thank you to Vladimir Paley and Professor Galina Barchukova in Russia.

In the United States, many thanks to Keith Cowan and Sandy Lechtick, to Rufford Harrison and Connie and Dell Sweeris, to Tim Boggan and Judy Bochenski-Hoarfrost. Many thanks to Doug Spelman, Marcia Burick, Rory Hayden, Victor Li, and Perry Link for sharing their memories of the 1972 return tour. Special thanks to

Acknowledgements

Jan Berris, who opened up her prodigious phone book to help, as well as allowing me access to the archives of the National Committee on United States–China Relations. Thank you to Herbert Levin, Ambassador Winston Lord, and Seymour and Audrey Topping. Thanks to Professor Hongshan Li and Professor Minxin Pei for taking their time to talk to me. Thanks to Kai Chen.

To an American original, Marty Reisman, who sadly passed away in 2012, the only person I've ever interviewed who kept the same conversation going over phone, coffee, phone, lunch, phone, phone, phone.

Very special thanks to William J Cunningham, an invaluable resource. He allowed me to study his own collection of papers he'd been gathering in the forty years since he found himself picking up the phone in the Tokyo Embassy in April 1971. He was ever patient with me, going over the events of those days almost hour by hour.

In New Zealand, many thanks to the veteran players Alan Tomlinson, Bryan Foster, and Murray Dunn, who were all kind enough to go through scrapbooks and cast their minds back to the Beijing of more than fifty years ago.

Many thanks to all who helped me at the Bentley Historical Library at the University of Michigan, those at the National Archives in Kew, and the archivists at the People's History Museum in Manchester, England, most especially Darren Treadwell.

I'd like to thank Sim Smiley in Washington for her help in dealing with the National Archives. Thanks also to Sunil Joshi and Susan Lee in New York for their help in the early days of this project. Thank you, New York Public Library. You might just be the best place in the world to read, to write, to stare at the ceiling.

An enormous thank you to Sunny Yang in Beijing. She saved me again and again from asking the wrong questions in the wrong order to the wrong people and was invaluable in helping me navigate along paths that were barely visible to me. To Lijia Zhang, so many thanks for your kindness that made a city of around 20 million seem smaller than it is and ever more fascinating.

The initial person I interviewed for this project was Robert Oxnam, former president of the Asia Society, who first wrote out the characters for table tennis in Mandarin for me. His explanation that the two characters of Ping-Pong are deliberately mirrored to suggest a poetic, yet military form of diplomacy was something I kept in mind through every subsequent trip or interview.

Thanks to Rob de Salle at the American Museum of Natural History. His revelation of the strange benefits that table tennis brings to both brain and body lent an extra dimension to my research and made me take up the game again.

I'd like to thank everyone at Scribner for rolling the dice on an idea that spanned espionage, famine, détente, and table tennis. Brant Rumble is the rare editor who knows how to operate without anesthesia and yet causes no pain. John Glynn helped wield that sharp knife.

Many thanks to my agent, David Kuhn, and the team at Kuhn Projects. Every writer needs an expert dowser, and David sorted through a mountain of my jumbled ideas to make me focus on this particular subject.

I'd like to thank those who gave me invaluable feedback as I approached the end of the project. To Lea Carpenter, Amanda Shuman, Bill Luers, Mike Meyer, Lijia Zhang, and Bill Cunningham. Sincerest thanks to you all. All remaining errors are my own.

Thanks to my parents for encouraging this from the start, for putting a roof over my head on London research trips, and for proofreading version one. Thanks to my sister and brother-in-law for hosting me on my swing toward Hastings and to Gabriel for his vocal support.

Thanks to Patty and Gustavo, who treated me to table tennis tickets in Beijing in 2008. That afternoon changed the next five years of my life.

OB, I've never written anything you haven't read first. There's a reason; you have no mercy.

I thank my wife, Adriana, because even though I went around the world for this book, she travelled double the distance most months for her own work and could still be wife, mother, superwoman, and always my first adviser.

To my children, Tomás and Eva, this book is for you. Mostly because for years you kept opening the door to my room to see how this was going. Also, I thank you both for believing that the entire New York Public Library was your dad's office and that it was much, *much* bigger than everyone else's.

Notes

Prologue

1   *a form of war waged for world revolution*: Shih Pen-shan, as told to Lester Velie, 'I Fought in Red China's Sports War,' *Reader's Digest*, June 1967.

Chapter 1 | Not-So-Humble Beginnings

5   *felt thoroughly cheated*: Montagu, *Youngest Son*, 35.

5   *casting a warmth and amber glow*: Levine, *Politics, Religion and Love*, 8.

5   *Ivor played in the garden*: Interview with Sidney Cole, IWM, 15618 (Reel 1), recorded 3 May 1995.

6   *solemnly . . . dropped it*: Montagu, *Youngest Son*, 67.

6   *the thin one was the family pedigree*: Ibid., 17.

6   *born to an observant Jew*: Levine, *Politics, Religion and Love*, 16.

7   *the current Lord Montagu would agree*: Montagu, *Youngest Son*, 20.

7   *Lord Swaythling, whom the people knew*: Levine, *Politics, Religion and Love*, 14.

7   *Three miles divided*: Report of Lord Swaythling's funeral, *Financial Times*, 17 January 1911.

7   *obsessed with breeding cows*: Author interview with Jennifer Montagu.

8   *used for bridge*: Michael Davies, 'Ping-Pong Diplomats,' *The Observer*, 3 April 1977.

8   *Oh what's this very funny game*: Estes, *A Little Book of Ping-Pong Verse*, 34.

8   *The Ping-Pong face*: Ibid., 91.

9   *suffered no slow lingering agonies*: Bergmann, *Twenty-One Up*, 5.

9   *Apparently the Ping-Pong nets*: Steve Grant, 'When Ping-Pong Came to Asia,' *Table Tennis Collector* (autumn 2008), quoting *Daily Mirror*, 4 February 1904.

9   *like all great men*: 'The Death of Lord Swaythling,' *Financial Times*, 13 June 1927.

Notes

Chapter 2 | Gentlemanly Rebel

10 *several hours on hands*: 'Seven Men,' *Daily Express*, 24 April 1971.

10 *give a lecture*: Montagu, *Youngest Son*, 17. Between his idyllic country wanderings, Montagu attended school in London. His parents had wanted him to board in the city, but within days he ended up before the headmaster. There were only four boarders, and as soon as lights were out, the older two ordered the younger pair 'to tickle one of our older companions in strange places' (p. 78). From then until his admission to Cambridge, he remained, at his parents' insistence, a 'day boy.'

10 *he'd leave the hat*: 'Dynamo and Man of Peace,' *Daily Worker*, 19 May 1959.

11 *minestrone and wobbly pink blancmange*: Montagu, *Youngest Son*, 134.

12 *the Spillikins*: Swann and Aprahamian, *Bernal: A Life*, 206.

13 *were political . . . I saw in Table Tennis*: Montagu, *Youngest Son*, 220.

13 *chess on steroids*: Author interview with Rob Desalle, January 2011.

13 *it's much more intense*: Ibid.

Chapter 3 | Roast Beef and Russia

15 *juicy roast beef and crackly roast potatoes*: Montagu, *Youngest Son*, 282.

15 *futuristic costumes*: Ibid., 301.

16 *thoroughly infested with worms*: Ivor Montagu, 'Like It Was,' unpublished autobiography, 108, Box 2.3, Montagu Collection, Labour History Archive and Study Centre, Manchester, UK.

16 *Sicilian pole-cat who died*: 'Dynamo and Man of Peace,' *Daily Worker*, 19 May 1959.

16 *One of his first jobs*: Ivor Montagu, 'Working with Hitchcock,' *Sight and Sound* 49 (summer 1980).

16 *I suppose I could leave tonight*: Montagu, 'Like It Was,' 22, Box 2.3.

17 *a letter of this kind*: Crossman, *God That Failed*, 56.

18 *in Montagu's wake*: Notes from ITTF Conference, London, March 1946.

Chapter 4 | The Dangers of Derision

19 *Before his life in Ping-Pong*: Ivor Montagu, 'Table Tennis and South Africa,' *Table Tennis* VIII, no. 6 (February 1950).

20 *Montagu's parents were proud*: Michael Davies, 'Ping-Pong Diplomats,' *The Observer*, 3 April 1977.

20 *the* Times *suggested*: 'Table Tennis: European Championships,' *The Times* (London), 13 December 1926.

20 *Can you imagine the training*: *Singapore Free Press and Mercantile Advertiser*, 18 February 1928.

21 *Is she a Jewess?*: interview with Ivor and Hell Montagu, undated, Box 12.9, Montagu Collection, Labour History Archive and Study Centre, Manchester, UK.

22 *I would pay*: Montagu, *Youngest Son*, 375.

22 *Montagu's share*: Ivor Montagu, 'Like It Was,' unpublished autobiography, Box 2.3, Montagu Collection, Labour History Archive and Study Centre, Manchester, UK.

Notes

Chapter 5 | Table Tennis and Trotsky

23 *his bright-red face*: Ivor Montagu, 'Like It Was,' unpublished autobiography, Box 2.3, Montagu Collection, Labour History Archive and Study Centre, Manchester, UK.

23 *No foreigner had ever won*: Henderson, *Last Champion*, 30.

24 *The greatest attacking stroke*: Ibid., 29.

24 *To get Perry safely inside*: Montagu, 'Like It Was,' Box 2.3.

24 *Perry tried a drop shot*: Henderson, *Last Champion*, 30.

24 *The crowd stood and cheered*: Ibid., 32.

24 *I have finished*: Terry Coleman, 'Ping-Pong,' *The Guardian*, 24 April 1963.

24 *Montagu had written to Trotsky*: Ivor Montagu to Leon Trotsky, letter, July 1929, Box 4.10, Montagu Collection, Labour History Archive and Study Centre, Manchester, UK.

24 *Montagu would confess*: Box 4.10, Montagu Collection, Labour History Archive and Study Centre, Manchester, UK.

25 *Communist Party had*: Carr, *Twilight of the Comintern*, 208.

Chapter 6 | Culture and the Coming War

26 *perfected a special shot*: 'The King and Table Tennis,' *Table Tennis*, April 1937.

26 *showing very great interest*: 'HM the Queen and Table Tennis,' *Table Tennis*, March 1937.

26 *table tennis is a distinct asset*: 'A Letter of Advice from Baroness Swaythling,' *Table Tennis Collector* 57 (summer 2010).

26 *'hate parties'*: McGilligan, *Alfred Hitchcock*, 76.

26 *Hitchcock had great regard*: Ibid., 157.

27 *Hitchcock had his favourite book*: Ivor Montagu, 'Working with Alfred Hitchcock,' *Sight and Sound* 49 (summer 1980).

27 *the unremarkable Ivor Montagu*: Ibid.

27 *something like* Potemkin: Ivor Montagu, 'Like It Was,' unpublished autobiography, 101, Box 2.3, Montagu Collection, Labour History Archive and Study Centre, Manchester, UK.

27 *devotes the whole of his energies*: US Department of Labour to New York Police Department, letter, 7 July 1930, Box 1.1, Montagu Collection, Labour History Archive and Study Centre, Manchester, UK.

27 *having betrayed the United States*: Montagu, 'Like It Was,' Box 2.3.

28 *as a teenager had dined*: Ebon, *Soviet Propaganda Machine*, 53.

28 *with a long list of introductions*: Montagu, *Youngest Son*, 301.

28 *Munzenberg was in charge*: Boris Volodarsky calls him the de facto director of the Soviet Union's covertly directed propaganda operations in the West in his 2010 master's thesis, 'Soviet Intelligence Services in the Spanish Civil War, 1936–1939.'

28 *he'd also invented the concept*: Ebon, *Soviet Propaganda Machine*, 50.

28 *And if he is a Jew*: Miles, *Dangerous Otto Katz*, 108.

29 *victim of a pair of agents*: This is the accepted point of view. Boris Volodarsky argued that though Munzenberg would have been of interest to the

NKVD, the Fascist troops invading France, and the French government, a local doctor near Montagne believed Munzenberg had hanged himself.

29 *the sound of a descending bomb*: Interview with Sidney Cole, IWM, 15618 (Reel 4), recorded 1978.

30 *an unintended explosion*: Miles, *Dangerous Otto Katz*, 171.

Chapter 7 | Suspect

31 *Haldane, a 'massive, towering' man*: Montagu, *Youngest Son*, 233.

31 *wearing a floppy hat*: Ibid., 233.

31 *intellectually sub-human*: Clark, *J. B. S.*, 21.

31 *the bravest and the dirtiest officer*: West, *Venona*, 77.

31 *exactly a year before*: Clark, *J. B. S.*, 41.

32 *The result of one of these experiments*: Ibid., 61.

32 *so many things to do*: Ibid., 123.

33 *The reason of our tentative interest*: Letter to Major Valentine Vivian, 9 November 1932, KV2/599, Montagu Files, National Archives, Kew, UK.

33 *declined an offer by Lenin*: Ivor Montagu, 'Like It Was,' unpublished autobiography, 61, Box 2.3, Labour History Archive and Study Centre, Manchester, UK.

33 *what were they saying?*: Letter to Major Valentine Vivian, 12 December 1932, KV2/599, Montagu Files, National Archives, Kew, UK.

33 *having answered him*: Ibid.

34 *all trussed up like a horse*: Evans, *Coloured Pins on a Map*, 4.

34 *spoke in English, French and German*: Bergmann, *Twenty-One Up*, 18.

34 *one hand in his pocket*: Reid, *Victor Barna*, 38.

35 *as table tennis players a menace*: 'Ought We To Boo Them?' *Table Tennis*, April 1936.

35 *let his hand drop off*: Ibid.

35 *to set up a chessboard*: Kersi Meher-Homji, 'Believe It or Not: A Table Tennis Match That Lasted 59 Hours,' The Roar, 7 July 2010, http://www.theroar.com.au/2010/07/07/a-table-tennis-match-that-lasted-59-hours/.

35 *the patted ball*: Bergmann, *Twenty-One Up*, 21.

36 *a palm full of pepper*: Tim Boggan, speech inducting Ruth Aarons into the US Table Tennis Hall of Fame, transcript, http://216.119.100.169/organization/halloffame/aarons1.html.

Chapter 8 | Brothers

37 *curious circles*: Unsigned letter from MI5 regional officer in Cambridge, UK, to Major Valentine Vivian, 20 February 1928, HW 15/43, National Archives, Kew, UK.

37 *particularly unpleasant Communist*: Unsigned letter from MI5 regional officer in Cambridge, UK, to Major Valentine Vivian, 3 March 1942, KV2/599, National Archives, Kew, UK.

37 *megaphone to the home games*: Montagu, *Youngest Son*, 167.

38 *but also Lady Swaythling's*: Conversation between Lady Swaythling and Lord Semphill, 9 February 1941, transcript, National Archives, Kew, UK.

Notes

38 *We have considerable information*: Letter from Ministry of Labour and National Service, 8 May 1941, HW 15/43, National Archives, Kew, UK.

38 *permanent suspension*: Letter to Ministry of Labour and National Service, 21 May 1941, HW 15/43, National Archives, Kew, UK.

38 *A local captain*: Captain Barratt to Major Cumming, letter, 22 February 1942, HW 15/43, Montagu Files, National Archives, Kew, UK.

38 *the well being of this country*: Unsigned letter from MI5 regional officer in Cambridge, UK, to Major Valentine Vivian, 3 March 1942, KV2/599.

38 *comically menial job*: F. Wilson to Ivor Montagu, letter, March 1942, HW 15/43, Montagu Files, National Archives, Kew, UK.

39 *no real formal written agenda*: Ewen Montagu to Ms. Filby, letter, 3 February 1979, RNVR 97/45/2, Imperial War Museum Archives, London.

39 *The goal was to deceive*: For the full, extraordinary tale, see the absorbing account in Macintyre, *Operation Mincemeat*.

40 *we shall have to get the body back*: Macintyre, *Operation Mincemeat*, 124.

40 *whose official post*: Top secret Venona intercept from London to Moscow, 16 August 1940, HW 15/43, Montagu Files, National Archives, Kew, UK.

40 *known by the moniker*: It's also possible that Montagu was NOBILITY and his friend Haldane was INTELLIGENTSIA. Haldane's father was Lord Haldane; Montagu's was Lord Swaythling. Both sons were members of the intelligentsia. Macintyre, in *Operation Mincemeat*, opts for Montagu as INTELLIGENTSIA. Nigel West believes it was Haldane. Christopher Andrew, MI5's official historian, wrote in his book *The Defence of the Realm*, that 'The Service devoted no significant further resources to unraveling either the connection between Montagu and the rest of the X Group or the identity of NOBILITY, which remains unknown'; this seems to imply that Montagu headed X group as INTELLIGENTSIA. Boris Volodarsky, historian and former captain of the GRU, implies that it was more likely that Haldane was INTELLIGENTSIA. All studied the same handful of decrypted telegrams. Until the GRU opens its doors to historians, the confusion cannot be resolved.

40 *by a concert pianist*: West, *Venona*, 54–60.

41 *relished the prospect*: Venona report, 25 July 1940, HW 15/43, Montagu Files, National Archives, Kew, UK.

41 *a man of different calibre*: Venona decryption, 16 August 1940, HW 15/43, Montagu Files, National Archives, Kew, UK.

41 *difficult to contact him*: Venona decryption, 6 September 1940, HW 15/43, Montagu Files, National Archives, Kew, UK.

41 *delayed-action bombs*: Venona decryption, 11 October 1940, HW 15/43, Montagu Files, National Archives, Kew, UK.

41 *was a matter of exceptional importance*: Venona decryption, 2 October 1940, HW 15/43, Montagu Files, National Archives, Kew, UK.

Chapter 9 | The End of the Game?

42 *One RAF flyer*: Leslie Bennett, 'Chiselling through the Tropics,' *Table Tennis*, May 1948.

42 *generations of unborn chickens*: Chris Clark, 'They Knew What They Wanted,' *Table Tennis*, January 1947.

42   *Their standard package*: Alan Duke, 'Table Tennis as an Escape Aid!' *Table Tennis Collector* 54 (fall 2009).

43   *leaned across the table*: Montagu, *Beyond Top Secret Ultra*, 49.

43   *He is simply enormous*: Ewen Montagu to Iris Montagu, letters, August–December 1940, quoted in Macintyre, *Operation Mincemeat*.

43   *a shoulder holster*: Montagu, *Beyond Top Secret Ultra*, 68.

43   *really bad on this war*: Macintyre, *Operation Mincemeat*, 88.

43   *got up at all hours*: Report from Hunton Bridge Station, Watford, UK, May 1940, HW 15/43, Montagu Files, National Archives, Kew, UK.

44   *very keen to listen*: Report on Ivor Montagu from Watford C Division, 21 November 1940, HW 15/43, Montagu Files, National Archives, Kew, UK.

44   *the captured documents*: Montagu, *Man Who Never Was*, 131.

Chapter 10 | The Jewish Question

46   *Scottish hammer-throwers*: Bergmann, *Twenty-One Up*, 88.

46   *Bergmann had also qualified*: Ibid., 94.

47   *a dump of human corpses*: Ibid., 102.

47   *domain of Central European Jews*: Ivor Montagu, quoted in Reid, *Victor Barna*, 107.

47   *by leaping from a moving train*: 'The Inspiring Zoltan,' *Table Tennis*, May 1951.

47   *father and sister died*: Matthew Surrence, 'Table Tennis Champion Retires His Game But Not His Memories,' JWeekly.com, 30 August 1996, accessed July 2010.

47   *Finding a beehive*: Charyn, *Sizzling Chops and Devilish Spins*, 23.

48   *only two memories*: Author interviews with Jeremy Montagu and Jennifer Montagu.

49   *strained through a bag*: Ivor Montagu to Hell Montagu, letters, Box 11.1, Montagu Collection, Labour History Archive and Study Centre, Manchester, UK.

49   *are worse than raisin bread*: Hell Montagu to Ivor Montagu, letters, Box 11.1, Montagu Collection, Labour History Archive and Study Centre, Manchester, UK.

50   *really world-embracing*: Notes from London ITTF Conference, 19–23 March 1946, available at http://www.ittf.com/museum/archives/index.html.

50   *ran smoothly*: Reports to HAR Philby, 26 November 1946, and 3 December 1946, KV2/599, National Archives, Kew, UK.

50   *politically influenced*: 'Shock Squads of Young Tories Told to Convert East Whitehall Files Reveal Conservatives Were Encouraged to Disrupt Soviets with "Inspired Speeches and Awkward Questions,"' *The Independent*, 26 July 2001.

Chapter 11 | Table Tennis Bandits

54   *bubonic plague*: Snow, *Red Star Over China*, 41.

54   *heavily bearded*: 'Behind the Red Star Over China,' *China Daily*, 22 October 2006, http://www.chinadaily.com.cn/china/2006-10/22/content_713979.htm. Huang was China's first ambassador to the United Nations in the wake of Ping-Pong diplomacy.

54   *a face so striking*: Suyin, *Eldest Son*, 57.

54 *a vast piece of farmland*: 'Behind the Red Star Over China.'

54 *probably the only seat*: Snow, *Red Star Over China*, 114.

55 *table tennis by the river*: Ibid., 116.

55 *W. H. Auden came to China*: They worked together in the 1930s on the translation of poems extolling both Stalin and Lenin; see http://www.guardian.co.uk/books/2009/may/22/unpublished-auden-poems-film-archive.

55 *hairy, meat-pink men*: Auden and Isherwood, *Journey to a War*, 31.

56 *take part in an All-China meet*: Programme Notes, World Table Tennis Championships, Bombay, 1952.

56 *Many people had been amused*: Snow, *Red Star Over China*, 281.

56 *poker was politicised*: Ibid., 282.

56 *when he was exiled in Berlin*: Suyin, *Eldest Son*, 57.

56 *a good game of table tennis*: Snow, *Red Star Over China*, 338.

57 *be immune to bullets*: Ibid., 338.

57 *could disappear among his troops*: Smedley, *Great Road*, xx.

57 *fellow Ping-Pong enthusiast*: The two men left Europe in 1924 and 1925, respectively. Since they both lapped up cultural activities in their time in Germany, France, and England, it's entirely possible that they were exposed to some of Ivor Montagu's early efforts to spread the gospel of table tennis.

57 *they painted slogans*: Smedley, *Great Road*, 267.

57 *the famous red star*: Ibid., 251.

58 *a fireworks display*: Belden, *China Shakes the World*, xii.

58 *be good enough for the thousands*: Jonathan Spence, 'Portrait of a Monster: Review of *Mao – The Unknown Story*,' *New York Review of Books*, 3 November 2005, http://www.nybooks.com/articles/archives/2005/nov/03/portrait-of-a-monster/?pagination=false.

58 *required five reprints*: In the United States, the book sold 23,500 copies but affected an entire generation of China watchers.

59 *bring some Ping-Pong balls*: Sues, *Shark's Fins and Millet*.

59 *In August 1937*: Unsigned letter, 9 August 1937, HW 15/43, Montagu Files, National Archives, Kew, UK.

59 *visited Japan in 1927*: Michael Davies, 'Ping-Pong Diplomats,' *The Observer*, 3 April 1977.

59 *She strongly objected*: Letters to the Editor, *The Times* (London), 27 and 29 February 1932.

59 *when Edgar Snow visited*: Jarvie, Dong-Jhy, and Brennan, *Sports, Revolution and the Beijing Olympics*, 56.

59 *Ping-Pong had ranked twelfth*: Morris, *Marrow of the Nation*, 120.

59 *China must have her own athletes*: Suyin, *Eldest Son*, 220.

60 *identify sport with the workplace*: Jarvie, Dong-Jhy, and Brennan, *Sport, Revolution and the Beijing Olympics*, 69.

Chapter 12 | The Trojan Dove

61 *regarded with amazement*: Editorial, *Table Tennis*, October 1954.

61 *benevolent monarchy*: 'Life Members,' *Table Tennis*, February 1958.

62 *correspondence had taken place*: Minutes of the Annual General Meeting of the ITTF, Vienna, 1951, 4, ITTF Archives.

Notes

62 *family shame*: Brownell, *Training the Body for China*, 300.

63 *the now-dissolved Comintern*: The Comintern officially ceased to exist in 1943.

63 *Sports relations are well worth while*: Montagu, *East–West Sport Relations*, 22.

64 *woke up to find themselves surrounded*: 'The Germ War Cannot Be Denied,' *Daily Worker*, 6 October 1952.

64 *Both the International Red Cross*: Guillemin, *Biological Weapons*, 99.

64 *it was Russian*: 'Investigator for Reds Admits No Proof of Germ Warfare,' *Washington Post*, 27 September 1952.

64 *Trojan Dove*: Philip Deery, 'The Dove That Flies East: Whitehall, Warsaw and the 1950 World Peace Congress,' *Australian Journal of Politics and History* 48, no. 4 (2002): 436–57.

64 *lanterns illuminated the political slogans*: Starobin, *Paris to Peking*, 173.

65 *Long Live Peace!*: 'All Peking Cheers the Fighters for Peace,' *Daily Worker*, 14 October 1952.

65 *20 million former idle landlords*: 'Peking Is Gay for National Day Festival,' *Daily Worker*, 1 October 1952.

65 *as sure as the sunrise*: 'In a Peking Street Market,' *Daily Worker*, 15 October 1952.

65 *We love peace, and smash all our enemies*: 'Pilgrims to Peking,' *The Economist*, 11 October 1952.

65 *the exploits of Hong Kong*: '7000 at All-China Final,' *Table Tennis*, December 1952.

65 *They weren't much good*: Michael Davies, 'Ping-Pong Diplomats,' *The Observer*, 3 April 1977.

66 *for decades to come*: A typical effort from Taiwan can be found in the 1959 *Honorable General Secretary Report* from the ITTF Museum.

66 *only if they accepted the name*: Lijuan, *He Zhenliang*, 46.

66 *dictated directly to him*: Ibid., 160.

66 *a historical opportunity*: Yaping, *From Bound Feet*.

66 *after twenty yards*: Ivor Montagu, 'Sports and Pastimes in China,' *United Asia – The Chinese Scene* 8, no. 2 (1956).

Chapter 13 | The Rise of Asia

67 *the gym was tended to*: Jojima, *Ogi*, 15.

68 *Table tennis is for girls*: Ibid., 13.

68 *Until the Japanese joined*: ITTF *Handbook*, 4.

68 *names of the winners*: 'The Game in Japan,' *Table Tennis*, October 1936.

68 *The MacArthur Cup*: 'Latest News from Abroad,' *Table Tennis*, November 1948.

68 *Mac the Devil*: Hung, *Mao's New World*, 162.

69 *a kind of salvation*: Jojima, *Ogi*, 18.

69 *he didn't chew*: Ibid., 36.

69 *all the cells in the human body*: Ibid., 58–59.

70 *It hit my racquet in a new way*: Author interview with Marty Reisman, 7 March 2012.

71 *suddenly everything was lit up*: 'Shizuka Narahara,' *Table Tennis News*, November 1953.

71 *bullet like forehand*: Leslie Nakashima, 'Survivor of Atomic Blast Seeks Table Tennis Title,' *Coshocton Tribune*, 3 January 1952.

Chapter 14 | Tiny Tornadoes

72 *he hopped for four kilometres*: Jojima, *Ogi*, 107.

72 *he begged on the streets*: Ibid., 120.

72 *finally had enough*: Ibid., 120.

73 *a class for translators*: Ogimura, *Ichiro Ogimura in Legend*, 92.

74 *atomic effort*: 'World Championship Report,' *Table Tennis Topics*, April 1954.

74 *miss an easy slam*: Ogimura, *Ichiro Ogimura in Legend*, 102–4.

74 *tiny tornadoes*: 'World Championships,' *Daily Express*, 15 April 1954.

74 *Her Majesty the Queen*: Editorial, *Table Tennis*, April 1954.

74 *brainy, superbly fit*: Jojima, *Ogi*, 138, quoting *Daily Express*, April 1954.

74 *battery of photographers*: *Times of India*, 16 April 1954.

74 *regard them with contempt*: Ogimura, *Ichiro Ogimura in Legend*, 105.

75 *much to the astonishment*: *Nippon Times*, 3 May 1954.

75 *help him back to his feet*: Ogimura, *Ichiro Ogimura in Legend*, 158.

76 *limb from glistening limb*: 'The Crowds Were Screaming,' *Daily Mirror*, 9 April 1956.

Chapter 15 | Reconnaissance

77 *It was only twenty-five miles*: Zhiyi, *Champion's Dignity*, chap. 4.

78 *the fishmonger was operating*: Li Yu-wen, 'Table Tennis World Champion,' *China Reconstructs*, July 1959.

78 *Rong found himself part*: Zhiyi, *Champion's Dignity*, chap. 4.

78 *in a solemn ceremony*: de Beauvoir, *Long March*, 374.

78 *in charge of over a million soldiers*: Lijuan, *He Zhenliang*, 111.

79 *a stevedore at the Seine quays*: Suyin, *Eldest Son*, 55.

79 *and a worker at a Michelin*: Lescot, *Before Mao*, 278.

79 *his true passion was Go*: Ibid., 277.

79 *kill a chicken for dinner*: Bosshardt, *Restraining Hand*, 120.

79 *Pay no attention to them!*: Smedley, *Battle Hymn of China*, 158.

80 *deported to remote areas*: Frank Dikötter, notes for the World's Greatest Famine: Witnessing, Surviving, Remembering conference, 9, Laogai Research Foundation, Washington, DC, 15 February 2012.

80 *would you be willing to return*: Zhiyi, *Champion's Dignity*, chap. 3.

80 *Rong's best friend*: Steven Cheung would become one of Canada's top economists before returning to Hong Kong in 1982.

81 *he'd have liked to head*: Steven Cheung, *Remembering Rong Guotuan*, Chung Lau, trans., http://home.covad.net/chunglau/021002.htm.

81 *fed rice and vegetables*: Li, *Bitter Sea*, 231.

81 *installed in a large house*: Zhiyi, *Champion's Dignity*, chap. 5.

Notes

Chapter 16 | The Golden Game

83   *electric cards to take a bus*: Author interview with Xu Yingsheng, May 2011.

84   *kept a bust on his mantelpiece*: Tim Boggan, speech inducting Dick Miles into the US Table Tennis Hall of Fame, transcript, http://216.119.100.169/organization/halloffame/miles2.html.

84   *To be honest*: Author interview with Marty Reisman, 7 March 2012.

85   *What were we going to do?*: Reisman, interview.

85   *the top foreign delegations*: Author interview with Zhuang Jiafu, 10 November 2011.

85   *I'm the premier*: Ibid.

85   *spiritual nuclear weapon*: 'Playing the Numbers Game,' *South China Morning Post*, 31 July 2008.

86   *much more than*: Frank Dikötter, notes for the World's Greatest Famine: Witnessing, Surviving, Remembering conference, Laogai Research Foundation, Washington, DC, 15 February 2012.

86   *when there is not enough to eat*: Dikötter, *Mao's Great Famine*, 134.

86   *Foreign friends visiting*: 'How China Gets High Farm Yields,' *China Reconstructs*, April 1959.

86   *It's easy to mock*: 'Jung Kuo-tuan,' *Daily Mirror*, 2 April 1959.

86   *In three months*: 'First National Games,' *China Reconstructs*, December 1959, 34–36.

Chapter 17 | Setting the Table

87   *a monstrous villain*: *Daily Worker*, 7 November 1948.

88   *Lysenko gained three chauffeured cars*: Becker, *Hungry Ghosts*, 64.

88   *desired requirements*: Clark, J. B. S., 174.

89   *he first shook Lysenko's hand*: Box 11.5, Montagu Collection, Labour History Archive and Study Centre, Manchester, UK.

89   *This tickles Lysenko*: Ibid.

89–90   *personally drew up*: Becker, *Hungry Ghosts*, 66–71.

Chapter 18 | The End of Brotherhood

91   *they released balloons*: 'Peking Ovation for Tibetans,' *Daily Worker*, 1 May 1959.

91   *caterpillars wrapped the foliage*: Suyin, *My House Has Two Doors*, 266.

92   *Among the buildings*: Brownell, *Training the Body for China*, 131.

92   *Brilliant sunshine*: 'May Day,' *Daily Worker*, 1 May 1959.

93   *considerable contribution to the consolidation*: 'International Lenin Peace Prize Presented to Ivor Montagu,' *Moscow News*, 1 May 1959.

93   *for about four hours*: Evans, *Coloured Pins on the Map*, 46.

93   *looking at the plans*: Author interview with Wang Ding Hua, November 2011.

94   *The forces of war*: 'International Lenin Peace Prize Presented to Ivor Montagu.'

94   *signed off on forty-four hectares*: Hung, *Mao's New World*, 46.

Notes

94 *margarine Marxist*: Montefiore, *Stalin*, 523.
94 *control China's seacoasts*: Burr, *Kissinger Transcripts*, 197.
94 *This friendship will live*: Moscow News, 30 September 1959.
95 *Nigerian speakers*: Moscow News, 29 April 1961.
95 *vigorous advocacy*: Tien-min, *Chou En-Lai*.

Chapter 19 | Preparation

96 *the emperor's garden*: Nai'an and Luo, *All Men Are Brothers*, x.
96 *with no windows*: Jiang, *Small Ball Spins the Big Ball*, chap. 6.
97 *half a dozen Ping-Pong tables*: Chang, *Wild Swans*, 267.
97 *took on the dual propaganda role*: 'Millions Take Up Table Tennis,' *China Reconstructs*, March 1960, 35.
97 *every athlete was expected*: Chen, *One in a Billion*, 78.
97 *We weren't encouraged*: Author interview with Xu Shaofa, May 2011.
98 *The new life*: Author interview with Xi Enting, 6 May 2011.
98 *downing ten bottles*: Author interview with Han Zhicheng, 8 November 2011.
99 *The two men would face off*: Author interview with Marty Reisman, 7 March 2012.
99 *no other apparent source*: Ibid.
99 *Everyone came to trade*: Ibid.
100 *The Buy Policy*: Author interview with Wang Ding Hua, November 2011.
100 *Whoever came up*: Author interview with Robert Oxnam, 19 May 2011.
101 *We were so nervous*: Author interview with Zhuang Jiafu, 10 November 2011.
101 *had all attended*: Sports column, *China Reconstructs*, January 1956, 30.

Chapter 20 | Sacrifice

102 *bumper harvest*: Wu with Li, *Single Tear*, 108.
102 *The men were reduced*: Dikötter, *Mao's Great Famine*, 288–90, gives the death rates in the Chinese gulags as ranging wildly. The best-case scenario was a 4 to 8 per cent chance of death in the North; at worst, an approximately 70 per cent chance in an area near the Gobi Desert.
102 *muddy rags*: Wu with Li, *Single Tear*, 146.
102 *deliberate murder on a mass scale*: Jasper Becker, notes for the World's Greatest Famine: Witnessing, Surviving, Remembering conference, 6, Laogai Research Foundation, Washington, DC, 15 February 2012.
103 *How bold the peasants*: 'Scientists Learn from Peasants,' *China Reconstructs*, October 1958.
103 *open invitation*: Zhisui, *Private Life of Chairman Mao*, 280.
103 *Grain should be taken*: Mao gave this speech in October 1958; it is included by Frank Dikötter in his notes for the World's Greatest Famine: Witnessing, Surviving, Remembering conference, Laogai Research Foundation, Washington, DC, 15 February 2012.
103 *17 million*: McGregor, *The Party*, 259.
104 *between two and three million*: Frank Dikötter, notes for the World's

Greatest Famine: Witnessing, Surviving, Remembering conference, 11, Laogai Research Foundation, Washington, DC, 15 February 2012.

104 *swell during the famine*: Ibid., 20.
104 *the people urgently demand*: Domes, *Peng Te-huai*, 86.
104 *Putting politics in command*: Ibid., 92–93; direct quote from Peng's letter.
105 *he had once glorified in poetry*: Ibid., 44.
105 *Mao's favourite movie*: Zhisui, *Private Life of Chairman Mao*, 374.

Chapter 21 | Nourishing the Team

106 *plenty of goat meat*: Author interview with Wang Dinghua, 9 November 2011.
106 *a roof that leaked*: Author interview with Qiu Zhonghui, 4 May 2011.
106–7 *there was little to buy*: Author interview with Li Furong, May 2011.
107 *the glory of our unit*: Author interview with Han Zhicheng, 8 November 2011.
107 *were very nervous*: Author interview with Zheng Chuan Qiang, 9 November 2011.
108 *If you lose a game*: Author interview with Liang Youneng, 11 November 2011.
108 *Mao stopped by*: Yaping, *From Bound Feet*, 25.
108 *the stadium was packed*: Zheng Chuan Qiang, interview.
108 *All 108 stayed*: Author interview with Qi Da Zheng, 8 November 2011.
108 *At the theatre*: Suyin, *My House Has Two Doors*, 318.
108 *she was chastised*: Ibid., 306.
108 *affected roughly 10 per cent*: Becker, *Hungry Ghosts*, 199.
108 *their heads well within*: Suyin, *My House Has Two Doors*, 362.
108 *for no more than two hours*: Ibid., 388.
108 *his wife served tea*: Becker, *Hungry Ghosts*, 240.
109 *a scene of booming prosperity*: Programme for the 1961 World Championships in Peking.
109 *Fu was trying to create*: Author interview with Shen Ji Chang, 7 November 2011.
109 *the sweat and the blood*: Qiu Zhonghui, interview.
110 *these special brooches*: Ibid.
110 *Let me tell you another story*: Author interview with Zhuang Jiafu, 10 November 2011.

Chapter 22 | Ping-Pong Espionage

112 *The most studied of all*: Author interview with Liang Youneng, 7 November 2011.
112 *He was amazed*: Ibid.
112 *was a very boastful article*: Ibid. Much of the rest of this chapter is based on an extensive interview with Zhuang Jiafu.

Notes

Chapter 23 | Cheery Martial Music

117 *seen five hundred cases of train robbery*: Frank Dikötter, notes for the World's Greatest Famine: Witnessing, Surviving, Remembering conference, 29, Laogai Research Foundation, Washington, DC, 15 February 2012.

117 *incredibly depressing*: Author interview with Alan Tomlinson, 10 September 2011.

117 *an absolute book*: Ibid.

118 *seeing a Chinese blonde*: 'Chou's Chaps Doing Us Proud,' *Daily Mirror*, 5 April 1961.

118 *recommended limits*: 'Sidelights on the Table Tennis Meet,' *China Reconstructs*, June 1961.

118 *statues of athletes*: Programme for the 1961 World Championships in Peking.

118 *I must admit the copy*: 'Chou's Chaps Doing Us Proud.'

119 *Don't throw anything away*: Tomlinson, interview.

119 *best sports journalists*: 'Ban That Shames Us All,' *Daily Mirror*, 22 February 1966.

119 *mourning bands*: Lescot, *Before Mao*, 299.

119 *legs of female dragonflies*: Yuan, *Born Red*, 90.

119 *The bitter joke*: Cao, *The Attic*, 90.

119 *a long, agonising process*: Oddly, cocklebur was also the inspiration for the creation of Velcro, a nylon imitation of cocklebur's tiny hooks invented by a Swiss engineer in the 1940s.

119 *What are you looking at?*: Author interview with Qiu Zhonghui, 4 May 2011.

Chapter 24 | The Chance to Shine

120 *It was like Cirque du Soleil*: Author interview with Murray Dunn, 19 September 2011.

120 *looked like the cat*: J. L. Manning, 'Ping Pang on the Avenue of Perpetual Peace,' *Daily Mail*, 5 April 1961.

120 *the premier and Mao's wife*: Evans, *Coloured Pins on the Map*, 42.

120 *something of a drawing-room Communist*: Chargé d'Affaires in Peking to Alec Douglas-Home, letter, undated (presumably April 1961), FO 371/158437, National Archives, Kew, UK.

120 *remarks were in lockstep*: File 117-01285-01, number 26, Ministry of Foreign Affairs Archive, Beijing, PRC.

121 *your reaction could be misconceived*: Author interview with Bryan Foster, 19 September 2011.

121 *Had they done that in Europe*: Ibid.

121 *lowly, grey tiled resting places*: 'Chou's Chaps Doing Us Proud,' *Daily Mail*, 5 April 1961.

121 *It was hard to tell*: Dunn, interview.

121 *British Railway engine drivers*: Desmond Hackett, *Table Tennis Topics*, May 1961.

122 *we'll have to have a coffee*: Dunn, interview.

122 *British sense of fair play*: Brownell, *Training the Body for China*, 291.

122 *Even though Major Gagarin*: 'Sidelights on the Table Tennis Meet,' *China Reconstructs*, June 1961.

122 *When are we going*: Foster, interview.

123 *in his own home*: 'My Boy Chaung Tse-tung, By His Mother, Le Chung-Ju,' *China Reconstructs*, June 1961.

123–24 *didn't know a thing about table tennis*: Author interview with Xu Yinsheng, 4 May 2011.

124 *no fleet worth speaking of*: Suyin, *Eldest Son*, 292.

124 *a sweat pit*: 'So Gentle Jap Rocks Diane,' *Daily Express*, 14 April 1961.

124 *big brother loud-speaker*: 'Chinese Crackers As They Win the Swaythling Cup,' *Daily Express*, 10 April 1961.

124 *every shot against the Japanese*: Guoqi, *Olympic Dreams*, 71.

124 *It was genuine happiness*: Author interview with Yao Zhenxu, 9 November 2011.

124 *China was champion of the world*: 'Chinese Crackers As They Win the Swaythling Cup.'

124 *technician flashed the stadium's lights*: Ibid.

125 *reverberated to the banging of drums*: Author interview with Shen Ji Chang, 7 November 2011.

125 *Everyone stood up to clap in his honour*: Dunn, interview.

125 *Zhou Enlai hosted a good-bye party*: Chargé d'Affaires in Peking to Alec Douglas-Home, FO 371/158437.

125 *reelected without any other nominations*: 'Behind the Championships,' *Table Tennis*, May 1961.

125 *China's fledglings*: Hua Wen, 'New Horizons for Table Tennis,' *China Reconstructs*, June 1961.

Chapter 25 | Fallout

126 *not entirely negligible fillip*: Chargé d'Affaires in Peking to Alec Douglas-Home, letter, undated (presumably April 1961), FO 371/158437, National Archives, Kew, UK.

126 *the great roar of China*: 'Cheering Chinese Hail Harrison the Great,' *Daily Express*, 6 April 1961.

126 *a lotus blossom drop*: 'Chinese Silent As Harrison Slams Russia,' *Daily Express*, 7 April 1961.

126 *no room for doubt*: *Daily Mirror*, 7 April 1961.

127 *and failed to find a single pub*: 'Play? It's All Work for the Chinese,' *Daily Mirror*, 3 May 1961.

127 *seem to be well within*: 'The Three Generals Leading China,' *Daily Worker*, 20 April 1959.

127 *the swollen faces*: Suyin, *My House Has Two Doors*, 373.

127 *no scruples in shattering world peace*: *Times of India*, 20 April 1961.

127 *Almost all the people in their fifties*: 'People Behind the Bamboo Curtain,' *New York Times*, 30 July 1961.

128 *weighed every pig and chicken*: Author interview with Herbert Levin, 5 October 2012.

128 *a genuine democrat*: *Sydney Morning Herald*, 23 April 1961.

128 *the number of American advisers*: Less than twenty Americans had been killed in Vietnam by May 1962. It was still thought of as a 'great continuing war game' (Sheehan, *Bright Shining Lie*, 58).

Chapter 26 | Heroes of the Nation

129 *down the back of people's trousers*: Author interview with Zhuang Jiafu, 10 November 2011.

129 *good luck to touch the world champion*: Author interview with Zhuang Xieling, May 2011.

130 *to tour Guinea, Mali, Ghana*: Chi-wen, *Sports Go Forward in China*, 50.

130 *also happened to be the minister of defence*: 'They Tip Ghana as Future Champs,' *Ghanaian Times*, 16 May 1962.

130 *was propelled into the air*: Ti Chiang Hua, 'In Peking: A Sports Horror,' Emily Wang, translator, *Free China Review*, 1 January 1986.

130 *the Mao suits would have to be returned*: Chen, *One in a Billion*, 185.

131 *were immediately suspended*: 'Peking's Envoys Ousted by Tunis,' *New York Times*, 24 September 1967.

131 *he was the crowd favourite*: 'Complete Oriental Domination,' *Table Tennis*, May 1965.

131 *a contingent of forty*: Dick Miles, 'No Defence against Murder,' *Sports Illustrated*, 5 May 1969.

131–32 *otherwise elusive government leaders*: Yaping, *From Bound Feet*, 100.

132 *The only guests*: Author interview with Qiu Zhonghui, 4 May 2011.

132 *a visit to one's own family*: Suyin, *My House Has Two Doors*, 212.

132 *small wooden twin beds*: Ibid.

132 *these special little meatballs*: Qiu Zhonghui, interview.

132 *close to both forests*: Zhisui, *Private Life of Chairman Mao*, 174.

132 *kept her feet covered with rubber shoes*: Ibid.

133 *danced alone in place*: Lescot, *Before Mao*, 285.

133 *accused of favouring a turn to the right*: Suyin, *Eldest Son*, 202.

133 *the leader of world revolution*: Shuman, 'Elite Competitive Sport in the People's Republic of China 1958–1966,' 22.

133 *already famous for his part*: 'New Era in Asian Sports History,' *China Reconstructs*, January 1967.

Chapter 27 | Spreading the Gospel

135 *was known for his fanatical love*: Jojima, *Ogi*, 201.

136 *Ogi lunched with Zhou Enlai*: Ogimura, *Ichiro Ogimura in Legend*, 165.

136 *There's another reason*: Jojima, *Ogi*, 202.

136 *That's why I want you*: Ibid.

137 *and fallen to his knees*: Ibid., 204–5.

137 *The Japanese were humiliated*: Ibid., 201–8.

137 *Flowers sometimes bloom*: David Wilson to David Timms, letter, 4 June 1964, FO 371/175966, National Archives, Kew, UK.

138 *I never thought anyone*: Author interview with Xu Yinsheng, 4 May 2011.

138 *not read anything so good for years*: Mao Zedong, 'Comment on the Article

Notes

"How to Play Table Tennis" by Comrade Xu Yingsheng,' *Selected Works of Comrade Mao Tse-Tung*, http://www.marxists.org/reference/archive/mao/selected-works/volume-9/mswv9_46.htm.

138 *Mao made everyone read Xu Yinsheng*: Author interview with Shen Ji Chang, 7 November 2011.

138 *To rely entirely on the team*: Hsu Yin-Sheng (Xu Yinsheng), 'On How to Play Table Tennis,' *Editorial Board of China's Sports*, 1964.

139 *dwelled on the failures*: Rice, *Mao's Way*, 185–86.

139 *In the middle of the room*: Author interview with Han Zhicheng, 8 November 2011.

Chapter 28 | The Grinding Halt

140 *If others attack me*: Domes, *Peng Te-huai*, 94.

141 *Only the lightness of traffic*: Chang, *Wild Swans*, 288.

142 *because the purpose of the training*: 'Sports Education,' *China Reconstructs*, April 1962, 40.

142 *Every restaurant's opened its doors*: Author interview with Xi Enting, 6 May 2011.

143 *at the forced pace*: Heng and Shapiro, *Son of the Revolution*, 101.

143 *their battered travel bags*: Xi Enting, interview.

143 *a man in a three-cornered hat*: Jojima, *Ogi*, 214.

143 *phlegm and saliva*: Ibid., 215.

143 *classic European composers*: Ibid.

143 *Even the hillsides of China*: Anthony Grey, 'Hostage in Peking,' *Reader's Digest*, January 1971.

144 *the crowd seemed to respond*: Jojima, *Ogi*, 216.

144 *you had to go along with it*: Author interview with Qi Da Zheng, 8 November 2011.

144 *they tied Mao slogans to their table tennis nets*: Shih Pen-shan (as told to Lester Velie), 'I Fought in Red China's Sports War,' *Reader's Digest*, June 1967.

144 *You may be able to help me now*: Jojima, *Ogi*, 217.

144 *Ogi sat silently thinking*: Ogimura, *Ichiro Ogimura in Legend*, 171.

Chapter 29 | Under Pressure

145 *Soldiers wept as the Chairman*: Heng and Shapiro, *Son of the Revolution*, 123–24.

145 *high jumpers held up the Little Red Book*: Shih Pen-shan (as told to Lester Velie), 'I Fought in Red China's Sports War,' *Reader's Digest*, June 1967.

146 *I followed the Red Guards*: Author interview with Liang Geliang, 5 May 2011.

146 *The local doctor had diagnosed her*: Ibid.

147 *forced themselves into Zhuang's house*: Ibid.

147 *they busied themselves writing*: Ibid.

147 *pointed interest in who*: Yan and Gao, *Turbulent Decade*, 262.

296

Notes

Chapter 30 | House of Cards

148 *Jiang called He Long a traitor*: Suyin, *Phoenix Harvest*, 74.

148 *more than 1000 confidential documents*: Salisbury, *Long March*, 331.

148 *beaten regularly*: Suyin, *Phoenix Harvest*, 68.

149 *a sure process of medical murder*: Salisbury, *Long March*, 331.

149 *ignorant children*: Suyin, *Phoenix Harvest*, 81.

149 *why don't you go and fight*: Suyin, *Eldest Son*, 345.

149 *Dealt with as counter-revolutionary*: Ibid., 336.

150 *The necklace was a personal touch*: Chang and Halliday, *Mao*, 551.

150 *he suffered a minor heart attack*: Wenqian, *Zhou Enlai*, 175.

150 *were rumoured to have defected*: William Cunningham interview with William Brown, William J Cunningham Papers.

151 *led by an ageing Zhu De*: Yuan, *Born Red*, 194.

151 *who had dared to declare himself*: Salisbury, *Long March*, 336.

151 *sports system was suddenly accused*: Zhiyi, *Champion's Dignity*, chap. 8.

151 *dragged their Ping-Pong tables*: Author interview with Qing Jiang, 3 May 2011.

151 *was made to stand up*: Author interview with Zheng Minzhi, 3 May 2011.

152 *Every now and then we'd be ordered*: Author interview with Xi Enting, 6 May 2011.

Chapter 31 | Death to the Doubters

153 *I felt like a piece of bamboo*: Author interview with Xi Enting, 6 May 2011.

153 *The more honour you'd brought*: Author interview with Dong Jinxia, 5 May 2011.

154 *the position of a swimmer*: Anthony Grey, 'Hostage in Peking,' *Reader's Digest*, January 1971.

154 *to collude with the enemy*: Ti Chiang Hua, 'In Peking: A Sports Horror,' Emily Wang, translator, *Free China Review*, 1 January 1986.

154 *yin-yang head*: Xi Enting, interview.

154 *When you're in the truck*: Ibid.

155 *hung over a tree branch*: Jicai, *Ten Years of Madness*, 7.

155 *duck swims on dry land*: Ibid., 183.

155 *Beaten by team-mates*: Yan and Gao, *Turbulent Decade*, 263.

155 *humiliated and slapped*: Author interview with Liang Youneng, 7 November 2011.

155 *emblazoned with a Japanese flag*: Yan and Gao, *Turbulent Decade*, 262.

156 *Though she was only thirty-five*: Jinxia, *Women, Sport and Society in Modern China*, 76.

156 *Rong Guotuan is dying*: Author interview with Qiu Zhonghui, 4 May 2011.

156 *I checked his neck*: Ibid.

156 *I am not a spy*: Yan and Gao, *Turbulent Decade*, 263.

157 *I felt miserable*: 'Cultural Revolution Villain or Victim? Zhuang Pleads His Case Forty Years On,' *The Times* (London), 17 February 2007.

157 *Katz had been arrested*: Miles, *Dangerous Otto Katz*, 9.

157 *We'll bury you*: Ibid., 16.

Notes

157 *Katz had been jailed*: Ibid., 18.
158 *on all points of indictment*: Ibid., 303.
158 *the longest ever handed down*: '42 Year Sentence – Longest Ever Known in Britain,' *Daily Worker*, 4 May 1961.
158 *a breach of hospitality*: 'March Row,' *Daily Express*, 13 July 1962.
158 *the game with the little white ball*: Quoted in *Table Tennis*, April 1966. Originally published in German in *Deutscher Tischtennis Sport*.

Chapter 32 | Down to the Country

159 *could influence many people*: Hong and Weikang, *Apocalypse of Pingpong*.
159 *promoting revisionist policy*: Jarvie, Hwang, and Brennan, *Sports, Revolution and the Beijing Olympics*, 88.
160 *the right hand grasped*: Hong and Weikang, *Apocalypse of Pingpong*.
160 *They ended up in Shanxi*: Author interview with Wang Ding Hua, 8 November 2011.
160 *art of the grenade toss*: 'Athletes in the Countryside,' *China Reconstructs*, September 1971.
160 *In truth, they depended*: Chen, *One in a Billion*, 81.
160 *a table tennis net from straw and leaves*: Author interview with Zheng Mingzhi, November 2011.
161 *she vomited at his feet*: Ti Chiang Hua, 'In Peking: A Sports Horror,' Emily Wang, translator, *Free China Review*, 1 January 1986.

Chapter 33 | The World at War

165 *Thanks to new satellite televison technology*: Smith, *Moondust*, 177.
165 *peaceful coexistence*: 'Peaceful coexistence' was a loaded term in China, an echo of Soviet terminology and Zhou Enlai's speech in 1955 in which he'd tried to construct a separate space for countries to cohere around China away from the US and Russia. To use it in reaching out to America was a further slap in the face to the Soviets.
166 *would shout insults*: Tyler, *Great Wall*, 48.
166 *It was a calculated attack*: Ibid., 48–50.
166 *the smashing of windows*: Kissinger, *White House Years*, 172.
167 *China was everyone's problem*: Ibid.
167 *challenge to Khrushchev's bid*: Zhisui, *Private Life of Chairman Mao*, 270–71.
167 *exploring rapprochement with the Chinese*: Nixon to Kissinger, memo, 1 February 1969.
167 *the whole of China could be underground*: Author interview with Seymour Topping, 27 April 2011.
167 *massive nuclear strikes*: Tyler, *Great Wall*, 61.
167 *diplomats seldom venture*: Sydney Liu, 'Watching Russia's China Watcher,' *Newsweek*, 21 July 1969.
168 *We have the Soviet Union to the north*: Zhisui, *Private Life of Chairman Mao*, 514.
169 *the longest continual talks*: Kissinger, *White House Years*, 684.

Notes

169 *so compromised electronically*: Pratt, *China Boys*, 58.

169 *Mao ordered two hydrogen bomb tests*: Tyler, *Great Wall*, 73.

170 *the ambassador would come in*: Author interview with Winston Lord, 16 December 2011.

170 *China lifted a restriction*: Tyler, *Great Wall*, 81.

170 *In a wide-ranging interview*: Snow, *Long Revolution*, 10.

170 *must be working for the CIA*: Zhisui, *Private Life of Chairman Mao*, 532.

170 *We thought he was a Communist propagandist*: Henry Kissinger, speech, 1997, the United Nations, New York, NY, transcript, William J Cunningham Papers.

170 *nothing to do but wait*: Kissinger, *White House Years*, 704.

171 *We hadn't heard anything*: Lord, interview.

171 *The only mention of table tennis*: 'Table Tennis Players from Vietnam,' *China Reconstructs*, February 1971, 43.

171 *fresh from the battlefront*: Ibid.

171 *Intrepid Fighters against the US*: Ibid.

171 *That same month*: Vincent Canby, 'Bob Hope, Comedic Master and Entertainer of Troops, Dies at 100,' *New York Times*, 28 July 2003.

172 *working in woodchip factories*: Author interview with Xu Shaofa, 3 May 2011.

Chapter 34 | The Seeds of Peace

173 *target for US bombing raids*: Itoh, *Origin of Ping-Pong Diplomacy*, 49.

173 *Ogi had immediately fired off a telegram*: Jojima, *Ogi*, 228.

173 *This liquor has a high alcohol content*: Ibid., 231.

173 *Suppose we were to send a team*: Ibid., 232.

174 *immediately banged his head*: Ibid., 234.

174 *had been sent to their deaths*: Ogimura, *Ichiro Ogimura in Legend*, 172.

175 *suddenly, in January 1971*: The invitation was delivered by Ogimura. The two men had never liked each other. Back in 1954, when Ogimura had seized the World Championship in London, Goto had led the team. He'd singled out Ogimura for criticism before they'd left Japan, calling him particularly ungracious and ordering him to practise smiling.

175 *Goto's second trip to China*: Itoh, *Origin of Ping-Pong Diplomacy*, 46.

175 *On his flight to Beijing*: Ibid., 91.

176 *Montagu's astonishing clout*: Evans, *Coloured Pins on a Map*, 22. Once, during the 1953 World Championships in Bucharest, two English women evaded their chaperones and meandered freely through the streets. They came back to their hotel, where they shared their adventures with the rest of the team. They had seen beggars behind the Iron Curtain. Evans overheard Montagu calling them liars and chastising them for spreading undiplomatic rumours. According to Evans, beggars in Bucharest were imprisoned for the remainder of the championships.

176 *applications have not been received*: 'They Still Swing a Mean Bat,' *Sports Illustrated*, 12 April 1971.

176 *the best thing Zhou could do*: Though Evans liked to take credit for what was about to happen, a year later he would write in an introduction to Tim

Boggan's self-published *Ping-Pong Oddity*, 'I am convinced that the Chinese did exactly what the Chinese planned to do.'

177 *A group from the Ministry*: Author interview with Xu Shaofa, 3 May 2011.

177 *What were they supposed to say*: Author interview with Zheng Mingzhi, November 2011.

177 *to prepare for death*: Author interview with Wang Ding Hua, 8 November 2011.

177 *We should be prepared to lose*: Zhaohui Hong and Yi Sun, 'The Butterfly Effect and the Making of Ping-Pong Diplomacy,' *Journal of Contemporary China* 9, no. 25 (2000): 429–48.

Chapter 35 | Long Hair, Light Heart

178 *We were crew-cut kids*: Author interview with Keith Cowan, 29 June 2011.

178 *won the next seventeen*: 'Move Over, Aunt Mildred – Sandpaper Paddles Are OUT,' *Los Angeles Times*, 11 July 1971.

178 *His father put a table*: Cowan, interview.

178 *on an uneven floor*: 'Opening Volley,' *Sports Illustrated*, 11 June 2008.

178 *This small white ball I hit*: Tim Boggan, 'In Memoriam,' *USA Table Tennis*, 2004.

179 *It belonged to Cowan's future mentor*: Tim Boggan, Review of 'Sizzling Chops,' *USATT News*, 15 January 2002.

179 *playing poker with men*: Yosi Zakarin, *Family Pong: A Table Tennis History of the Zakarin Family (1965–1983)*, http://yzakarin.tripod.com/Family_Pong_Part_1.pdf.

179 *skid row type locations*: Chris Faye, 'At McGoo's,' *Table Tennis Topics*, September–October 1970, 7.

179 *if you've got to do swimming*: Glenn Cowan, appearance on *Dinah's Place*, 25 May 1971.

179 *After high school*: 'Table Tennis Whiz to Try Outdoor Courts,' *Los Angeles Times*, 28 July 1966.

179 *died abruptly*: 'Opening Volley.'

180 *a small florist business*: Cowan, interview.

180 *over a hundred trophies*: David Davis, 'Broken Promise,' *Los Angeles Magazine*, 1 August 2006.

180 *El Mongol, a not-so-famous wrestler*: Boggan, *History of US Table Tennis*, Vol. VI, 106.

181 *raised her funds at a high school*: Author interview with Judy Bochenski, 9 August 2012.

181 *semi-retired engineering executive*: 'Player Almost Ruled Out by His Long Hair,' *Los Angeles Times*, 13 April 1971.

181 *recognised the derisive tone*: Boggan, *Ping-Pong Oddity*, chap. 1.

181 *there were no expectations*: Author interview with Tim Boggan, 18 November 2010.

182 *How the fuck were we going*: Ibid.

182 *from the hotel to the Aichi Gymnasium*: Boggan, *Ping-Pong Oddity*.

182 *The Chinese entered*: Boggan, interview.

182 *hadn't provided him*: Boggan, *History of US Table Tennis, Vol. VI*, chap. 10.

Notes

182 *reading copies of Ogimura's books*: 'Nagoya Worlds,' *Table Tennis Topics*, May–June 1971.

183 *out of a spaceship*: Boggan, interview.

Chapter 36 | Could the Great Wall Crumble?

184 *chosen a decorated air force*: Jiang, *Small Ball Spins the Big Ball*.

184 *rejoin the international family*: Author interview with Zheng Minzhi, 10 November 2011.

184 *Among the advance party*: Author interview with Liang Youneng, 7 November 2011.

184 *as the team tried to sleep*: Author interview with Xi Enting, 6 May 2011.

185 *To ensure their safety*: Chuang Tse-Tung, 'Friendship First, Competition Second,' *China Reconstructs*, September 1971.

185 *a handful of Japanese Communists*: Once Coach Liang was sure that he saw an anti-China protester being paid at the end of a demonstration: 'He had been shouting at us, and then he smiled at me. I didn't worry so much after that.'

185 *two patriotic films*: The plot revolves around a small group of Chinese villagers inspired to fight against the occupying Japanese after witnessing the invaders burn villages to the ground. See http://en.wikipedia.org/wiki/Tunnel_War.

185 *20 million civilians*: Clodfelter, *Warfare and Armed Conflicts*, 956.

185 *We all stood and started*: Xi Enting, interview.

186 *Ogimura seemed bemused*: Ibid.

186 *The radio commentator*: Jiang, *Small Ball Spins the Big Ball*, chap. 7.

186 *Those that rolled left or right*: Peyrefitte, *The Chinese*, 275.

186 *except for a cartoon*: Xi Enting, interview.

187 *was about to step away*: Author interview with Liang Geliang, 5 May 2011.

187 *puppets of US imperialism*: Boggan, *History of US Table Tennis*, Vol. VI, chap. 10.

187 *pure strategy, devised a month before*: Zhaohui Hong and Yi Sun, 'The Butterfly Effect and the Making of Ping-Pong Diplomacy,' *Journal of Contemporary China* 9, no. 25 (2000): 429–48.

Chapter 37 | A Measured Coincidence

188 *I was invited actually*: Glenn Cowan, appearance on *Dinah's Place*, 25 May 1971.

188 *It was really weird*: Boggan, *Ping-Pong Oddity*, chap. 5.

188 *I know all this*: Ibid.

189 *orders had been strict*: Zhaohui Hong and Yi Sun, 'The Butterfly Effect and the Making of Ping-Pong Diplomacy,' *Journal of Contemporary China* 9, no. 25 (2000): 429–48.

189 *the naïve smile on his face*: 'Opening Volley,' *Sports Illustrated*, 11 June 2008.

189 *he was willing to go against*: Interview with Zhuang Zedong for the US–China International Exchange Programme, September 2007, http://www.youtube.com/watch?v=s7VE26-Qs1A.

190   *I went to a warehouse*: Ibid.

190   *very carefully graded*: Author interview with Herbert Levin, 12 October 2012.

190   *always decided in advance*: Little had changed since England's first mission to Beijing back in 1793. The Englishman Lord McCartney noted how all his men were given the lowliest of gifts – small pieces of cloth. It was worse than he knew: they were actually re-gifted from a Korean tribute.

191   *increase from three to five times*: Guoqi, *Olympic Dreams*, 131.

191   *the idea had been discarded*: Itoh, *Origin of Ping-Pong Diplomacy*, 141. While it's a lovely idea, I have found no evidence to support this claim other than its inclusion in Jiang, *Small Ball Spins the Big Ball*.

192   *gave me a big hug*: Zhuang Zedong, 'The Small Ball Pushes Forward the Big Ball: Going to Peace Harmoniously,' speech, USC US–China Institute, Los Angeles, CA, 25 September 2007.

192   *one of the most remarkable gifts*: Kissinger, *White House Years*, 709.

Chapter 38 | An Invitation Home

193   *general secretary*: Chen, *One in a Billion*, 116.

193   *Song had previously worked*: Jiang, *Small Ball Spins the Big Ball*, chap. 2.

193   *if he could finagle*: Rufford Harrison, interview, 16 November 1977, transcript, Box 19, National Archive on Sino-American Relations, University of Michigan, Ann Arbor, MI.

193   *iron hand in a velvet glove*: Author interview with Rufford Harrison, 7 April 2011.

194   *the pinko-commie bastards*: Ibid.

194   *long inured to the Chinese*: Graham Steenhoven, interview, transcript, Box 20, National Archive on Sino-American Relations, University of Michigan, Ann Arbor, MI.

194   *He'd noted that the quality*: Rufford Harrison, 'A Meeting Is a Meeting Is a . . . ,' *Table Tennis Topics*, July–August 1971.

194   *I heard you Chinese people*: Jiang, *Small Ball Spins the Big Ball*.

195   *Song Zhong was really like a spy*: Author interview with Qian Jiang, 3 November 2011.

195   *one of their female players*: Author interview with Xu Yinsheng, 4 May 2011.

195   *Glad to meet you*: Qian Jiang, interview.

195   *only if it was 'progressive'*: 'Ping-Pong Diplomacy,' China through a Lens, 8 July 2004, http://www.china.org.cn/english/features/olympics/100660.htm.

195   *never gambles – without four aces*: Snow, *Long Revolution*, 184.

196   *having taken the pills*: Chang and Halliday, *Mao*, 602–3.

196   *emergency message arrived*: According to my interview with Tim Boggan, he had been told by Zhuang Zedong that Mao had called Zhuang Zedong directly.

196   *Considering the fact that*: Zhaohui Hong and Yi Sun, 'The Butterfly Effect and the Making of Ping-Pong Diplomacy,' *Journal of Contemporary China* 9, no. 25 (2000): 429–48.

196   *insists the message*: Tim Boggan, 'Ping-Pong Diplomacy's Reunion in

Beijing,' 2005, http://www.bumpernets.com/store/index.php?option=com_content&view=article&id=53&Itemid=70-.

196 *At 10.45am*: Rufford Harrison, interview by William Cunningham, 14 June 1999, transcript, tape 2, 1, William J Cunningham Papers.

197 *How would you respond*: Harrison, interview.

197 *'Don't worry,' said Song*: Harrison, interview, National Archive on Sino-American Relations.

197 *"everybody-goes-to-China"*: Harrison, interview by Cunningham, tape 2, 3.

197 *out shopping with his wife*: Ibid., tape 2, 10.

197 *with administrative matters*: Steenhoven, interview, National Archive on Sino-American Relations.

197 *he was livid*: Harrison, interview by Cunningham, tape 2, 9.

198 *rather horrible people*: Harrison, interview.

Chapter 39 | Surprise

199 *the story of the year*: Rufford Harrison, interview by William Cunningham, 14 June 1999, transcript, tape 1, 3, William J Cunningham Papers.

200 *Twelve Americans spent*: Kahn, *China Hands*, 103.

200 *Sometimes they'd play Ping-Pong*: Carter, *Mission to Yan'an*, 41.

200 *favoured anything starring*: Author interview with Seymour Topping, 27 April 2011.

200 *to make* The Great Dictator: 'The Fears of a Clown,' *The Guardian*, 11 October 2002.

200 *Dixie Mission be made permanent*: Carter, *Mission to Yan'an*, 99.

200 *the world's worst leadership*: Topping, *On the Front Lines*, 47.

200 *illiterate, peasant son of a bitch*: Kahn, *China Hands*, 82.

201 *code name was* ALBATROSS: Carter, *Mission to Yan'an*, 131.

201 *the weakness of the American foreign policy*: 'China Hands,' US Diplomacy, http://www.usdiplomacy.org/history/service/history_chinahands. php.

201 *a school friend of Chen Yi's*: Kahn, *China Hands*, 117.

201 *to posts as incongruous*: Ibid., 10.

201 *was a 'wasteland' that came*: Ibid., 275.

201 *guerilla warfare may continue*: Ibid., 191.

201 *closer to astrophysics*: Author interview with Robert Oxnam, 11 February 2011.

201 *any time the PRC gained*: Conversation between Alan Carter and Bill Cunningham, audiotape, William J Cunningham Papers.

202 *the United States is open*: William J Cunningham, interview, Frontline Diplomacy series, Library of Congress, Washington, DC.

202 *Tell them we know*: William J Cunningham, interview, 17 March 1997, Foreign Affairs Oral History Collection, Association for Diplomatic Studies and Training, Arlington, VA.

202 *you've gone awfully far*: Cunningham, interview, Frontline Diplomacy series.

202 *I haven't the slightest idea*: William J Cunningham, audiotape, recorded June 1988, William J Cunningham Papers.

Notes

Chapter 40 | Decisions to Be Made

203 *barricaded in his hotel room*: William J Cunningham, interview, 17 March 1997, Foreign Affairs Oral History Collection, Association for Diplomatic Studies and Training, Arlington, VA.

203 *pounding down his door*: Author interview with William J Cunningham, 12 May 2012.

203 *rebuilt his question*: Cunningham, interview, Foreign Affairs Oral History Collection.

204 *in a windowless room*: Graham Steenhoven, interview, transcript, Box 20, National Archive on Sino-American Relations, University of Michigan, Ann Arbor, MI.

204 *the only thing he had control*: Ibid.

204 *We were all nincompoops*: Author interview with Tim Boggan, 18 November 2010.

204 *pigtails, satin pyjamas*: Steenhoven, interview, National Archive on Sino-American Relations.

204 *quick breakfast of beer*: Rufford Harrison, 'A Meeting Is a Meeting Is a . . . ,' *Table Tennis Topics*, July–August 1971.

205 *like everyone's grandpa*: Author interview with William J Cunningham, 23 May 2012.

205 *had he seen Glenn Cowan*: Author interview with Rufford Harrison, 7 April 2011.

205 *who were these fellows?*: Herbert Levin, interview by William Cunningham, 13 May 2006, transcript, William J Cunningham Papers.

205 *Never call a Chinese*: Rufford Harrison, interview, 16 November 1977, transcript, Box 19, National Archive on Sino-American Relations, University of Michigan, Ann Arbor, MI.

205 *young Californian*: Rufford Harrison, interview by William Cunningham, 14 June 1999, transcript, tape 2, 17, William J Cunningham Papers.

205 *Steenhoven's first worry*: Harrison, interview.

Chapter 41 | The Worries

207 *There was no avoiding the media*: Author interview with Rufford Harrison, 7 April 2011.

207 *He carried four cameras*: Boggan, *Ping-Pong Oddity*, chap. 8.

208 *a fairy godmother*: US Department of State, 'Invitation to US Table Tennis Team.'

208 *To Steenhoven's relief*: Eckstein, 'Ping Pong Diplomacy.'

208 *going to look like an asshole*: Author interview with Tim Boggan, 18 November 2010.

208 *Gusikoff called him back*: Boggan, *Ping-Pong Oddity*, chap. 6.

208 *Don't worry, baby*: Ibid., chap. 7.

208 *flushed the last of his stash*: Ibid., chap. 6.

209 *he could play chess*: Author interview with Dell Sweeris, 15 June 2011.

209 *giving him a blow job*: Boggan, interview.

209 *being dressed down by his captain*: Boggan, *Ping-Pong Oddity*, chap. 7.

209 *guy's still on something*: Boggan, interview.

Notes

210 *given explicit directions*: Boggan, *Ping-Pong Oddity*, chap. 8.

210 *there was music*: Author interview with Judy Bochenski, 9 August 2012.

210 *Am I going to come out*: George and Madeline Buben, interview, transcript, Box 19, National Archive on Sino-American Relations, University of Michigan, Ann Arbor, MI.

210 *crossed the border*: NARA College Park, RG 59, SNF 1970–73, Entry 1613 POL CHINCOM US, Box 2188, National Archives, Washington, DC.

210 *hit the front page*: 'GI Toll in Week at 9-Month High,' *New York Times*, 9 April 1971.

211 *China's quiet surge*: 'China Is Quietly Renewing an Active Role in Africa,' *New York Times*, 9 April 1971.

211 *life is simple*: Boggan, *Ping-Pong Oddity*, chap. 8.

211 *playing chess against himself*: Ibid.

211 *one of the best books*: Ibid.

212 *fear that they would be torn*: Rufford Harrison, interview by William Cunningham, 14 June 1999, transcript, William J Cunningham Papers.

212 *a vat of vomit*: Boggan, *Ping-Pong Oddity*, chap. 9.

212 *tried to get on bikes*: John Tannehill, interview, transcript, Box 19, National Archive on Sino-American Relations, University of Michigan, Ann Arbor, MI.

212 *The only way we could stop*: Ibid.

212 *there was only the usual*: 'Chinese Greet Americans with Smiles and Curiosity,' *New York Times*, 12 April 1971.

212 *whistling at the girls*: Tannehill, interview, National Archive on Sino-American Relations.

213 *stoned to death*: Boggan, *Ping-Pong Oddity*, chap. 9.

213 *crept into officials' offices*: Author interview with Xu Shaofa, 3 May 2011.

213 *Roderick was among*: 'China Has Made Huge Gains in 25 Years, Newsman Finds,' *Los Angeles Times*, 19 April 1971.

214 *Early on, he heard one player*: 'China: A Whole New Ballgame for Newsmen,' *Washington Post*, 16 April 1971.

214 *He thought they were going*: Boggan, *Ping-Pong Oddity*, chap. 9.

214 *muscled aside Roderick*: Ibid., chap. 10.

214 *the Harlem Globetrotters*: Ibid.

214 *making small speeches of thanks*: Ibid.

214 *stream of oncoming Mongolian ponies*: 'Americans Visit Great Wall,' *New York Times*, 13 April 1971.

215 *Cowan thought that the country*: Boggan, *Ping-Pong Oddity*, chap. 10.

215 *Tannehill taped a silk-screen*: Ibid., chap. 11.

216 *don't leave me here!*: Ibid.

216 *rolled past him in a wheelchair*: Tannehill, interview, National Archive on Sino-American Relations.

216 *From his sick bed*: John Roderick, 'Chinese Tact Lets U.S. Lose Gracefully,' *New York Times*, 14 April 1971.

216 *What else was he supposed to do*: Graham Steenhoven, interview, transcript,

Box 20, National Archive on Sino-American Relations, University of Michigan, Ann Arbor, MI.

Chapter 43 | All Eyes on America

217 *grander than Madison Square Garden*: 'The Play and the Meals Are Tough on US Team,' *New York Times*, 12 April 1971.
217 *the ailing Tannehill*: John Roderick, 'Chinese Tact Lets U.S. Lose Gracefully,' *New York Times*, 14 April 1971.
217 *The interpreter just smiled*: Graham Steenhoven, interview, transcript, Box 20, National Archive on Sino-American Relations, University of Michigan, Ann Arbor, MI.
217 *a twist-like shuffle*: 'Mao's Thoughts Greet English Sports Team,' *The Times* (London), 14 April 1971.
218 *the timing of the applause*: Guoqi, *Olympic Dreams*, 137.
218 *Steenhoven listened as laughter*: Steenhoven, interview, National Archive on Sino-American Relations.
218 *Eight hundred million people*: Boggan, *Ping-Pong Oddity*, chap. 11.
218 *probably being reeducated*: Roderick, 'Chinese Tact Lets US Lose Gracefully.'
219 *Hippies aren't rude*: Boggan, *Ping-Pong Oddity*, chap. 12.
219 *Had you ever seen an American before?*: Ibid.
220 *big bulky chairs*: Steenhoven, interview, National Archive on Sino-American Relations.
220 *A chagrined Canadian player*: 'Canada's Ping-Pongers Admit Political Use Made of China Trip,' *Globe and Mail* (Toronto), 19 April 1971.
220 *was quite the tea party*: Joe Schlesinger, 'What China's Ping-Pong Diplomacy Taught Us,' *CBC News* (Canada), 11 April 2011.
220 *What joy it is*: Boggan, *Ping-Pong Oddity*, chap. 12.
220–21 *the first person in purple*: 'Chou and "Team Hippie" Hit It Off,' *New York Times*, 15 April 1971.
221 *also the rest of the Americans*: Ibid.
221 *more time with Cowan*: Ibid.
221 *could have been a top executive*: Steenhoven, interview, National Archive on Sino-American Relations.

Chapter 44 | Tension

222 *his forgotten toothbrush*: George and Madeline Buben, interview, transcript, Box 19, National Archive on Sino-American Relations, University of Michigan, Ann Arbor, MI.
223 *his long-haired hippie*: Boggan, *Ping-Pong Oddity*.
223 *racquets as teething tools*: Graham Steenhoven, interview, transcript, Box 20, National Archive on Sino-American Relations, University of Michigan, Ann Arbor, MI.
223 *extremely upset*: Department of State, telegram, 16 April, NARA RG59, Entry 1613 CUL 16 US Box 382-20120924-1071, National Archives, Washington, DC.

223 *The great leader Chairman Mao*: Ibid.

223 *very special treatment*: John Tannehill, interview, transcript, Box 19, National Archive on Sino-American Relations, University of Michigan, Ann Arbor, MI.

224 *was the exact antithesis*: Ibid.

224 *Get some yellow paint*: Ibid.

224 *behaved very properly*: Ibid.

224 *Look, this is silly*: Boggan, *Ping-Pong Oddity*, chap. 12.

224 *Steenhoven finally silenced him*: Author interview with Tim Boggan, 18 November 2010.

225 *'I was getting into the chickens'*: Boggan, *Ping-Pong Oddity*, chap. 14.

225 *he'd smuggled drugs*: Tannehill, interview, National Archive on Sino-American Relations.

225 *Why the hell do you keep talking*: Boggan, *Ping-Pong Oddity*, chap. 14.

225 *Dick Miles interviewed Tannehill*: Ibid.

225 *an art form of stupefying boredom*: Kissinger, *White House Years*, 779.

226 *Boggan estimated*: Boggan, *Ping-Pong Oddity*, chap. 15.

226 *There are the vultures*: Ibid.

226 *Chinese had carefully analyzed each member*: Embassy in Kabul to Department of State, telegram, 19 May 1971, NARA RG59, Entry 1613 POL CHICOM-USSR, Box 2192, National Archives, Washington, DC.

226 *cameras and elbows in our faces*: Author interview with Judy Bochenski, 9 August 2011.

226 *ordered the consulate*: William J. Cunningham, interview, Frontline Diplomacy series, Library of Congress, Washington, DC.

226 *'No repeat no contacts'*: Department of State to FBI/CIA/Joint State/DIA/Justice, telegram, 16 April 1971, NARA RG56, Entry 1613: SNF 1970–73, CUL 16 US, National Archives, Washington, DC.

227 *Cunningham looked at Steenhoven*: Cunningham, notes to author, 29 April 2013.

227 *Was Steenhoven working for the CIA?*: William Cunningham, audiotape, recorded June 1988, William J Cunningham Papers.

227 *'Our kids will just be delighted'*: Mrs Cunningham does not remember calling Steenhoven 'Fred,' only explaining to their children that he was 'an uncle from home travelling around Asia.' Cunningham, notes to author.

227 *Cunningham didn't want*: Cunningham, notes to author.

227 *unsophisticated youth*: Department of State, telegram, 19 April 1971, NARA RG56, Entry 1613: SNF 1970–73, CUL 16 US, National Archives, Washington, DC.

227 *Zhou Enlai told me*: Cunningham, audiotape, June 1988.

227 *Sometimes, one single event*: Ross and Changbin, *Re-examining the Cold War: US–China Diplomacy, 1954–1973*, 344.

227 *conscious if limited diplomatic initiative*: 'US Table Tennis Team to Visit China for the Week,' *New York Times*, 8 April 1971.

227 *For the first time ever*: Zhaohui Hong and Yi Sun, 'The Butterfly Effect and the Making of Ping-Pong Diplomacy,' *Journal of Contemporary China* 9, no. 25 (2000): 429–48.

Notes

Chapter 45 | Nixon's Game

228 *recovering from a serious bout*: Kissinger, *White House Years*, 739.

228 *rose at 3.30am*: Holdridge, *Crossing the Divide*, 53.

228 *herself so high-ranking*: Kissinger, *White House Years*, 793.

228 *every line had a symbolic meaning*: Boggan, *Ping-Pong Oddity*, chap. 15.

228 *Lord secured his position*: Author interview with Winston Lord, 16 December 2011.

229 *toward the end of a ranging conversation*: Richard Nixon, conversation, April 8, 1971, 9.18am to 10.07am, conversation no. 475-16B, www.nixontapes.org, http://bit.ly/fUyLIb.

229 *I had never expected*: David Davis, 'Broken Promise,' *Los Angeles Magazine*, 1 August 2006.

229 *screwed up all these back channel plans*: Jan Berris, speech, Chinese Consulate, New York, NY, 28 August 2012.

229 *learned to play Ping-Pong*: Tyler, *Great Wall*, 91.

229 *The last time the game*: Steve Grant, *Ping-Pong Fever*, 28, quoting *Waterloo Times-Tribune*, 23 May 1902.

230 *Be sure we get the tone*: Richard Nixon, conversation, 13 April 1971, 10.16am to 10.21am, conversation no. 001-076, www.nixontapes.org.

230 *US did not understand*: NARA College Park, RG 59, SNF 1970–73, Entry 1613 POL CHINCOM US, Box 2188, National Archives, Washington, DC.

230 *made big show of demonstrating*: Ibid.

230 *He facetiously told*: Ibid.

230 *Nixon was seeking reassurance*: Richard Nixon, conversation, 16 April 1971, 11.22pm to 11.27pm, conversation no. 001-119, www.nixontapes.org.

231 *the Jane Fondas of the world*: Lord, interview.

231 *was overheard explaining that*: NARA College Park, RG 59, SNF 1970–73, Entry 1613 POL CHINCOM US, Box 2188, National Archives.

231 *a propaganda beating*: 'Agnew Sees China Visit as Propaganda Defeat for US,' *Los Angeles Times*, 20 April 1971.

231 *veterans marched on Washington*: Robbins, *Against the Vietnam War*, 31.

231 *contact with the Chinese was finally re-established*: Kissinger, *White House Years*, 713.

231 *anxiety that had dated*: Ibid., 714.

232 *reaffirms its willingness*: Ibid.

232 *the mystery man*: Tyler, *Great Wall*, 107.

232 *preferably at some location*: Kissinger, *White House Years*, 725.

233 *The first question*: Winston Lord to Henry Kissinger, memo, 29 July 1971, National Security Archives, White House, Washington, DC.

233 *You saw just throwing a Ping-Pong ball*: MacMillan, *Nixon and Mao*, 198.

Notes

Chapter 46 | Political Ping-Pong

234 *the lead item on television*: Richard Nixon, conversation, 14 April 1971, 8.05pm to 812pm, conversation no. 001-091, www.nixontapes.org.

234 *As Nixon would soon write*: MacMillan, *Nixon and Mao*, 262.

234–35 *You would get the Taiwan seat now*: Chang and Halliday, *Mao*, 604.

235 *It is extremely difficult to capture*: Henry Kissinger to Richard Nixon, memo, 14 July 1971, Foreign Relations of the United States, 1969–1976, Volume E-13, Documents on China, 1969–1972, Document 9, http://history.state.gov/historicaldocuments/frus1969-76ve13/d9.

235 *'With this move by the Chairman'*: MacMillan, *Nixon and Mao*, 203.

235 *In his mother's house*: Author interview with William Cunningham, 23 May 2012.

235 *exquisite nerve twitching*: Department of State, telegram, 14 April 1971, NARA RG59, Entry 1613 CUL 16 US Box 382-20120924-1071, National Archive, Washington, DC.

235 *threw the barber out of his office*: Armin Meyer, interview by William Cunningham, 18 May 2006, William J Cunningham Papers.

235 *Nixon's tiny loop*: Herbert Levin, interview by William Cunningham, 13 May 2006, transcript, William J Cunningham Papers.

236 *tons of equipment*: MacMillan, *Nixon and Mao*, 208.

236 *State Department's official record*: McGregor, *The Party*, 20.

236 *rat running across the street*: Tyler, *Great Wall*, 57.

236 *Hoxha, Albania's dictator*: MacMillan, *Nixon and Mao*, 158.

237 *'I saw you were right'*: Tyler, *Great Wall*, 133.

237 *Later that night he confided*: MacMillan, *Nixon and Mao*, 284.

237 *had played a huge role*: Speech, 28 August 2012, Chinese Consulate, New York, NY.

237 *an instrument of subversion*: Shih Pen-shan (as told to Lester Velie), 'I Fought in Red China's Sports War,' *Reader's Digest*, June 1967.

Chapter 47 | Return Game

241 *pulled out a piece of paper*: Author interview with Marcia Burick, 28 March 2011.

242 *Bandit Table Tennis*: Department of State, telegram, 13 April 1971, NARA RG59, National Archives, Washington, DC.

242 *attention-seeking projects*: Carl McIntire, 'What Is the Difference between Capitalism and Communism?' http://www.carlmcintire.org/booklets-capitalismVcommunism.php.

242 *had been given a list of talking points*: Department of State to Henry Kissinger, memo, April 20, 1971, NARA RG59, National Archives, Washington, DC.

243 *not the turn for the officials*: Author interview with Zheng Mingzhi, November 2011.

243 *a brassy version*: English-language CCTV documentary, Central Newsreel and Documentary Film Studio, People's Republic of China, September 1972.

243 *professor from Columbia*: Jose Yglesias, 'Chinese Ping-Pong Players vs. the Press: Love All,' *New York Times*, 14 May 1972.

243 *check for explosive devices*: 'Detroit Gives Subdued Welcome to China's Table Tennis Team,' *Los Angeles Times*, 13 April 1972.

243 *Each member of the Chinese delegation*: Ruth Eckstein, 'Ping Pong Diplomacy: A View from Behind the Scenes,' report, 16 April 1990, William J Cunningham Papers.

244 *kind of awkward*: Author interview with Perry Link, 19 April 2011.

244 *everyone carried a gun*: Author interview with Li Furong, May 2011.

244 *of the American consumer society*: 'Detroit Gives Subdued Welcome to China's Table Tennis Team.'

244 *combination of different people*: Author interview with Liang Geliang, 5 May 2011.

244 *extraordinarily quick to feel condescension*: Link, interview.

244 *an act of 'coldness'*: Eckstein, 'Ping Pong Diplomacy.'

245 *Don't you find it ironic*: Yglesias, 'Chinese Ping-Pong Players vs. the Press: Love All.'

245 *spectacular kind of sport*: *Wide World of Sports*, ABC TV, April 1972.

245 *Send us our POWs*: Eckstein, 'Ping Pong Diplomacy.'

245 *had a red coat on it*: Boggan, *Grand Tour*, chap. 2.

245 *didn't want to take a chance*: Ibid.

245 *a motherfucking racist bastard*: Author interview with Tim Boggan, 18 November 2012.

245 *Sweeris over George Brathwaite*: John Tannehill, interview, transcript, Box 19, National Archive on Sino-American Relations, University of Michigan, Ann Arbor, MI.

246 *Hitler Killed Jews*: Author interview with Judy Bochenski, 9 August 2012.

246 *How do you like American food*: Boggan, *Grand Tour*, chap. 2.

Chapter 48 | Capital Performance

247 *served by candlelight*: English-language CCTV documentary, Central Newsreel and Documentary Film Studio, People's Republic of China, September 1972.

247 *thought it was beautiful*: Author interview with Zheng Huaiying, 10 November 2011.

247 *Every morning, when Edwards*: Vee-ling Edwards, interview, transcript, Box 19, National Archive on Sino-American Relations, University of Michigan, Ann Arbor, MI.

248 *stood up in a Virginia restaurant*: 'Chinese Team Arrives in DC,' *Washington Post*, 17 April 1972.

248 *Home on the Range*: 'Bless the Beasts and the Ping-Pong Players,' *Los Angeles Times*, 19 April 1972.

248 *Merrily, merrily, merrily*: Edwards, interview, National Archive on Sino-American Relations.

248 *Would you believe it!*: Jose Yglesias, 'Chinese Ping-Pong Players vs. the Press: Love All,' *New York Times*, 14 May 1972.

248 *Kill Mao!*: Author interview with Jan Berris, 13 March 2011.

Notes

248 *bought a block of seats*: Bob Kaminsky, interview, transcript, Box 19, National Archive on Sino-American Relations, University of Michigan, Ann Arbor, MI.

248 *heckled the team*: Ruth Eckstein, 'Ping Pong Diplomacy: A View from Behind the Scenes,' report, 16 April 1990, William J. Cunningham Papers.

248 *inscrutable and imperturbable*: Yglesias, 'Chinese Ping-Pong Players vs. the Press: Love All.'

249 *called out the National Guard*: 'Bombs on Hanoi; Explosions at Home,' *New York Times*, 23 April 1972.

249 *as rock-throwing student groups*: '200 Are Arrested Near White House,' *New York Times*, 16 April 1972.

249 *White House was surrounded*: Author interview with Rory Hayden, 12 June 2011.

249 *Rose Garden was in bloom*: 'Chinese Team Greeted by President,' *New York Times*, 19 April 1972.

249 *the first group from the People's Republic*: 'Chinese Team Arrives in DC.'

249 *the course of your contest*: Boggan, *Grand Tour*, chap. 5.

249 *Come enter the free world!*: Author interview with Zhuang Xielin, 6 May 2011.

249 *the American way of doing things*: Author interview with Li Furong, May 2011.

250 *didn't know you were here*: Boggan, *Grand Tour*, chap. 5.

250 *I wondered who you were*: Yglesias, 'Chinese Ping-Pong Players vs. the Press: Love All.'

250 *It was awful*: Author interview with Marcia Burick, 28 March 2011.

250 *the bombing of Haiphong*: Author interview with Perry Link, 19 April 2011.

250 *we'd like you to come*: Edwards, interview, National Archive on Sino-American Relations.

Chapter 49 | United Nations

251 *accompanied by circling helicopters*: Vee-ling Edwards, interview, transcript, Box 19, National Archive on Sino-American Relations, University of Michigan, Ann Arbor, MI.

251 *more than two hundred*: 'China Table Tennis Lights Up Cole Field House,' *Washington Post*, 17 April 1972.

251 *followed the Chinese bus*: Jan Berris, speech, 28 August 2012, Chinese Consulate, New York, NY.

251 *weren't interested in covering the American*: Author interview with Marcia Burick, 28 March 2011.

252 *cause more countries*: Lijuan, *He Zhenliang*, 235.

252 *world headquarters of Holiday Inn*: Jose Yglesias, 'Chinese Ping-Pong Players vs. the Press: Love All,' *New York Times*, 14 May 1972.

253 *this grand design*: Edwards, interview, National Archive on Sino-American Relations.

253 *their antebellum costumes*: Burick, interview.

253 *reminder of the Vietnam war*: Yglesias, 'Chinese Ping-Pong Players vs. the Press: Love All.'

253 *a dolphin named Peppy*: Herman Wong, 'Chinese Players Turn from Table Tennis to Fun,' *Los Angeles Times*, 26 April 1972.

253 *were greeted by Mickey Mouse*: 'Disneyland Shatters Chinese Stoic Calm,' *Los Angeles Times*, 27 April 1972.

253 *swirling giant teacups*: 'China's Ping-Pong Team Gets Warm Disney Welcome,' *Los Angeles Times*, 26 April 1972.

253 *large, fat man standing right there*: Author interview with Doug Spelman, 20 March 2011.

253 *the middle of a mystery*: Boggan, *Grand Tour*, chap. 8.

254 *not a golfer among them*: Author interview with Zhuang Xielin, 6 May 2011.

254 *We don't have peasants*: Rufford Harrison, interview by William Cunningham, 14 June 1999, transcript, tape 3, 14–15, William J Cunningham Papers.

254 *interpreter spoke no Spanish*: English-language CCTV documentary, Central Newsreel and Documentary Film Studio, People's Republic of China, September 1972.

254 *with a sacred song*: Ruth Eckstein, 'Ping Pong Diplomacy: A View from Behind the Scenes,' report, 16 April 1990, William J. Cunningham Papers.

255 *the majority of Americans*: Alexander Eckstein, Letter to the Editor, *New York Times*, 20 August 1972.

255 *Do you know what a "sacrifice" is*: Burick, interview.

Chapter 50 | The Hippie Opportunist

256 *at least Cowan was still representing*: Graham Steenhoven, interview, transcript, Box 20, National Archive on Sino-American Relations, University of Michigan, Ann Arbor, MI.

256 *I could mediate*: Boggan, *Ping-Pong Oddity*, chap. 15.

256 *being cold-shouldered*: Department of State to Henry Kissinger, memo, NARA RG59, National Archives, Washington, DC.

257 *turn into a money-maker*: 'Move Over, Aunt Mildred – Sandpaper Paddles Are OUT,' *Los Angeles Times*, 11 July 1971.

257 *asked to shoot a pilot*: 'A Ping-Pong Star's Get-Rich Plans,' *Business Week*, 8 May 1971.

257 *a hippie opportunist*: Boggan, *Ping-Pong Oddity*, chap. 1.

257 *We're so proud of you*: Glenn Cowan, appearance on *Dinah's Place*, NBC, 25 May 1971.

258 *followed by a reporter*: *Table Tennis Topics*, July–August 1971.

258 *interviewed by Barbara Walters*: Author interview with Judy Bochenski, 9 August 2012.

258 *He'd be invited onto talk shows*: John Tannehill, interview, transcript, Box 19, National Archive on Sino-American Relations, University of Michigan, Ann Arbor, MI.

258 *Orange County Teen-Age Fair*: 'Variety Feature at Teen Fair,' *Los Angeles Times*, 7 July 1971.

258 *judging a fashion show*: 'Show Staged on Bicycles,' *Los Angeles Times*, 20 September 1971.

259 *he was caught on film swearing*: Boggan, *History of US Table Tennis, Vol. VI*, chap. 11.

259 *bipolar and schizophrenic*: David Davis, 'Broken Promise,' *Los Angeles Magazine*, 1 August 2006.

259 *Russian spies planting stuff*: Author interview with Keith Cowan, 29 June 2011.

259 *Pot was his thing*: 'Opening Volley,' *Sports Illustrated*, 11 June 2008.

259 *he had freaked out*: Ibid.

259 *declared bankruptcy*: Tannehill, interview, National Archive on Sino-American Relations.

260 *the toughest guy*: Author interview with Sandy Lechtick, 26 June 2011.

260 *nothing in the world*: 'Opening Volley.'

260 *you've got to give up*: Cowan, interview.

260 *he sold shoes*: Ibid.

260 *attempt at a comeback*: Davis, 'Broken Promise.'

260 *asking about an ivory carving*: Author interview with Qian Jiang, 2 May 2011.

261 *Cowan had had to explain who he was*: Boggan, *Ping-Pong Oddity*, chap. 15.

261 *After China, everything seemed*: Davis, 'Broken Promise.'

261 *what the Paris peace talks*: Ibid.

261 *When I die*: Boggan, *History of US Table Tennis, Vol. VI*, chap. 24.

Chapter 51 | The Heights

262 *an anonymous building*: 'Cultural Revolution Villain or Victim? Zhuang Pleads His Case Forty Years On,' *The Times* (London), 17 February 2007.

262 *murmuring niceties*: William Johnson, 'Gentle Tigers of the Tables,' *Sports Illustrated*, April 1972.

262 *treated Bush to a long harangue*: Bush, *China Diary*, 211.

262 *I like the man*: Bush, *China Diary*, 60.

263 *red flags fluttered*: 'Peking Cheers US Victors; AAU Stars May Not Try,' *New York Times*, 28 May 1975.

263 *meditating by the side*: 'China Plans a Leap Forward in Track and Field,' *New York Times*, 8 June 1975.

263 *Chairman Mao approached*: Author interview with Zheng Minzhi, 10 November 2011.

264 *until later in the year*: Ibid.

264 *omnipresent shadows*: Chen, *One in a Billion*, 68.

Chapter 52 | The Costs

265 *dragging carts of manure*: Susan Brownell, 'Globalisation Is Not a Dinner Party,' paper presented at Conference on Globalisation and Sport in Historical Context, University of California, San Diego, March 2005.

265 *decadent bourgeois habits*: Chen, *One in a Billion*, 73.

265 *receiving blood transfusions*: Zhisui, *Private Life of Chairman Mao*, 593.

265 *overseeing all sports*: Lijuan, *He Zhenliang*, 131. Deng Xiaoping was put in charge of all sports work in January 1974.

Notes

265   *main rival in the race*: 'Zhuang Zedong,' *Newsweek China*, 3 June 2011.

266   *only one centre of power*: Reuters, 'Ping-Pong Diplomat Left Out in the Cold,' 7 August 2008.

266   *where he was filmed playing*: Witke, *Comrade Chiang Ch'ing*, 400.

266   *become Jiang's 'cat's paw'*: 'Table Tennis Champ Loses in Politics,' *Los Angeles Times*, 14 December 1976.

266   *was a huge honour*: 'Cultural Revolution Villain or Victim? Zhuang Pleads His Case Forty Years On,' *The Times* (London), 17 February 2007.

266   *beaten around the head*: Ibid.

267   *didn't know whether to laugh*: Susan Brownell, 'A Look Back at the Tangshan Earthquake and the Montreal Olympics,' The China Beat blog, 14 May 2008, http://thechinabeat.blogspot.com/2008/05/look-back-at-tangshan-earthquake-and.html, quoting from the censored material in the English edition of He Zhenliang's memoir.

267   *most miserable victim*: Kai Chen, *My Way*, New Tang Dynasty TV, 2009, http://www.youtube.com/watch?v=Yh_OH3KSwUE&list=PL540F8E044E B115C&index=10.

267   *You keep on having to wake people up*: Ivor Montagu, interview, London Broadcasting Corporation, September 1976.

267   *When he said "Bite," I bit*: MacMillan, *Nixon and Mao*, 281.

267   *paraded on the streets*: Heng and Shapiro, *Son of the Revolution*, 264.

267   *forced to appear*: 'Table Tennis Champ Loses in Politics.'

268   *a fascist dictatorship*: 'Purge of Chiang China and Three Other Chinese Leaders Being Extended to the Culture and Sports Agencies,' *New York Times*, 7 December 1976.

268   *spending five peaceful minutes*: Author interview with Marcia Burick, 28 March 2011.

268   *in a cramped room*: 'Cultural Revolution Villain or Victim?'

268   *not allowed to play table tennis*: Reuters, 'Ping-Pong Diplomat Left Out in the Cold.'

268   *The book taught me to hope*: 'Cultural Revolution Villain or Victim?'

268   *He was exiled to Shanxi*: Zedong, *Deng Xiaoping Approved Our Marriage*, 18.

269   *a lifetime in second place*: Author interview with Liang Youneng, 7 November 2011.

269   *he had turned down*: Author interview with Xu Shaofa, 3 May 2011.

269   *against all three*: Ibid.

269   *caused anybody to die*: 'Zhuang Zedong.'

269   *sparring partner*: *Table Tennis Topics*, November–December 1972.

269   *Tan found himself in Macau*: Shih Pen-shan (as told to Lester Velie), 'I Fought in Red China's Sports War,' *Reader's Digest*, June 1967. Shih Pen-shan is an alias confirmed to be used by Tan Cho Lin by both Tim Boggan (author interview, 18 November 2010) and Graham Steenhoven (interview, transcript, Box 20, National Archive on Sino-American Relations, University of Michigan, Ann Arbor, MI).

269   *an ancient scooter*: J. D. Ratcliff, 'Out through the Bamboo Curtain,' *Reader's Digest*, August 1966.

269   *not be included in any friendly matches*: *Table Tennis Topics*, November–December 1972.

270 *keep him company*: *Table Tennis Topics*, September–October 1973.

270 *we need to find a bigger room*: Author interview with anonymous source.

270 *Zhuang Zedong was allowed*: Author interview with Qian Jiang, 3 May 2011.

270 *The midnight shadows*: Author interview with Liang Geliang, 5 May 2011.

271 *not with Zhuang Zedong*: Youneng, interview.

271 *seemed cool to him*: Tim Boggan, 'Ping-Pong Diplomacy's Reunion in Beijing,' 2006, http://www.bumpernets.com/store/index.php?option=com_content&view=article&id=53&Itemid=70.

271 *Cowan's mother wept*: Ibid.

272 *Can you imagine*: 'China's Ping-Pong Diplomat, Zhuang Zedong,' October 2009, http://en.showchina.org/03/audio/200910/t429748.htm.

272 *be funding his ongoing treatments*: Patrick Tan, 'Zhuang Zedong Struggling against Cancer,' 19 September 2012, http://tabletennista.com/2012/9/zhuang-zedong-struggling-against-cancer-ph/.

272 *often ignored Zhuang*: Author interview with anonymous source.

272 *list of Zhuang's hospital visitors*: China News Agency, 15 October 2012, http://www.chinanews.com/shipin/cnstv/2012/10-15/news107658.shtml.

272 *The Cold War*: Elaine Woo, 'Zhuang Zedong Dies at 72,' *Los Angeles Times*, 12 February 2013.

272 *the whole country won*: 'China's Pingpong Diplomat, Zhuang Zedong.'

Epilogue

273 *a weapon for peace*: Ivor Montagu, 'The Task of the Sportsmen for Peace,' undated, Box 3.4, Montagu Collection, Labour History Archive and Study Centre, Manchester, UK.

274 *Few men have achieved*: C. M. Woodhouse, Book Review, *TLS*, 9 July 1970.

274 *told more lies*: 'Red Ping-Pong Blue,' *The Observer*, 7 June 1970.

274 *the squad to London Zoo*: 'The Chinese Tour,' *Table Tennis*, January 1972.

274 *pottering about*: 'Ivor Goldsmid Samuel Montagu,' *Oxford Dictionary of National Biography*, http://www.oxforddnb.com/view/printable/31459.

274–75 *the only one of his relatives*: Author interview with Nicole Montagu, 7 July 2011.

275 *so many injustices*: Ibid.

275 *never forget Ivor Montagu*: Author interview with Yao, 9 November 2011.

Selected Bibliography

Books

Andrew, Christopher. *The Defence of the Realm*. London: Penguin, 2010.

Auden, WH and Christopher Isherwood. *Journey to a War*. New York: Paragon House, 1990.

Becker, Jasper. *Hungry Ghosts: Mao's Secret Famine*. New York: Owl Books, 1998.

Belden, Jack. *China Shakes the World*. New York: Monthly Review Press, 1970.

Benton, Gregor, and Lin Chun, eds. *Was Mao Really a Monster?* New York: Routledge, 2010.

Bergmann, Richard. *Twenty-One Up*. London: Sporting Handbooks, 1950.

Bo, Ma. *Blood Red Sunset: A Memoir of the Chinese Cultural Revolution*. New York: Viking, 1995.

Boggan, Tim. *History of U.S. Table Tennis, Vol. VI: 1970–1973*. Self-published, 2006.

———. *History of US Table Tennis, Vol. V: 1971–1975*. Self-published, 2005.

———. *The Grand Tour*. Self-published, 1972.

———. *Ping-Pong Oddity*. Self-published, 1971.

Bosshardt, RA *The Restraining Hand*. London: Hodder & Stoughton, 1936.

Braun, Otto. *A Communist Agent in China, 1932–1939*. Stanford, CA: Stanford University Press, 1982.

Brownell, Susan. *Training the Body for China: Sports in the Moral Order of the People's Republic*. Chicago: University of Chicago Press, 1995.

Burr, William, ed. *The Kissinger Transcripts: The Top-Secret Talks with Beijing and Moscow*. New York: New Press, 1998.

Bush, George HW. *The China Diary of George H. W. Bush: The Making of a Global President*. Princeton, NJ: Princeton University Press, 2008.

———. *All the Best, George Bush: My Life in Letters and Other Writings*. New York: Scribner, 1999.

Cao, Guanlong. *The Attic: Memoir of a Chinese Landlord's Son*. Berkeley: University of California Press, 1996.

Carr, EH. *Twilight of the Comintern, 1930–1935*. New York: Pantheon, 1982.

Selected Bibliography

Carter, Carolle J. *Mission to Yan'an: American Liaison with the Chinese Communists, 1944–1947.* Lexington: University Press of Kentucky, 1997.

Chang, Jung. *Wild Swans: Three Daughters of China.* New York: Touchstone, 2003.

Chang, Jung and Jon Halliday. *Mao: The Unknown Story.* London: Jonathan Cape, 2005.

Charyn, Jerome. *Sizzling Chops and Devilish Spins: Ping-Pong and the Art of Staying Alive.* New York: Four Walls Eight Windows, 2002.

Chen, Kai. *One in a Billion: Journey toward Freedom.* Bloomington, IN: Authorhouse, 2007.

Clark, Ronald. *J.B.S.: The Life and Work of JBS Haldane.* Oxford: Oxford University Press, 1968.

Clodfelter, Micheal. *Warfare and Armed Conflicts: A Statistical Reference to Casualty and Other Figures, 1500–2000.* Vol. 2. Jefferson, N.C.: McFarland, 2002.

Cowan, Glenn. *The Book of Table Tennis: How to Play the Game.* New York: Grosset & Dunlap, 1972.

Crayden, Ron. *The Story of Table Tennis: The First 100 Years.* Hastings, UK: Battle Instant Print, 1995.

Crossman, Richard, ed. *The God That Failed: Six Studies in Communism.* New York: Columbia University Press, 2001.

de Beauvoir, Simone. *The Long March: An Account of Modern China.* London: Phoenix Press, 2001.

Dikötter, Frank. *Mao's Great Famine: The History of China's Most Devastating Catastrophe, 1958–1962.* New York: Walker & Co., 2010.

Ding Shu De, Zhu Qing Zuo, Wang Lian Fang, and Yuan Hai Lu. *The Chinese Book of Table Tennis: The Definitive Book on Techniques and Tactics from the World's Top Table Tennis Nation.* New York: Atheneum, 1981.

Domes, Jürgen. *Peng Te-huai: The Man and the Image.* Stanford, CA: Stanford University Press, 1985.

Ebon, Martin. *The Soviet Propaganda Machine.* New York: McGraw-Hill, 1987.

Estes, Dana. *A Little Book of Ping-Pong Verse.* Boston: Colonial Press, 1902.

Evans, Roy. *Coloured Pins on a Map: Around the World with Table Tennis.* Cardiff, UK: Aureus, 1997.

Foote, Alexander. *Handbook for Spies.* Darke County, OH: Coachwhip Books, 2011.

Grant, Steve. *Ping-Pong Fever: The Madness That Swept 1902 America.* Self-published, 2012.

Guillemin, Jeanne. *Biological Weapons: From the Invention of State-Sponsored Programmes to Contemporary Terrorism.* New York: Columbia University Press, 2004.

Guoqi, Xu. *Olympic Dreams: China and Sports, 1895–2008.* Cambridge, MA: Harvard University Press, 2008.

Guttman, Allen. *Games and Empires: Modern Sports and Cultural Imperialism.* New York: Columbia University Press, 1994.

Hahn, Emily. *China Only Yesterday: 1850–1950, A Century of Change.* Garden City, NY: Doubleday, 1963.

Haldane, Charlotte. *Truth Will Out.* New York: Vanguard Press, 1950.

Haynes, John Earl and Harvey Klehr. *Venona: Decoding Soviet Espionage in America.* New Haven, CT: Yale University Press, 1999.

Selected Bibliography

Henderson, Jon. *The Last Champion: The Life of Fred Perry*. London: Yellow Jersey Press, 2009.

Heng, Liang and Judith Shapiro. *Son of the Revolution*. London: Fontana, 1988.

Holdridge, John H. *Crossing the Divide: An Insider's Account of Normalisation of US–China Relations*. Lanham, MD: Rowman and Littlefield, 1997.

Hong, Guan and Huang Weikang. *Apocalypse of Pingpong: Zhuang Zedong in the Culture Revolution*. Nanjing: Jiangsu Art Publishing House, 1986.

Hua, Huang. *Memoirs*. Beijing: Foreign Language Press, 2008.

Hung, Chang-tai. *Mao's New World: Political Culture in the Early People's Republic*. Ithaca, NY: Cornell University Press, 2011.

International Table Tennis Federation. *ITTF Handbook*. Baden, Switzerland: International Table Tennis Federation, 1937.

Itoh, Mayumi. *The Origin of Ping-Pong Diplomacy: The Forgotten Architect of Sino–US Rapprochement*. New York: Palgrave Macmillan, 2011.

Jackson, John. *Ping-Pong to China*. Melbourne: Sun Books, 1971.

Jacobson, Howard. *The Mighty Walzer*. London: Vintage, 2000.

Jarvie, Grant, Dong-Jhy Hwang, and Mel Brennan. *Sports, Revolution and the Beijing Olympics*. Oxford, UK: Berg, 2008.

Jiang, Qian. *Small Ball Spins the Big Ball: Behind the Curtain of Pingpong Diplomacy*. Beijing: Dongfang Publishing, 1997.

Jicai, Feng. *Ten Years of Madness: Oral Histories of China's Cultural Revolution*. San Francisco: China Books, 1996.

Jinxia, Dong. *Women, Sport and Society in Modern China: Holding Up More Than Half the Sky*. London: Frank Cass, 2003.

Jisheng, Yang. *Tombstone: The Great Chinese Famine 1958–1962*. New York: Farrar, Straus and Giroux, 2012.

Kahn, EJ *The China Hands: America's Foreign Service Officers and What Befell Them*. New York: Viking Press, 1975.

Kissinger, Henry. *On China*. New York: Penguin, 2011.

———. *White House Years*. Boston: Little, Brown, 1979.

Kolatch, Jonathan. *Is the Moon in China Just as Round? Sporting Life and Sundry Scenes*. New York: Jonathan David, 1992.

———. *Sports, Politics and Ideology in China*. New York: Jonathan David, 1972.

Lescot, Patrick. *Before Mao: The Untold Story of Li Lisan and the Creation of Communist China*. New York: HarperCollins, 2004.

Levine, Naomi. *Politics, Religion and Love: The Story of H. H. Asquith, Venetia Stanley and Edwin Montagu*. New York: New York University Press, 1991.

Li, Charles N. *The Bitter Sea: Coming of Age in a China before Mao*. New York: HarperCollins, 2008.

Liang, Lijuan, *He Zhenliang and China's Olympic Dream*. Beijing: Foreign Language Press, 2007.

Liu, Peter (Liu Naiyuan). *Mirror: A Loss of Innocence in Mao's China*. Bloomington, IN: Xlibris, 2001.

Lung, Ho (He Long). *Democratic Tradition of the Chinese People's Liberation Army*. Beijing: Foreign Language Press, 1965.

Macintyre, Ben. *Operation Mincemeat: How a Dead Man and a Bizarre Plan Fooled the Nazis and Assured an Allied Victory*. New York: Harmony Books, 2010.

Selected Bibliography

MacMillan, Margaret. *Nixon and Mao: The Week That Changed the World*. New York: Random House, 2008.

Mann, James. *About Face: A History of America's Curious Relationship with China, from Nixon to Clinton*. New York: Vintage, 2000.

Masterman, JC. *The Double-Cross System in the War of 1939 to 1945*. New York: Avon Books, 1972.

McGilligan, Patrick. *Alfred Hitchcock: A Life in Darkness and Light*. New York: HarperCollins, 2010.

McGregor, Richard. *The Party: The Secret World of China's Communist Rulers*. New York: HarperCollins, 2010.

Miles, Jonathan. *The Dangerous Otto Katz: The Many Lives of a Soviet Spy*. New York: Bloomsbury, 2010.

Montagu, Ewen. *The Man Who Never Was: World War II's Boldest Counterintelligence Operation*. Annapolis, MD: US Naval Institute Press, 2001.

———. *Beyond Top Secret Ultra*. New York: Coward, McCann and Geoghegan, 1978.

Montagu, Ivor. *With Eisenstein in Hollywood*. New York: International Publishers, 1974.

———. *The Youngest Son*. London: Lawrence and Wishart, 1970.

———. *Film World*. London: Pelican Books, 1964.

———. *Land of Blue Sky*. London: Camelot Press, 1956.

———. *East–West Sports Relations*. London: National Peace Council, 1951.

Montefiore, Simon Sebag. *Stalin: The Court of the Red Tsar*. London: Weidenfeld & Nicolson, 2003.

Morris, Andrew D. *Marrow of the Nation: A History of Sport and Physical Culture in Republican China*. Berkeley, CA: University of California Press, 2004.

Nai'an, Shi and Luo Guanzhong. *All Men Are Brothers*. Pearl Buck, trans. New York: Moyer Bell, 2006.

Ogimura, Ichiro. *Ichiro Ogimura in Legend*. Tokyo: Takkyu Okoku, 2009.

Palmer, James. *Heaven Cracks, Earth Shakes: The Tangshan Earthquake and the Death of Mao's China*. New York: Basic Books, 2012.

Peyrefitte, Alain. *The Collision of Two Civilisations: The British Expedition to China 1792–4*. London: Harvill, 1993.

———. *The Chinese: Portrait of a People*. New York: Bobbs-Merrill, 1977.

Philby, Kim. *My Silent War: The Autobiography of a Spy*. New York: Modern Library, 2002.

Pięta, Wiesław. *Table Tennis among Jews in Poland (1924–1949)*. Częstochowy, Poland: Stowarzyszenie Przyjaciół Gaude Mater, 2009.

Pratt, Nicholas. *China Boys: How U.S. Relations with the PRC Began and Grew*. Washington, DC: Vellum Books, 2009.

Reid, Philip. *Victor Barna*. Suffolk, UK: Eastland Press, 1974.

Rice, Edward. *Mao's Way*. Berkeley: University of California Press, 1974.

Riordan, James and Robin Jones. *Sport and Physical Education in China*. London: ISCPES, 1999.

Robbins, Mary Susannah, ed. *Against the Vietnam War: Writings by Activists*. Syracuse, NY: Syracuse University Press, 1999.

Ross, Robert S and Jiang Changbin, eds. *Reexamining the Cold War: US-China Diplomacy, 1954–1973*. Cambridge, MA: Harvard University Press, 2001.

Salisbury, Harrison E. *The Long March: The Untold Story*. New York: Harper & Row, 1985.

Schneider, Laurence, ed. *Lysenkoism in China: Proceedings of the 1956 Qingdao Genetics Symposium*. New York: M. E. Sharpe, 1986.

Sheehan, Neil. *A Bright Shining Lie: John Paul Vann and America in Vietnam*. New York: Vintage Books, 1989.

Shih, Chi-wen. *Sports Go Forward in China*. Beijing: Foreign Language Press, 1963.

Smedley, Agnes. *The Great Road: The Life and Times of Chu Teh*. New York: Monthly Review Press, 1956.

———. *Battle Hymn of China*. New York: Alfred A. Knopf, 1943.

Smith, Andrew. *Moondust: In Search of the Men Who Fell to Earth*. London: HarperPerennial, 2005.

Snow, Edgar. *The Long Revolution*. New York: Vintage, 1973.

———. *Red China Today*. New York: Vintage, 1971.

———. *Red Star Over China*. New York: Grove, 1968.

Snow, Helen Foster. *Inside Red China*. New York: Da Capo Books, 1979.

Spence, Jonathan D. *Mao Zedong*. New York: Lipper/Penguin, 1999.

———. *To Change China: Western Advisers in China*. New York: Penguin, 2002.

———. *The Gate of Heavenly Peace: The Chinese and Their Revolution, 1895–1980*. New York: Penguin Books, 1982.

Starobin, Joseph. *Paris to Peking*. New York: Cameron Associates, 1955.

Su, Yang. *Collective Killings in Rural China during the Cultural Revolution*. Cambridge, UK: Cambridge University Press, 2011.

Sues, Ilona Ralf. *Shark's Fins and Millet*. Boston: Little, Brown and Company, 1944.

Suyin, Han. *Eldest Son: Zhou Enlai and the Making of Modern China, 1898–1976*. New York: Kodansha International, 1995.

———. *The Crippled Tree*. London: Triad Grafton, 1989.

———. *My House Has Two Doors*. London: Triad Grafton, 1988.

———. *Phoenix Harvest*. London: Triad Grafton, 1986.

Swann, Brenda and Francis Aprahamian, eds. *JD Bernal: A Life in Science and Politics*. New York: Verso, 1999.

Syed, Matthew. *Bounce: Mozart, Federer, Picasso, Beckham and the Science of Success*. New York: HarperCollins, 2010.

Tien-min, Li. *Chou En-lai*. Republic of China: Institute of International Relations, 1970.

Topping, Seymour. *On the Front Lines of the Cold War: An American Correspondent's Journal from the Chinese Civil War to the Cuban Missile Crisis and Vietnam*. Baton Rouge: Louisiana State University Press, 2010.

———. *Journey between Two Chinas*. New York: Harper & Row, 1972.

Tyler, Patrick. *A Great Wall: Six Presidents and China: An Investigative History*. New York: PublicAffairs, 2000.

Uehara, Hisae, Motoo Fujii, and Koji Oribe. *Ogi's Dream*. Tokyo: Takkyu Okoku, 2006.

Van Bottenburg, Maarten. *Global Games*. Chicago: University of Illinois Press, 2001.

Vogel, Ezra F. *Deng Xiaoping and the Transformation of China*. Cambridge, MA: Harvard University Press, 2011.

Wenqian, Gao. *Zhou Enlai: The Last Perfect Revolutionary*. New York: PublicAffairs, 2007.

West, Nigel. *Venona: The Greatest Secret of the Cold War*. London: HarperCollins, 1999.

Whitson, William and Chen-hsia Huang. *The Chinese High Command: A History of Communist Military Politics, 1927–71*. New York: Praeger, 1973.

Winchester, Simon. *Bomb, Book and Compass*. London: Viking, 2008.

Witke, Roxanne. *Comrade Chiang Ch'ing*. Boston: Little, Brown, 1977.

Worden, Minky, ed. *China's Great Leap: The Beijing Games and the Olympian Human Rights Challenges*. New York: Seven Stories Press, 2008.

Wright, Patrick. *Passport to Peking: A Very British Mission to Mao's China*. Oxford, UK: Oxford University Press, 2010.

Wu, Ningkun and Yikai Li. *A Single Tear*. Boston: Back Bay Books, 1993.

Xiao, Xiaoda. *The Visiting Suit: Stories from My Prison Life*. Columbus, OH: Two Dollar Radio, 2010.

Xinran. *China Witness: Voices from a Silent Generation*. New York: Anchor Books, 2010.

Yan, Jiaqi and Gao Gao. *Turbulent Decade: A History of the Cultural Revolution*. Daniel W. Y. Kwok, trans. Honolulu, HI: University of Hawaii Press, 1996.

Yaping, Deng. *From Bound Feet to Olympic Gold in China: The Case of Women's Table Tennis*. Beijing: Beijing Publishing House, 2004.

Yu, Siao. *Mao Tse-tung and I Were Beggars*. Syracuse, NY: Syracuse University Press, 1959.

Yuan, Gao. *Born Red: A Chronicle of the Cultural Revolution*. Stanford, CA: Stanford University Press, 1987.

Zedong, Zhuang. *Deng Xiaoping Approved Our Marriage*. People's Republic of China: Red Flag Press, 1991.

Zhisui, Li. *The Private Life of Chairman Mao*. New York: Random House, 1994.

Zhiyi, He. *A Champion's Dignity*. Guangdong, China: Guangdong People's Publishing House, 2009.

Archives

British Library Newspaper Archive, Colindale, UK.

Imperial War Museum Archives (IWM), London.

Labour History Archive and Study Centre (People's History Museum), Manchester, UK.

Marx Memorial Library, London.

Ministry of Foreign Affairs, People's Republic of China.

National Archive on Sino-American Relations Records, 87260 Bimu C539 2; Bimu C539 Outsize, Bentley Historical Library, University of Michigan, Boxes 1–20.

National Archives, Kew, UK.

National Archives, Washington, DC.

National Committee on United States–China Relations.

Nixon Presidential Library and Museum.

William J Cunningham Papers (courtesy of William J Cunningham).

Video

The Glory of China's Table Tennis Game (1959–1999). Beauty, Culture, Communication, Guangzhou, China.

China Central Television (CCTV) coverage of both the US trip to China in April 1971 and the Chinese trip to the US in 1972, courtesy of the National Committee on United States–China Relations.

My Way, New Tang Dynasty TV, 2009.

Index

Index

Index

Index

Index

World War I, 10, 28, 31, 38–39, 87

World War II, 27, 28, 42, 71
 and Britain, 38–40, 43–45, 73
 and death camps, 47, 109
 and Dixie Mission, 200, 213
 and Nuremberg Trials, 48–49
 Operation Mincemeat, 39–40, 44–45

X Group, 40–41

Xi Enting, 143, 146, 152, 153, 185

Xinhua News Agency, 244, 255

Xu Shaofa, 213, 269

Xu Yinsheng, 123–24, 137–39, 141, 142, 146, 269

XX Committee, 39, 43, 50

Yan'an, China, Dixie Mission in, 200, 213

Yan Fumin, 66

Young, York, 121–22

Zhenbao/Damansky Island, 166

Zheng Huaiying, 247

Zheng Mingzhi, 151–52, 263–64

Zhongnanhai, China, 135–36

Zhou Enlai:
 and Africa, 211
 and Cultural Revolution, 140, 146, 148, 149–50, 160, 161, 266
 death of, 267
 exile in France, 79
 and famine, 107, 108
 foreign policy of, 130, 133, 168, 195
 and Gang of Four, 266
 and Great Leap Forward, 91, 93
 and Japan, 9, 174–75
 and Long March, 87, 139, 272
 and Montagu, 64, 66
 and Nixon's visit, 236–37
 and Ogimura, 67, 135–36, 173–74
 and Pakistani back channel, 170

and Ping-Pong diplomacy, 2, 66, 85, 130, 175–77, 187, 192, 195, 202, 203, 217–18, 227, 234–35, 263

and reciprocity, 237

and recreation, 133

and Russia, 134, 166, 167

and Snow, 54, 252

and table tennis, 56, 57, 58, 59, 92, 95, 101, 107, 120, 124, 125, 126, 132, 135–36, 146, 161, 173, 184–87, 192, 193, 213, 219–21, 229, 231, 233, 237, 243

and Third World, 95, 101, 130, 133

and US connection, 170, 192, 193, 194, 195, 201, 202, 203, 210, 215, 227, 228–33, 234

and Vietnam, 195

Zhuang Jiafu, 101, 113–16, 154–55

Zhuang Xieling, 129

Zhuang Zedong, 138, 174
 and arranged victories, 131
 and Cowan, 188–92, 261, 271, 272
 and Cultural Revolution, 145, 146–47, 154, 157, 158, 159–60, 189–90, 263, 266–67, 269, 270
 death of, 272
 and Jiang Qing, 150, 160, 265–66, 267, 269
 and Ogimura, 136–37
 and Ping-Pong diplomacy, 187, 193, 196, 237, 263
 rise and fall of, 154, 159–60, 185, 262–63, 265–72, 275
 and US visit, 242–43, 245, 248, 249, 252, 253, 254, 262, 268, 271
 and World Championships, 116, 123, 124–25, 129, 131, 158, 183, 187
 and Zhou Enlai, 160, 187

Zhu De, 56–57, 58, 59, 101, 133, 151, 267, 272

336

Commu